Building the English Classroom

NCTE Editorial Board

Building the English Classroom

Foundations, Support, Success

Bruce M. Penniman
Amherst Regional High School

NCTE
NATIONAL COUNCIL OF TEACHERS OF ENGLISH
1111 W. KENYON ROAD, URBANA, ILLINOIS 61801-1096

Copy Editor: Theresa Kay

Production Editor: Carol Roehm

Interior Design: Jenny Jensen Greenleaf

Cover Design: Pat Mayer

Cover Images: Jerry Thompson at Thompson-McClellan Photography. iStockphoto.com images: iStockphoto.com/Kameleon007, iStockphoto.com/deanm1974, iStockphoto.com/urbancow, and iStockphoto.com/konradlew.

NCTE Stock Number: 03869

It is the policy of NCTE in its journals and other publications to provide a forum for the open discussion of ideas concerning the content and the teaching of English and the language arts. Publicity accorded to any particular point of view does not imply endorsement by the Executive Committee, the Board of Directors, or the membership at large, except in announcements of policy, where such endorsement is clearly specified.

Every effort has been made to provide current URLs and email addresses, but because of the rapidly changing nature of the Web, some sites and addresses may no longer be accessible.

Library of Congress Cataloging-in-Publication Data

Penniman, Bruce M., 1949–
    Building the English classroom : foundations, support, success / Bruce M. Penniman.
        p. cm.
    Includes bibliographical references and index.
    ISBN 978-0-8141-0386-9 (pbk)
    1. English language—Study and teaching (Secondary) I. Title.
    LB1631.P36 2009
    428.0071'2--dc22
                                                                            2009032479

Contents

Permission Acknowledgments

Acknowledgments

I owe so much to so many.

First, I would like to thank Kurt Austin, division director of publications, at NCTE, who has encouraged and assisted me since I first pitched the idea for this project to him several years ago. NCTE's anonymous peer reviewers, copyeditor Theresa Kay, and book editor Carol Roehm have also been enormously helpful throughout the process of writing and revising the manuscript. Also, I am indebted to fellow members of NCTE and its regional affiliate the New England Association of Teachers of English who have shared their teaching strategies in publications and conference sessions and inspired me to do the same.

Closer to home, I am grateful to my wife, Val, who read every word of every draft and provided supportive criticism, as well as to my Western Massachusetts Writing Project colleague Susan Connell Biggs, who thoughtfully reviewed the manuscript and made several pivotal suggestions. Michael Braidman, Kristen Iverson, and Erin Smith also read major portions of the text and offered constructive feedback and advice. More broadly, I would like to acknowledge all of the teacher-consultants and leaders of WMWP, who have taught me so much about teaching and learning, as well as the University of Massachusetts Amherst Department of English and the College of Humanities and Fine Arts, which have given me invaluable opportunities for leadership and professional growth. I am especially appreciative of the mentoring and support I have received from professors Charles Moran and Anne Herrington.

I would also like to thank the National Writing Project for allowing me to attend its 2006 Professional Writing Retreat, where I drafted the introduction for the book and received some important early response, and for the chance to participate in other programs, such as Project Outreach, the National Reading Initiative, and the State and Regional Networks, all of which have contributed substantially to my thinking about equity and efficacy in literacy instruction.

Many of the strategies presented in this book were borrowed from or developed in collaboration with my colleagues and friends in the Department of English at

Amherst Regional High School and Amherst Regional Middle School, whose ideas and example have shaped my development as a teacher. Some of them are mentioned by name in the chapters that follow, but all of them are here. I offer this work as a tribute to their commitment, passion, and generosity, and I hope that it pays forward some portion of their wisdom.

Finally, and most important, I want to express my appreciation to the students who graciously allowed me to include their work in this book—and to the thousands of others I have had the honor to work with over the past forty years (including my daughters, Becky and Abby). My students have taught me—and continue to teach me—how to teach effectively, and with profound gratitude I dedicate this book to all of them.

Introduction

Getting Organized

M y wife, Val, finds the title of this introduction amusing. "They should see your study," she says. It's true. Or my desk at school. Or my bookshelves. My neatness impairment notwithstanding, I do have a reputation among my Amherst Regional High School (ARHS) colleagues for being well organized: for seeing the big picture, for planning ahead, and for fitting all of the pieces together. And through involvement in NCTE, the National Writing Project, and other professional groups, I have become an active teacher-leader in curriculum and instruction.

It wasn't always so. For much of my first decade in the classroom—and regularly thereafter—I often felt overwhelmed by the demands of teaching, which seemed to grow in number and complexity every year. Through almost forty years in the classroom, I have learned how to determine what is really important to my students and to me—and what I can safely set aside. I have also learned to work *smart* as well as *hard*.

Teaching English is challenging in part because it is many subjects in one—traditionally, writing, literature, public speaking, and grammar, but now all of those plus media literacy, computer technology, social justice, and much more. Not to mention that as the primary locus of formal literacy instruction, English also provides the foundation for student achievement in all other subjects—and on high-stakes tests. The job of organizing all of these demands can be overwhelming, especially to a teacher still developing a repertoire of management strategies. Even the most creative, committed teachers struggle with feelings of inadequacy because they can't do it all—plan units and lessons, comment on student papers, address individual student needs—to their own satisfaction, despite working ten or twelve hours a day and half the weekend.

If you are one of those teachers, *Building the English Classroom: Foundations, Support, Success* is addressed to you. Reading this book won't reduce your workload or eliminate your job stress. But it may help you to manage the myriad responsibilities you face every day and thus feel more satisfied with the results of your efforts. Take the paper load, for example—every English teacher's greatest burden (literally and figuratively). I can't promise an end to taking home stacks of papers, but I will offer an assessment strategy that abolishes agonizing over grades, leaving more time to focus on coaching for improvement. I will encourage you to step back from the daily blur to where you can see issues broadly, think about your essential goals, and adopt teaching practices that will help you achieve them. There are already many fine books treating all of the topics addressed here, and I will recommend several of them in the chapters that follow. But if you are overworked, you probably don't have time to read these books, at least not all at once. What I hope to do is offer you a few key insights on a wide range of topics.

My goal is not to provide you with a comprehensive, foolproof, one-size-fits-all system but to share some helpful ideas and strategies, developed (read: borrowed from colleagues at my school and out in the field) and adapted over many years, that have worked effectively for me—and, most important, to prompt you to think about how best to organize language arts teaching and learning in your classroom situation. *Reflection* is a central theme in this book because meaningful change is impossible without it. *Flexibility* is another key theme. No system works for all or forever, so constructing the English classroom must be an ongoing process.

Where I'm From

Asking students to write "Where I'm From" poems, based on the original by George Ella Lyon, has become a popular assignment in English classes. It's a wonderful prompt: students get to explore their memories and heritages, and the results are nearly always poignant, compelling pieces. I'm not going to inflict any of my own verse on you here, but I would like to share some of my teaching story, to give you a sense of how the ideas in this book have evolved. I grew up in a working-class family in a small, homogeneous town in central Massachusetts. Inspired by my senior-year English and French teachers, who opened my eyes to the wonders of literature, I headed off to the University of Massachusetts determined to be just like them. Four years later, I took my first and only teaching job in the nearby Amherst Regional Schools. At first I taught in both the junior high and the senior high; when I became the newspaper advisor, I moved to the high school full-time and stayed until my recent retirement. I'm still working with a group of faculty to establish an interdisciplinary African Studies program and co-teaching a pilot course.

Amherst has always been an interesting place to teach. The presence of five colleges in the region creates a cosmopolitan atmosphere and guarantees a lively discourse on public affairs. The college "industry" also generates support for public education. But Amherst Regional High is by no means a prep school. Amherst is in the middle of a rural area where agriculture is still a key part of the economy, and the three other towns that are part of the regional schools are quite sparsely populated. When I first began teaching in the district, the student body was fairly homogeneous, mostly white, and working or middle class. The English as a Second Language program consisted of a dozen or so children of visiting professors and graduate students. Things have changed a lot since then. Circumstances ranging from refugee resettlement programs to a surplus of affordable apartments have made Amherst a much more diverse place. Currently more than 30 percent of the high school's 1,200-plus students are people of color, including roughly equal numbers of African Americans, Asians, and Hispanics. More than 16 percent are classified as low income, and 12 percent are not native English speakers ("School/District Profiles"). The English Language Learners program includes students whose first languages are Cape Verdean Creole, Khmer, Korean, Spanish, and twenty others. ARHS might be called a rural/suburban/urban school.

Long before it became a truly multicultural school system, Amherst was committed to multicultural education. Throughout my career I've had the opportunity to take courses and workshops on cultural diversity and antiracist teaching practices and to collaborate with knowledgeable colleagues on curriculum reform. These opportunities have profoundly affected my belief system and my teaching. As I'll explain in Chapter 9, it was multicultural thinking that eventually led several of us in the English department to challenge the practice of tracking. Making the change in 1990–1991 to teaching all students together in heterogeneous classes was a pivotal moment in my professional life. That transition and many others have been facilitated by the network of caring colleagues I have been privileged to work with.

Another career-changing event for me was participating in the Western Massachusetts Writing Project's Invitational Summer Institute in 1994 and thus becoming part of the National Writing Project's network of "teacher-consultants" committed not only to improving writing instruction but also to advancing social justice and promoting teacher leadership. It was through my writing project work, which has included participating in and leading workshops, institutes, and graduate courses, that I developed a deep understanding of student-centered pedagogy. The writing project also has also given me access to fellow educators in all grades in all kinds of communities, from whom I have learned a great deal about the myriad ways in which schools are conducted and the strategies that talented teachers use to provide for their students.

A third network of teachers that has influenced my career is NCTE. My participation started when two of my mentors introduced me to the New England affiliate, in which I've held a variety of positions. At the national level, I've been involved in the standards project and the Assembly on American Literature. Reading the publications, attending the conferences, and connecting with other teachers have enabled me to relate my work to ongoing developments in the field, including the latest theory and research.

Speaking of theory and research, my core understandings about language, literacy, and learning were profoundly influenced by my doctoral work in the University of Massachusetts School of Education. I was particularly affected by the writings of Lev Vygotsky. His concept of the "zone of proximal development," "*the distance between the actual developmental level as determined by independent problem solving and the level of potential development as determined through problem solving under adult supervision or in collaboration with more capable peers*" (86; emphasis original), clarified for me what had been somewhat vague beliefs about education. Over time I have also come to understand more and more the importance of "collaboration with peers" (for me, as a teacher, as well as for students), so group learning has played a larger and larger role in my classes, and my classroom now gets reconfigured regularly into groupings of different sizes and shapes, but rarely into forward-facing rows of student desks.

The experiences I've summarized here, plus years of learning from my students, have coalesced into a core philosophy that governs the way I think about my work and, I hope, the ways I carry it out. To borrow Herman Melville's words, I believe in a "ruthless democracy on all sides" (556–557). That is, I believe that *all* students can learn and want to learn and that they *all* are entitled to the best education we can offer. In English this means that *everyone* should have the opportunity to develop what Patrick J. Finn calls "powerful literacy" (ix), the kind that prepares people to be leaders and critical thinkers—as opposed to "functional literacy," which prepares them to follow. It also means that our curriculum and pedagogy should be *inclusive*, reflecting the rich diversity of our interconnected world, and *relevant* to the needs, desires, and hopes of our students. Everything that I recommend in this book is based on that philosophy.

I'm sure that most teachers agree with these ideas—making a difference for students is why we all went into education. But institutional inertia, insufficient resources, inadequate professional development, and sheer exhaustion sometimes prevent us from doing what we want to do and what we know is best. I hope that my suggestions on organizing the teaching of English can contribute to your becoming the educator you want to be.

Your turn. What's your teaching story? What educational and collegial experiences have influenced your ideas about education? What core beliefs inform your approaches to developing curriculum and conducting lessons? Reflect on these questions in writing.

How to Use This Book

Building the English Classroom can be used in a variety of ways. You may want to read it straight through and then return to the parts that apply most directly to your situation, or you may want to use it one chapter at a time as the stimulus for a deliberate, self-directed inquiry into your teaching practice. Even better, perhaps, the chapters could serve as discussion starters for English department or study group meetings. They are grouped into sections named for stages in the construction process. My father was a carpenter, so this metaphor comes to me naturally, but I think it works for organizing instruction: effective classrooms are *built*; they don't just happen. The chapters follow a logical sequence, but each can be read independently. I know that treating topics such as writing and literature in separate chapters is somewhat artificial, but I have done so to allow you to focus on one set of issues at a time. I have also included many cross-references.

The first section, **Laying the Foundation**, focuses on "big picture" topics, drawing attention to the fundamental decisions you need to make when organizing a whole course of study. Its chapters will encourage you to reflect on your overall approaches to teaching English.

Chapter 1: Planning for the Long Term. The day-to-day demands of teaching can be so consuming that it's easy to lose sight of the big picture and to end up feeling lost by the midpoint of a course or rushed at the end. Drawing on the principles of "backward design," this chapter describes a goal-driven planning process that includes developing comprehensive course outlines, managing the workload across teaching assignments, designing and publishing unit plans, monitoring progress, and making adjustments in the face of unexpected developments.

Chapter 2: Designing a Classroom Writing Program. No matter what kind of courses you teach—full-year comprehensive English courses or electives in composition or literature—student writing should be at the center of their organization. Using a table that draws together key ideas from a range of composition theorists, this chapter offers suggestions for planning a curriculum that includes expressive, poetic, and transactional modes and a range of genres; low-, medium-, and high-stakes assignments; and writing for a variety of audiences and purposes.

Chapter 3: Developing a Literature Curriculum. Organizing the study of literature to help students find relevance in great books, classic and contemporary, and to expose them to the diversity of experience these works represent is a huge and growing challenge. This chapter explores the *what* and the *why* of literature instruction and presents approaches to assembling a syllabus; methods of changing the pace of literary study throughout the term; and tips for coping with the limitations imposed by textbooks, curriculum mandates, and censorship.

Chapter 4: Creating an Assessment System. Handling the paper load is a key challenge for English teachers. Worse than spending an inordinate amount of time grading student papers, though, is suspecting that your effort isn't producing positive results. This chapter suggests ways to minimize grading and to maximize student reflection and growth through formative and summative assessment. It includes ideas for setting up writing folders and portfolios, using student- and teacher-generated evaluation criteria, and creating meaningful projects and tests.

The second section, entitled **Raising the Structure**, concentrates on instructional strategies, addressing the major components of most English courses. Its four chapters recommend principles and demonstrate methods for developing effective day-to-day lessons.

Chapter 5: Teaching Writing as a Process. By now the "process model" of writing instruction is well established in most high school English classrooms, but the ways in which it is implemented are sometimes inflexible and artificial and sometimes not explicit enough to ensure success for all. This chapter reviews some key findings of writing process research and presents several approaches to structuring them into classroom practice. Invention (prewriting/planning) strategies, peer and teacher feedback, revision, and publication are key topics in the chapter.

Chapter 6: Encouraging Response to Literature. A love of literature brings many people into the teaching of English, but it's easy to fall into traditional practices that kill the enjoyment of reading for some students—especially teacher-dominated "discussions" based on New Critical textual analysis. This chapter explores the possibilities of using other critical lenses (feminist, Marxist, psychoanalytical, etc.) with high school students and of incorporating small-group activities, such as literature circles and jigsaws. It also offers strategies for designing effective literature-based writing assignments and for teaching literary concepts and terms.

Chapter 7: Making the Most of Media and Technology. Many English teachers have embraced the use of electronic media and technology in the classroom—from videos and DVDs to word processing and PowerPoint to websites and blogs. But how can you be sure that the benefits of these activities are commensurate with the costs in time and resources? This chapter tries to prompt strategic thinking about the uses of media and technology, moving past "now that we've read the book, let's watch the movie" and "let's go to the computer lab to type our papers" to activities that provide students rich opportunities for skill building and critical thinking.

Chapter 8: Supporting Development of "Basic Skills." English teachers are obliged and duty bound to provide instruction in grammar, vocabulary, reading comprehension, and now often test-taking strategies. This chapter suggests ways to include the skills instruction that students need without letting exercises and worksheets take over the curriculum, using formats such as mini-lessons, conferences, peer tutoring, and group work. Also included are ideas for helping students develop the important but frequently neglected skill of public speaking.

The third section, **Opening the Door**, focuses on diversity, offering ideas for examining the curriculum through the lens of multiculturalism and for attending to the needs of individuals.

Chapter 9: Taking a Multicultural Stance. The social justice movements and "culture wars" of recent decades have had profound implications for the English classroom. An ever-broadening literary landscape makes possible a curriculum that reflects the diversity of the nation and the world. This chapter makes a case for applying principles of multicultural education to select and group course readings to create literary "conversations" and "contact zones" and to manage discussions of difficult subjects, such as race, religion, and sexual orientation.

Chapter 10: Embracing Diversity in the Classroom. The rapid growth of immigrant populations and changes in policies regarding inclusion of students with disabilities, among other factors, mean that English classes are more diverse than ever. The need to provide myriad individual accommodations can be a logistical challenge. This chapter promotes the idea of "universal design"—incorporating the most common special education and English language learner accommodations into the structure of the class—along with culturally responsive teaching practices and multiple intelligences theory, to make coursework accessible and relevant to all. The chapter also encourages a flexible approach to underachievement, focusing on recovery rather than failure, and it explores the benefits of co-teaching courses with specialists.

The afterword, *Growing Professionally through Teacher Leadership,* suggests some paths for pursuing a professional life outside the classroom, in the wider world of English education. School improvement plans, inhouse inservice training, state recertification requirements, and other mandates have narrowed the scope of professional growth for many teachers. This chapter makes the case for a diversified approach to career growth, explaining opportunities available through NCTE and the National Writing Project and their local affiliates and exploring possibilities for teacher leadership at the school, regional, and national levels.

The chapters are presented—to the extent possible in a paper publication—as if they were a series of interactive workshops. Each one begins with some observations about the challenge or problem on which it focuses, as well as an overview of the chapter's goals. Next comes a discussion of selected sources in the professional literature that I have found helpful in deepening my understanding of the topic. Several sections of each chapter comprise nuts-and-bolts descriptions of management strategies I have developed, on my own or with others, including teaching methods and materials, plus classroom anecdotes and/or samples of student work. Throughout these sections I try to let you in on my thinking process, and each one ends with a part that includes activities and questions to stimulate yours. At the end of each chapter I offer some final thoughts and some recommendations for further reading.

> **Your turn.** Before plunging into this book, take some time to consider your goals. What's working well in your classroom? What aspects of organizing English teaching are you struggling with? What do you hope to learn or improve? Make a list of priorities and refer to it as you work through the chapters. If possible, engage one or more of your colleagues in regular conversations about the topics in the book. Collaboration facilitates reflection and change.

A Word of Encouragement

There is nothing quite as exciting as a high school English class that is running smoothly. On the best days, when my students and I share a clear sense of purpose and direction, when everyone is engaged, learning new skills, thinking new thoughts, sharing new insights, I can't believe I get paid for teaching. Of course it will never be like that all the time. Bureaucratic snafus, reluctant learners, and heavy workloads will always be sources of stress. But I firmly believe that organization is the key to having more good days than bad. A well-organized English teacher (that's not an oxymoron!) is a more confident and effective English teacher, and one who is more satisfied with his or her work, as hard as it is. I hope that this book will help you to manage your professional life in pursuit of a long and rewarding career. I would love to hear from you as you work on building (or renovating) your own English classroom.

Bruce M. Penniman
http://blogs.umass.edu/Penniman

1

Laying the Foundation

Planning for the Long Term

Okay, I'll admit it: I'm a bit obsessive about long-range planning. My compulsion goes back to my first year of teaching when I was given a "surprise" class assignment right at the beginning of the school year: seventh-grade remedial reading. With no preparation for teaching such a course, I sought out the established curriculum. There was none. So, every Monday, after a weekend of scrambling, I would come to school with a new plan of action. By Wednesday it was in shambles, and I had to limp through the rest of the week and then come up with another approach the next weekend. I have never gotten over that experience.

During that first year of teaching—and well beyond it—I was concerned with establishing my authority in the classroom. Not *control*, exactly: more like a feeling that students trusted me to be in charge. Authority is closely related to confidence, and there is nothing that builds confidence more than good planning, especially long-range planning. New teachers—and experienced teachers, too—are often so preoccupied with what they are doing the next day that they lose sight of the big picture and in the process miss opportunities to boost their confidence and their authority with students and parents.

Several years ago I gave a workshop on long-range planning to a group of new teachers. I asked them what the barriers were to effective planning, and most of them said "stress." I then asked them what the consequences were of not planning well, and the answer was "more stress!" It's a vicious cycle, and if we can't break it, we resort to merely "covering the curriculum," which is not an effective way to teach. We move from one topic to another without making clear connections and always end up rushing at the end, cramming things in because we need to get a few more grades in our rank books. Instead, we should be *un*covering the curriculum for students, teaching for depth as well as breadth, moving toward carefully planned objectives.

In this chapter, I describe a goal-driven planning process that includes developing comprehensive course outlines, managing the workload across teaching assignments, designing and publishing detailed unit plans, and making adjustments in the face of unexpected developments. I encourage you to try out the process—or parts of it—as you are reading.

Backward Design

The idea of establishing long-range goals and designing instruction to meet them is not new. One of the first skills I had to learn as a new teacher in 1971 was how to write "measurable" performance objectives using Bloom's taxonomy (201–207). The method I was taught was clunky and sometimes felt forced, not an entirely comfortable fit for a subject that emphasizes appreciation and personal response. But the message of the inservice sessions was clear: if you don't know where you're going, you'll never know whether you get there.

More recently, Grant Wiggins and Jay McTighe have developed a more nuanced method of planning that many schools and districts have adopted. Called "backward design," their approach focuses on *understanding* rather than just *knowing* or *doing*. "To *understand*," they write, "is to make connections and bind our knowledge together into something that makes sense of things" and "to *apply* knowledge and skill effectively, in realistic tasks and settings" (7; emphasis original). To design instruction for understanding is to concentrate on outcomes and assessments, not merely on content or activities. The three stages of backward design signal this emphasis:

- **Stage 1: Identify desired results** (what students should know and be able to do, what enduring understandings they should develop).
- **Stage 2: Determine acceptable evidence** (the work samples and assessments that will show whether students have reached the desired results).
- **Stage 3: Plan learning experiences and instruction** (the activities, resources, and methods that will enable students to achieve the necessary knowledge and skills). (Wiggins and McTighe 17–19)

Most teachers understand the logic and power of backward planning, but the pressures of managing a full course load make shortcuts tempting. Designing a course around a reading list or a series of projects—or merely following an anthology's table of contents—is simple, but the results are never satisfying. Marching through a syllabus without clear aims is just marching.

Focusing on outcomes can actually help clear away the clutter from the planning process. Several years ago I was working with a student teacher whose final project was to design and implement a three-week poetry unit. A few weeks before the unit was to begin, she brought in a list of the lessons that she *really* wanted to include. She had brainstormed almost fifty activities, all potentially interesting and valuable, but far too numerous for the time available and without any clear connections to each other. I suggested that she winnow the list by clarifying for herself the *big ideas* and *essential questions* (two key terms used by Wiggins and McTighe) that she wanted students to grapple with and the knowledge and skills she wanted them to develop. These included, for example, the idea that poetry condenses experience into resonant images and the question of how form enhances meaning, as well as more concrete goals related to specific types of figurative language. Taking this step enabled her to decide which projects and assessments were the most relevant to her purposes and what process steps the students would need to take to complete them successfully. Soon she had a workable three-week plan.

The planning process that I have developed and refined over many years shares with Wiggins and McTighe's backward design a big-picture-first, ends-before-means orientation, but it focuses more on producing documents that students (and often parents) will use. I think of students as the primary audience for my planning activities because I have found that the better they understand what we're doing and why, the more likely they are to feel connected to the course and committed to helping it succeed. My planning process emphasizes three key words: *goals, agendas,* and *outcomes.* These are the elements of an effective plan. Where are we going? How are we going to get there? How will we know when we have made it? They seem obvious when stated so simply, but it is amazing how often these questions go unanswered—or even unasked—in many classrooms. In the discussion that follows, I'll refer to a junior/senior course called American Literature and Nature, but the process is adaptable to any subject or level.

A practical point: We can never *find* the time for long-range planning. We have to *make* the time. I prefer to plan when I am not facing the day-to-day work of teaching: in the summer, during school vacations, ideally after collaboration with colleagues teaching the same courses. Sometimes the conditions are less than ideal. I have friends who are constantly surprised by new teaching assignments and mandates. When time is short, I try to devote a Saturday or Sunday to thinking and planning ahead. This investment saves time (and certainly stress) in the long run.

Setting Goals

Long-range planning begins for me with setting up a course outline, including a course description, a list of major goals, a tentative syllabus, an explanation of core requirements and evaluation methods, and my general expectations of students. Working out these details takes a long time, especially when I'm teaching a course for the first time, but it's time well spent. I begin by reflecting on three broad sets of goals, using these questions to guide my planning:

- **Curricular goals:** What big ideas am I passionate about? What concepts, skills, or materials do I want to include in the curriculum? What school and/ or departmental mandates or agreements must I consider when developing the syllabus? What state and/or district curriculum frameworks apply to the course?

- **Pedagogical goals:** Are there particular approaches or projects that I want to try (or try again)? Have the district, school, department, and/or grade-level team adopted particular strategies that I need to include in my long-range planning?

- **Professional goals:** What aspects of my teaching was I *most* happy with during the previous year or semester? What was I *least* satisfied with? What do I need to get a better handle on? What do I want to accomplish?

Reflecting on these questions at the start of the planning process is like spreading out and examining the pieces of a jigsaw puzzle before attempting to put them together. Identifying all of my goals—those I set for myself and those that others set for me—helps me to frame my planning task, to assemble the edges of the puzzle.

Moving from goals to curriculum is a dialectical process. When I have developed a reasonably clear sense of my aims for a course, I think about how I can translate them into a coherent plan for my students—a plan that will be detailed enough to provide a road map for the course but flexible enough to accommodate inevitable adjustments. As my course plan emerges, I revisit my goals and refine them even further. A key part of this process is focusing on what *students* will do, not what I will do; what they will *learn*, not what I will teach. A typical result is my course outline for American Literature and Nature (see Figure 1.1).

When I was preparing the course outline for American Literature and Nature, I had much to consider. I knew the material well, having taught most of the texts many times. I was certainly familiar with all of the relevant state standards. But since the previous time I had taught the course, its title had been changed (from Foundations of American Literature), and its method had switched from chronological to thematic. I had been involved in this work, which had been part of a larger departmental revision of the literature program, but I had not yet tried the new approach myself. Thus one of my *curricular* goals was to build in a progression of ideas about nature and human beings' relationship to it. I chose to begin with *The Adventures of Huckleberry Finn*, not only because I knew that my students would enjoy it but

AMERICAN LITERATURE AND NATURE COURSE OUTLINE
Mr. Penniman

Spring 2007
E Period

Times available for conferences: Fourth lunch (English Office, 167), and after school (167 or 169)
Home telephone (for emergencies): 555-5555   **Email address:** penniman@arps.org (checked daily)

Goals of the Course

The relationship between human beings and the natural world has been an important theme in American literature from precolonial times until the present. American writers have viewed nature both as a wilderness to be feared and subdued and as a paradise to be sought and savored. American authors from all cultural traditions have associated great spiritual power and symbolic meaning with nature, and many have lamented the corruption of the natural world through slavery, careless development, and other forms of exploitation. American Literature and Nature explores these themes through the works of writers from a variety of periods, regions, and cultural backgrounds, with special emphasis on nineteenth-century New England.

All assignments in American Literature and Nature are connected to these major course goals:

1. To encourage you to develop your own understanding of the natural world and human beings' changing relationships to nature through literary analysis, discussion of current events, and firsthand experience.
2. To broaden your understanding of major themes in American literature, history, and culture, including issues of race, class, and gender; but also religion, philosophy, and politics.
3. To acquaint you with authors representing differing visions of the American experience with nature: majority and minority, male and female, classic and modern.
4. To improve your ability to read critically, make interpretive connections, and share ideas in discussions.
5. To develop your writing skills through informal responses, analytical essays, and creative pieces.
6. To increase your awareness of language and expand your vocabulary.

Course Readings

Mark Twain, *The Adventures of Huckleberry Finn***:** Our first novel will be Twain's humorous/serious story of a boy and a runaway slave escaping society on a raft.

Ralph Waldo Emerson, *Essays***, and Henry David Thoreau,** *Walden***:** After reading excerpts from Emerson's influential "Nature" essay, we will study Thoreau's experiment in living "as deliberately as nature" by Walden Pond in Concord, Massachusetts.

Narrative of the Life of Frederick Douglass **and Harriet Jacobs,** *Incidents in the Life of a Slave Girl***:** ˙
You will choose one of these autobiographical accounts of slaves' lives in the Southern plantation system.

Louise Erdrich, *Tracks***, and John Neihardt,** *Black Elk Speaks***:** These books (of which you will read one) depict American Indians' painful transition to life on the reservation.

Nathaniel Hawthorne, *Short Stories***, and Herman Melville,** *Moby-Dick***:** After reading some of the stories that helped inspire it, we will dive into what is arguably the greatest work of American literature, the story of Captain Ahab's pursuit of the white whale and Ishmael's search for meaning.

Poetry and Short Stories: Throughout the term we will sample works of poets and short-story writers who focus on nature such as Walt Whitman, Emily Dickinson, Robert Frost, Leslie Silko, and William Faulkner.

continued on next page

Figure 1.1. Course outline.

Course Requirements

CLASS PARTICIPATION: All students are expected to contribute to the best of their abilities, both in large-group and small-group activities. Participation also includes listening to and showing respect for others' ideas. Attendance, punctuality, daily preparation, effort, conduct, productivity, and notebook writing also count.

READING ASSIGNMENTS: Readings will total roughly 150 pages per week, not counting some poems and other pieces we will read in class. Set aside adequate "quality" time for reading assignments—don't put them off until the last minute or when you are half-asleep. Jot down important information, questions, and ideas in your notebook. Try to make connections among the readings, and between them and your own experience.

NOTEBOOK WRITING: Your notebook will also be a place for you to begin or end class, commenting on readings, ideas we are discussing, and relevant current issues and events, as well as for class notes.

RESPONSE PAPERS: Every two weeks or so, a two- or three-page paper based on current readings will be due. You will often choose your topics. Some pieces will be reader response, some analytical, and some creative.

MAJOR PROJECTS: Throughout the term you will be working on a nature journal about a particular outdoor place that you will visit often. There will also be a small class presentation based on library research. Students choosing to work at AP level will also develop an inquiry project based on independent reading and research.

QUIZZES AND TESTS: Major exams will be rare in this course, but you can expect unannounced quizzes on the readings and a few medium-sized tests on background material and readings. There will be a final exam.

EVALUATION AND GRADES: Most assignments **will not be graded individually**. I will assess most work over a period of several weeks. This process will include *self*-evaluation. *Progress* counts as much as *products*.

Class Participation/Notebook Evaluations	20%
Writing Folder Evaluations (includes AP project = 20%)	30%
Nature Journal Project and Research Presentation	15%
Quizzes and Tests	15%
Final Exam and Course Portfolio	20%

General Expectations (or Penniman's Pet Peeves)

ABSENCES/TARDINESS/PASSES: You need to be in class to learn. Period. The only exceptions should be for serious illness. Be in your seat before the bell rings with all of your materials ready and your mind engaged. Bathroom or locker visits during class should be extremely rare. Act like an adult, and I'll treat you like one.

MAKEUP OR LATE WORK: You will always have assignments in advance, so you will know what is due. Don't insult my intelligence or embarrass yourself with lame excuses. If you mess up, say so. I'll forgive you. There is a 10 percent penalty for late work (more if really late) unless you negotiate an extension ahead of time. Here's a little secret: I tend to be very flexible about due dates and requirements if (1) I can see that you're making a good-faith effort, (2) you communicate with me, and (3) you don't go to the well too often.

CONTRABAND: iPods, cell phones, etc. must not be seen nor heard. No food or drink other than water.

ACADEMIC INTEGRITY: You will collaborate on some projects, but work that you pass in as your own must be your own. If you use other sources for papers, you must cite them properly. Plagiarism is serious.

CARE OF MATERIALS: You share responsibility for keeping books, desks, and the room in good condition.

CONFERENCES: I'm here late almost every day. Ask for extra help if you need it. Don't suffer in silence!

Signatures: I've read this course outline. Student_____ Parent_____

Figure 1.1. *continued*

also because it presents clear contrasts between nature and society in both physical and moral terms and raises questions about race that would recur throughout the course, paving the way for the more challenging works and complex views of nature and human nature that would follow: *Walden,* slave narratives, Native American texts, poetry. I decided to end with *Moby-Dick,* the quintessence of associating "great spiritual power and symbolic meaning with nature" (a key idea in the course description) and to focus the unit on the stories of Ishmael and Ahab, just sampling a few of the whaling chapters.

I also had *pedagogical* goals in mind as I was developing this course outline. One was a schoolwide effort to make what our principal referred to as "high-status knowledge" accessible to all students, with particular emphasis on those with a history of underachievement. Designing curriculum and learning activities to meet the needs of a range of students wasn't new to me, but I wanted to be sure that I was including strategies that would reach out to the inexperienced or reluctant readers who might be drawn to the course because of its emphasis on the outdoors. I decided to include a nature journal as a major ongoing project. I had seen and been impressed by a presentation on nature journals at a conference several years earlier (Rous), and I had saved the handouts, from which I drew ideas as I developed my own plans.

A *professional* goal that affected my thinking about the American Literature and Nature course was to incorporate literature circles into one or more parts of the course. I had tried this technique in other courses with mixed success, and I wanted to get better at it. I thought that the unit on slave narratives might be a good place to start. I planned to offer students a choice of two readings and to set up small groups in which the participants would have specific, rotating roles (more on this in Chapter 6). I thought that if the strategy worked well, I could extend it into other units or into what I imagined might be weekly seminars on poets or short-story writers.

When I design a course outline, my goal is to provide students (and parents) a clear idea of the content and expectations of the course without overwhelming them with detail. I also try to leave some wiggle room to adjust the curriculum to meet changing circumstances and to accommodate the needs and interests of the class. I do try to be precise, however, about the requirements and basis for evaluation. Deciding in advance what assignments and projects students will be responsible for and their relative weight in the final grade ensures that I meet all school and department mandates and helps me with unit planning throughout the term. Besides, it would be unfair to withhold this information. I also like to be clear about my classroom rules and expectations so there's no confusion about whether I accept late work, for example.

I always distribute my course outline on the first day of the term, but I rarely "go over it" in class on that day. Instead, I give students a day or two to digest it and ask their parents to do the same (often with the incentive of a 100 percent quiz grade for getting it signed). Then I take some time in class to ask and respond to questions about the course goals, syllabus, requirements, and procedures. My goals in this discussion are to help students understand the thinking and planning I have put into the course and to welcome them into the work, hoping they will engage with the content and look forward to developing new knowledge and skills. Even if they aren't quite ready to embrace the mission, they should come away with a clear sense of what it is.

Your turn. If you are mapping out a course or major unit as you read this chapter, now would be a good time to do some reflecting and planning. What are your curricular, pedagogical, and professional goals, and how will your course design reflect these purposes? How will you describe the course content, goals, and expectations to students? Don't be afraid to experiment to find a comfortable form and style. Share your ideas with colleagues and get their feedback. But don't make a final draft of your course outline until you've considered the calendar.

Seeing the Big Picture

Just as important as establishing goals is crafting clear and workable agendas. I do this in two stages, the first of which is broad-stroke, big-picture planning. Once I have drafted a detailed course outline for each of my classes, I sketch out a full-term, cross-referenced schedule for *all* of my classes to improve organization and minimize work overload. I added this step after foolishly deciding one year that it would be a good idea to introduce a new topic in each of my classes on Monday that would culminate in a paper due on Friday. It didn't take too many weekends of bringing home over a hundred papers to see the flaw in that scheme. Now I map out the whole term using a grid with spaces for every class meeting (see Figure 1.2). A legal pad divided into columns works just as well. The idea is to be able to see the whole term at a glance, both within a particular class and across all classes.

This schedule is not very detailed at first—it's certainly not a full-course syllabus. (I tried that once, too, but a picture day and two fire drills messed up my plans by the second week of school.) This rough calendar does allow me to make strategic decisions (how many weeks to allow for each book, when to schedule special projects or field trips, when each class will submit papers). Making these decisions early reduces the likelihood of running out of time at the end of the course or of overloading myself with work during a particular week. Planning ahead does not mean that

Day/Date	Period _A_ Class _Study_	Period _B_ Class _W+L_	Period _C_ Class _Prep_	Period _D_ Class _Bible_	Period _E_ Class _AL+N_	Special Events
M 3/19		Intro		Intro	Intro	
Tu				Gen. 1-2		
W				History		
Th				Gen. 3	P1: Nat.	
F				P1: Bible		Sat. mtg.
M 3/26		P1: topics		Rap. Dau.	Song of My.	AP topic
Tu				"	**Huck F.**	
W		**Yellow**		Gen. 4-5	Nat. Jrl. 1	
Th		**Raft**		Gen. 6-8		
F		P1: draft		Gen. 9-11		Sat. conf
M 4/2				P2: draft		AP step 1
Tu		P1: per. n.		Quiz/refs.		
W					P2: Song	
Th				no class	HF test	late arr.
F		Quiz			**Emerson**	
M 4/9		P2: wksht			P3: draft	AP step 2
Tu		P2: plan		P2: RD an.		
W				**Pat./Mat.**		
Th		P2: ch. an.		**Legends**	**Walden**	
F				**Gen. 12-50**	P3: HF an.	
M 4/23		Voc. due				AP step 3
Tu		**Rom +Jul**		P3: creat.		
W				Ind. rdg.	NJ2/Quiz	DOE mtg
Th		Voc. Quiz				
F					**Slave Nar.**	

Notes: Spring break week of 4/16. | Writing folder evaluation #1 ~4/3.

Figure 1.2. Course planning sheet.

everything will go according to schedule, but it enables me to make better choices. If it turns out (as is often the case) that I have planned too many readings for a course, having a full-term schedule allows me to decide (with students) what to sacrifice rather than simply lop off the last unit, which is sometimes the most important.

Figure 1.2 shows how I use the schedule grid. In this illustration, I have included readings, paper topics and due dates, and other projects for three classes, Writing and Literature, Bible and Related Literature, and American Literature and Nature, for the first five weeks of the spring trimester. To fill in the grid, I find it helpful to start with fixed dates: holidays, grading deadlines, inservice days, assemblies, and such. These include personal and professional obligations, too: the family reunion that will take me away for an entire weekend, the two days of school I will miss for a conference, and so on. Then I set aside chunks of the calendar for major units and choose approximate dates for special projects. Finally, I fill in and highlight regular events, such as paper due dates and journal checks, always reading across the columns to make sure I won't be overwhelmed with work. As the term progresses, I add more detail to the schedule a few weeks at a time; it becomes, in effect, the rough draft of my unit plans.

Consistent with the backward design concept of determining "acceptable evidence" of "desired results," I tend to focus on student writing when building term schedules. One of my goals in every course is that students learn to write effectively and respond to literature in a variety of modes (see Chapter 2). In planning the junior/senior Bible and Related Literature and American Literature and Nature courses, I decided that by midterm each student should write a personal essay, an analytical essay, and a creative piece, one of which would be thoroughly revised for the first writing folder evaluation (see Chapter 4). I elected to begin with the personal essays in both classes—perceptions papers on the Bible and nature, respectively—because I knew that these would help me get to know the students and that I could respond to them fairly quickly. Teaching the analytical essay is always a challenging, labor-intensive process, so I made this assignment the second paper in one class and the third in the other and built in due dates for partial drafts and plenty of time for revision. I also planned the creative pieces as opportunities for students to deepen their understandings of the texts they were reading. In American Literature and Nature, for example, I decided that the best way for students to "get" Whitman's "Song of Myself" was to try writing a similar series of connected pieces about their own experiences and interests and beliefs, taking as many liberties as Whitman had in form and style. In the ninth-grade Writing and Literature section, the second half of a two-part course, I elected to begin with a personal narrative because students would be reading three first-person accounts in Michael Dorris's *A Yellow Raft on Blue Water*. The second assignment would be a character analysis, planned and written in class with a lot of support.

Putting in regular process steps for long-term projects is also an important part of building a full-term schedule. Otherwise, the final due dates tend to sneak up, leaving both students and teacher feeling rushed and unprepared. In American Literature and Nature, I decided to review and comment on students' nature journals every two weeks and was careful (for their sakes and mine) not to schedule these checkpoints the same weeks they had papers due. I also included regular due dates for students electing to take the AP option (see Chapter 6 for details).

Once I have the entire course "infrastructure" in place, I'm ready to get down to specifics—reading assignments, major quizzes and tests, library and computer lab visits, and other learning activities. At this point I sometimes discover that there isn't enough time for everything I want to include, so I have to start making choices. I would like to have allowed more time for reading *Walden*, for instance, but I didn't want to crowd the titles coming later in the course. So I opted to assign fewer chapters of the book than I had originally planned, leaving open the possibility of extending the unit if the students responded positively to Thoreau.

> **Your turn.** Using a grid like the one in Figure 1.2, plan out the major units, regular assignments, and key assessments and projects for all of the courses you will be teaching in the next term. Be sure to plan "horizontally" as well as "vertically"—look at your total workload when deciding on unit start dates and end dates, writing assignments, and other key elements of your professional and personal life. When you are satisfied with your term schedule, go back to your course outlines, adjust them as needed, and get them in publishable shape.

Devising Unit Plans

Goal-setting and "big-picture" planning culminate for me in the two- to three-week unit schedules that I write and publish for my students (parents, special education liaisons, and tutors find them useful, too). In these schedules I provide a day-by-day listing of assignments and class activities (see Figure 1.3). Knowing what is coming up helps students who have busy after-school lives to plan ahead and allows absentees to keep track of what they have missed. More important, unit schedules enable students to see the larger purposes of their daily work and to feel a part of the class endeavor. I love it when students ask in advance about upcoming assignments or activities—or better, when a less-than-attentive student comes into class and asks, "What are we doing today?" and a classmate gives the answer based on the published schedule. I rely on the schedules to keep me on track, too. At the end of a long day, I don't have to decide what I'm doing the next day; I just have to check to

AMERICAN LITERATURE AND NATURE ASSIGNMENT SHEET #1			
Date	Assignment DUE (check off when completed)	Class Activity	Notes
Mar. 19		Course intro: Americans and nature.	
Mar. 20	Read *The Adventures of Huckleberry Finn*, Chapters I–VI (pp. 13–42).	Notebook writing and discussion on *The Adventures of Huckleberry Finn*.	
Mar. 21	Read *The Adventures of Huckleberry Finn*, Chapters VII–XII (pp. 43–80).	Notebook writing and discussion on *The Adventures of Huckleberry Finn*.	
Mar. 22	Study course outline and get it signed; write 2-page **perceptions paper** on nature.	Quiz on course goals; projects and AP work; share papers in response groups.	
Mar. 23	Read *The Adventures of Huckleberry Finn*, Chapters XIII–XVI (pp. 81–116).	Notebook writing and discussion on *The Adventures of Huckleberry Finn*.	
Mar. 26	Read *The Adventures of Huckleberry Finn*, Chapters XVII–XX (pp. 117–150).	Notebook writing and discussion on *The Adventures of Huckleberry Finn*.	AP topic
Mar. 27	Read *The Adventures of Huckleberry Finn*, Chapters XXI–XXV (pp. 151–183).	View *American Passages* film and read from Whitman's "Song of Myself."	
Mar. 28	Complete first set of **nature journal** entries (see separate project sheet).	Share journal entries, read Whitman, begin drafting your "Song of Myself."	
Mar. 29	Read *The Adventures of Huckleberry Finn*, Chapters XXVI–XXIX (pp. 184–215).	Notebook writing and discussion on *The Adventures of Huckleberry Finn*.	
Mar. 30	Read *The Adventures of Huckleberry Finn*, Chapters XXX–XXXIV (pp. 216–245).	Notebook writing and discussion on *The Adventures of Huckleberry Finn*.	
Apr. 2	Read *The Adventures of Huckleberry Finn*, Chapters XXXV–XXXIX (pp. 246–274).	Notebook writing and discussion on *The Adventures of Huckleberry Finn*.	AP step 1
Apr. 3	Read *The Adventures of Huckleberry Finn*, Chapters XL–end (pp. 275–296); bring in draft of "Song of Myself" paper.	Notebook writing and discussion on *The Adventures of Huckleberry Finn*; share drafts of "Song of Myself" paper.	
Apr. 4	Complete and revise your own **"Song of Myself"** collection.	Review novel for unit test; begin work on analytical paper using critical lenses.	
Apr. 5	Review for unit test on *Huckleberry Finn*.	**Unit test on *Huckleberry Finn*.**	
Apr. 6	Work on draft of analytical essay on *Huckleberry Finn*.	Reading and discussion of excerpts from Emerson's "Nature."	
Apr. 9	Complete working draft (1–2 pages) of analytical essay on *Huckleberry Finn*.	Introduction to Henry David Thoreau's *Walden*.	AP step 2

NOTE: Response paper assignments are on the back. AP project assignments will be distributed on a separate handout.

Figure 1.3. Unit plan.

Response Papers

Every other week, a two- or three-page paper based on the previous unit's reading will be due. Besides class participation, these response papers will be your primary means of demonstrating your learning in this course. **Most papers will be shared in class.** It is important that you give these assignments your best effort, using a thorough, thoughtful writing process. These papers will not all be in strict essay form, but they should be well-organized and supported with adequate detail (including quotations from the readings when appropriate). Papers should be revised and checked for errors in mechanics. Final drafts should be word-processed, and sources should be documented in correct MLA form (author-page in parentheses, listed in works cited at the end). Ask for help in the English Study Center and/or from me when you need it. It is also critical that you get your work done on schedule. **Papers will not be graded individually.** You will keep them in your writing folder, monitoring your progress and revising as needed. Twice during the term you will submit your writing folder for evaluation, and at the end of the term, you will select and polish three pieces for your course portfolio.

Response Paper #1: Perceptions of Nature

Your first paper will be a personal essay about your perceptions of and experiences with nature. This topic is pretty open-ended, and you can shape it as you wish. Here are a few questions that you might consider:

- How would you define "nature"? What aspects of life as we understand it does it include? Not include?
- What kinds of relationships do human beings have with nature? Have they changed over time?
- What kinds of experiences have you had with nature—recreational, agricultural, or scientific? Good or bad?
- Do you think nature is symbolic or spiritual in any way? Does nature have anything to teach us?

Don't try to cover all of these questions, and ignore them if you have a better idea to write about. Aim for two pages or so of informal but well-crafted writing. Successful papers will include specific details as well as "big ideas."

Response Paper #2: Your Own "Song of Myself"

All of the authors we have studied so far emphasize individualism: Emerson wrote an essay on "Self-Reliance," Thoreau described his experiment in living independently in *Walden*, Whitman celebrated his uniqueness in "Song of Myself," and Twain embodied all of these qualities in the main character of *Huckleberry Finn*. Now it's your turn. What qualities make you a self-reliant, independent, unique individual? How do you assert your individuality and yet remain connected to others? How do you *express* who you are?

Using "Song of Myself" as a model (and perhaps even stealing Whitman's first line: "I celebrate myself, and sing myself . . ."), create a two- or three-page collection of poems or pieces in a variety of genres that get the essence of *you*—not just what you *do* but also what you *think about* and *care about*. Try to have some fun with this—don't be afraid to let loose your own "barbaric yawp"!

Response Paper #3: Analytical Essay on *Huckleberry Finn*

This paper will be more substantial than the first two and will go through more drafts. You will receive a separate assignment sheet for this essay on April 4.

Figure 1.3. *continued*

see what I've already planned. I can also look a few days ahead to make sure I have handouts and other materials ready on time.

The keys to developing a good unit schedule, like a good course plan, are to set aside adequate planning time (read: leave the papers at school for one weekend) and to work backward. Determining where students should be by the end of the unit simplifies decision making about day-to-day assignments and activities: if we are going to be at Point Z by the end of the unit, then we have to do X by this date and Y by that date. Working backward from the first analytical essay due date in American Literature and Nature, for example, helped me decide on the reading schedule for *Huckleberry Finn*. I also try to establish some rhythms in my lesson planning. After three or four reading assignments, I include a writing task for a change of pace. Once a week, when the class has a ninety-minute period (Tuesdays in this case), I plan an additional activity, such as a film or a peer-response session. Naturally, this process becomes a little easier and more refined each time I teach a particular unit.

In some classes I use a weekly schedule instead of a full unit plan (see Figure 1.4). I like this alternative (which I borrowed from a math teacher) for my younger students because it lays out the coursework in more digestible chunks and gives them a sense of closure every Friday.

Devising a clear and well-organized schedule is no guarantee that students will follow it, of course. When I distribute a new unit plan (three-hole punched for easy insertion into students' binders), I always take some time in class not only to highlight the upcoming assignments and activities but also to help students connect the work to the overall goals of the course. I post a copy of the schedule on the bulletin board and frequently ask a student to remind the class about the homework. Every few days I ask everyone to take out the schedules to review what we have accomplished so far and to preview what we will be doing in the next few days. These regular, brief check-ins allow me to bring anyone who has gotten lost or confused back on board and to identify those who need more extensive individual help.

Your turn. Using your course planning sheet as a guide, create a two- or three-week unit schedule like the one in Figure 1.3. Remember to work backward, starting with major projects or assessments, then filling in the process steps, reading assignments, and daily lessons that lead up to them. Publish the schedule for your students and take some time to review it with them.

This Week in English
December 5–9

Welcome to ninth-grade English! At the beginning of each week, you will receive a sheet explaining what will be happening in class that week and what your assignments will be. Always read the entire sheet right away so you'll know what to expect and so you can get your questions answered. Put the sheet in your three-ring binder and check it every day to make sure you know what is due. As you complete your assignments, check them off in the margin. Save all of these sheets, as they will help you review at the end of the term. Most daily assignments are *cumulative*, that is, they are steps toward a larger product. It's important that you complete all of the steps on time, keep them in order, and submit them together when the final draft is due.

Writing Assignment #1: Reading Journal
A reading journal is a collection of informal commentaries about a piece of literature, written in stages during the reading process. The goal is not to *summarize* the work but to *respond* to it in a variety of ways: finding connections to your own experience, reacting to particular passages, analyzing characters and relationships. You will keep a reading journal as we study Lorraine Hansberry's *A Raisin in the Sun*, one page per assignment, six pages in all. You will give special attention to one character.

<u>Monday</u>
Class activities: Review of the course outline, warm-up activity, and introduction to *A Raisin in the Sun.*
Assignment: Read *A Raisin in the Sun*, pp. 25–53, and write your first one-page reading journal entry: Explain your first impressions of the character you have chosen to study: Ruth, Walter, Beneatha, or Mama. Also, ask a parent to read and sign the course outline (return by Friday at the latest).

<u>Tuesday</u>
Class activities: Introduction to MUG shots (one-sentence exercises in mechanics, usage, and grammar), review of journal entries, and acting and discussion of play.
Assignment: Read *A Raisin in the Sun*, pp. 54–75, and write your second one-page reading journal entry: Explain the relationship between your character and one other character in the play.

<u>Wednesday</u>
Class activities: MUG shot sentence, review of journal entries, and viewing of the American Playhouse production of the play.
Assignment: Read *A Raisin in the Sun*, pp. 76–95, and write your third one-page reading journal entry: Choose an important speech by your character and comment on its importance in the play.

<u>Thursday</u>
(no class—late arrival day)

<u>Friday</u>
Class activities: MUG shot sentence, review of journal entries, and acting and discussion of the play.
Assignment: Read *A Raisin in the Sun*, pp. 96–109, and write your fourth one-page reading journal entry: Choose your own focus for your commentary. Students who wish to try honors level should decide on a second reading for the first enrichment project (see separate handout).

Figure 1.4. One-week plan.

Monitoring Progress, Adjusting Schedules, and Assessing Outcomes

Developing and publishing a unit plan is not the end of the process. Even the best-laid plans need—and should be open to—revision (hence the "Notes" column in my unit schedules). Some discussions may run longer than expected. Some concepts may need reteaching. Unexpected events may force changes in the school calendar. Or a class may simply want to pursue an interesting digression. Adjusting the unit schedule can become an exercise in class problem solving. Because students understand the larger purposes of their work and know its intended outcomes, they can help decide how to meet unit goals amid changing circumstances.

Schedule revising can be an effective class activity even when things are not going well. Several years ago I taught a section of American literature made up of nineteen boys and one girl, few of whom were motivated students of literature. They did fairly well with *Huckleberry Finn* and some of the writings of Emerson and Thoreau, but when it came time to read *The Scarlet Letter*, their passive resistance brought the class almost to a halt (maybe I had taught Thoreau's "Civil Disobedience" essay too well). Some just wouldn't read the novel beyond the first few chapters; others were reading but wouldn't talk. After a week of trying to muddle through, I convened a "town meeting" in class to discuss the problem. Several students presented their reasons for not liking Hawthorne, and I (aided by a few brave students) gave mine for wanting them to read his work. In the end, we agreed on a new plan that made finishing the novel optional but required reading several Hawthorne short stories that raised similar issues. Everyone was satisfied. Changing the required readings isn't always an option, but talking about why assignments are not working and making some useful adjustments to the schedule are possible in most courses.

Ongoing monitoring of students' progress should always drive decisions about fine-tuning the schedule, and evaluation of the unit as a whole should lead to adjustments in the next schedule. I find that a mix of informal and formal assessment tools works best—daily check-ins, observations of small-group work, writing assignments, open-response tests, and/or end-of-unit reflections. I will offer several specific suggestions in later chapters. Suffice it to say now that student learning should be assessed by the students themselves as well as by the teacher.

> **Your turn.** As you implement the unit plan you designed in the previous step, take a few minutes each day to reflect on your students' progress toward the unit goals. Solicit feedback and make use of informal assessments to monitor student learning. If it becomes apparent that some retooling of the schedule is needed, be sure to involve the students in the process.

A Final Thought

The approach to planning I'm recommending can be summed up in one phrase: macro to micro. Start with big ideas and lofty goals, and then work out the details. Don't be afraid to dream. As Thoreau put it, "If you have built castles in the air, your work need not be lost; that is where they should be. Now put the foundations under them" (215). You may develop planning steps other than the ones I have outlined that are more useful to you and your teaching situation, but whatever the method, I hope you can see that long-range planning should be a priority among the too-many tasks you face as a teacher. There is no more concrete way of showing students we care—and empowering them as learners—or of convincing parents and administrators that we know what we're doing. There is no better way of keeping our focus on what's most important or scaffolding work for success. For all teachers, new and veteran alike, long-range planning is the key to teaching with confidence and authority.

Recommended Reading

Hillocks, George, Jr. *Teaching Writing as Reflective Practice*. New York: Teachers College Press, 1995. Print.

> Hillocks offers a sophisticated, theory-driven approach to structuring learning activities to improve thinking and writing skills. His chapters on the art of planning, though focused on writing, are applicable to all parts of the English curriculum.

Smagorinsky, Peter. *Teaching English through Principled Practice*. Upper Saddle River, NJ: Merrill Prentice Hall, 2002. Print.

> This ample volume focuses on strategies for designing multiweek "conceptual units of instruction" and the principles of practice behind them. Smagorinsky provides a wealth of resources, teaching materials, and vignettes.

Stern, Deborah. *Teaching English So It Matters: Creating Curriculum for and with High School Students*. Thousand Oaks, CA: Corwin Press, 1995. Print.

> Stern provides a rationale and procedure for developing student-centered curriculum through a "cocreative" process as well as detailed examples of thematic units.

Wiggins, Grant, and Jay McTighe. *Understanding by Design*. Expanded 2nd ed. Upper Saddle River, NJ: Pearson Education, 2006. Print.

> This influential book is worth a careful study—preferably over several weeks to allow time for absorbing the theory and research that the authors present and for experimenting with their comprehensive model of instructional planning.

2

Designing a Classroom Writing Program

A love of great books is what drew me into the world of English, and during my first several years of teaching, I emphasized appreciation and analysis of literature above all other aspects of the discipline. But I gradually came to believe that writing should be at the center of the English curriculum, even in courses that have "literature" in their titles, for the same reasons that drawing and painting should be at the heart of the art program or lab experiments at the core of science. Language is the medium of our field, and students should learn how to use it creatively and thoughtfully for their own purposes, not just examine how others have used it.

When I say that writing should be at the center of the curriculum, I don't mean the all-too-common pattern of teaching a novel and then having students write an essay about it or even teaching the haiku and then asking students to try to create one, though those are both perfectly valid activities. It's easy to fall into a rut of assigning reading that leads to writing designed to assess understanding of the reading. I've been in that rut many times. Rather, I'm suggesting that the curriculum should be *organized* around writing, that students should use writing—all kinds of writing—every day to *develop* skills and knowledge as well as to *demonstrate* them.

Organizing English courses around writing presents tough challenges. Chief among them is *time*: finding time for students to write with so many curriculum mandates to be addressed and making time to respond to their work with too few hours in the day. There are no easy solutions to these problems. But placing writing at the center has enormous benefits. Most important, it focuses our attention on student work, rather than on our presentations or on the "material" that we have to "cover." In addition, writing activities can serve as powerful tools for planning.

The goal of this chapter is to help you design a writing program in which students can learn to write by writing to learn. Drawing together insights from my classroom experience and from a variety of composition theorists and researchers, I will offer suggestions for planning a curriculum that includes a range of modes and genres; low-, medium-, and high-stakes tasks; and writing for a variety of audiences and purposes. Two key considerations in this process are *authenticity*—creating opportunities for writing that serve real purposes for the students—and *manageability*—developing a system that facilitates the instructional goals of the teacher.

Learning from Writing Process Theory and Research

As I began my teaching career, a revolution was under way in the teaching of writing. The old paradigm of writing instruction, which focused almost entirely on learning discrete skills, such as sentence diagramming and paragraph organization, "was largely product-centered and print-based; that is, it focused on the finished exemplar of student work with little or no attention to the purpose or process of producing it" (National Writing Project and Nagin 19–20). The five-paragraph theme, a staple of many high school writing programs even today, exemplifies the traditional paradigm: assigned primarily as a skill-building exercise, it rarely serves as an authentic communication from a writer to a reader. In contrast, the process-based pedagogy that emerged in the 1960s and 1970s emphasized authenticity, deriving its approach from reflection on what real writers do when writing for real audiences and purposes. In the past four decades, composition researchers have explored all facets of the act of writing and explained many of its complexities. Their research has not produced consensus on every aspect of writing instruction, but this much is clear: students learn to write by writing—on a regular basis—on their own topics and viewpoints, for audiences and purposes they understand, to inquire into problems they care about, by exploring and planning and drafting and revising, in a variety of modes and styles.

Many studies of the composing process have influenced my thinking over the years, and I would like to mention a few that I have returned to again and again for inspiration and guidance. Among them is the work of James Britton, who authored and coauthored numerous books and articles on language, learning, and schooling. His essay "Writing to Learn and Learning to Write" is especially valuable for anyone engaged in designing a classroom writing program.

Britton distinguishes three kinds of language: *expressive, transactional,* and *poetic* (see Figure 2.1). Expressive language is "language close to the self" (96), and expressive writing is "primarily written-down speech," which makes it important "because in it, we make sure the writer stays in the writing and doesn't disappear" (97). Transactional language, in contrast, makes more explicit references to the outside world to enable the individual to *participate* in events. "Whenever we talk or write or read for some functional purpose—to get things done, to make things happen—we are using 'language in the role of participant'" (103), or transactional language. Poetic language is also distanced from the self, but its purpose is to *interpret* events, to cast

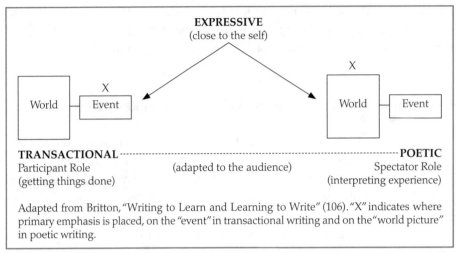

Adapted from Britton, "Writing to Learn and Learning to Write" (106). "X" indicates where primary emphasis is placed, on the "event" in transactional writing and on the "world picture" in poetic writing.

Figure 2.1. James Britton's delineation of language functions.

the individual in the role of spectator concerned about the total world picture. "We can take up the role of spectator of our own past experiences and . . . other people's experiences, real or unreal" (104). Poetic writing (which is not limited to poetry) is not designed to make things happen; rather, its language is an end in itself—an artifact, a work of art.

Paradoxically, in a subject devoted in large part to studying poetic language, students have too few opportunities to develop their own. Writing tasks in English, as in other classes, are more often than not transactional, where what's "getting done" is the student trying to convince the teacher that he or she has "learned the material"—what Britton would call a "dummy run," not a real communication. Transactional writing is important, but it should not dominate.

> Everyone wants children to learn language to get things done, you know—even politicians and economists. If we as English teachers do not foster the kind of language which represents a concern for the total world-picture, the total context into which every new experience that comes to a child—a man—has to be fitted, then I don't know who will. (109)

Britton argues for balance in students' development as writers. "Their explorations of the outer world demand the transactional; their explorations of the inner world demand the poetic, and the roots of it all remain in the expressive" (110).

Another key figure in the development of contemporary writing pedagogy is James Moffett, whose *Teaching the Universe of Discourse* was a seminal text in the writing process movement. In the chapter "Learning to Write by Writing," he argues that people learn primarily by feedback and response, so these should be the foundation of the writing program. Ideally,

> a student would write because he was intent on saying something for real reasons of his own and because he wanted to get certain effects on a definite audience. He would write only authentic kinds of discourse such as exist outside of school. A maximum amount of feedback would be provided him in the form of audience response. That is, his writing would be read and discussed by this audience, who would also be the coaches. (193)

The most important audience, in Moffett's view, is the student's peers, however inexperienced or uninformed they might be. "It is much easier for peers than for the teacher to be candid and thus to give an authentic response, because the teacher, usually aware of his special significance, is afraid of wounding his students" (194). Peers respond to each other on their own terms, "whereas the teacher is more likely to focus too soon on technique."

In Moffett's action-response model, learning to write is a process of trial and error. The teacher's role is "to propose meaningful trials (assignments) in a meaningful order" and to arrange for genuine feedback, but not to protect the student from making mistakes: "avoiding error is an inferior learning strategy to capitalizing on error" (199). For this reason, Moffett opposes using textbooks and writing exercises, which disrupt the natural learning process by preteaching solutions and offering unsolicited (and thus unhelpful) advice. Most writing problems arise not from a student's "ignorance of common-sense requirements" but from egocentricity, the writer's assumption that the reader shares his or her point of view. "What [the student] needs is not rules but awareness" (202), Moffett contends. Awareness grows as the writer listens to feedback from peers and the teacher helps to clarify the questions that they have raised. This feedback should come *during* the writing, not just *afterward* (200), and should lead to real revision. Papers should be collected to evaluate growth but not graded individually (198).

Feedback and evaluation are also key concerns of Peter Elbow, a leading thinker in composition studies since the 1970s, from whom I have learned a great deal about writing and the teaching of writing through publications and personal contact. Elbow's advocacy of freewriting, or "uncensored, generative writing" as a means to enhancing creativity, is well known (see, for example, "Teaching Two Kinds of Thinking by Teaching Writing"), but he has also contributed many provocative strategies for designing classroom writing programs. One compelling approach is to establish "evaluation-free zones," including ten-minute, nonstop freewrites composed in class; unrevised, unevaluated sketches or "quickwrites" assigned for homework; and even multiweek course "jump starts" with only evaluation-free activities ("Ranking, Evaluating, and Liking" 197–198). Frequent opportunities to engage in such low-stakes writing, Elbow argues, result in students' "investing and risking more, writing more fluently, and using livelier, more interesting voices," preparing them to move on "to more careful and revised writing tasks that involve more intellectual pushing" (199).

The goal of low-stakes assignments is "to get students to think, learn, and understand the course material" (Elbow, "High Stakes and Low Stakes" 351). Low-stakes writing frees them to explore new concepts in comfortable, informal language, without fear of judgment. These pieces also give the teacher a window into students' thinking without requiring huge outlays of time for evaluating and grading. Most important, perhaps, frequent low-stakes writing helps students lay a foundation for developing high-stakes pieces that require them to articulate clearly what they have learned. We all want students to reach the top of the writing pyramid—to produce polished essays—but they can't do so without first building a solid base through experimentation.

Considerations of *purpose, audience*, and *stakes* in the writing curriculum all lead eventually to the question of *genre*: what, ultimately, will students write in English class? Most teachers are accustomed to thinking of genres as static forms such as the comparison-contrast essay or the haiku. But since the 1980s, composition theorists have completely transformed the concept of genre. As Amy J. Devitt, who has published numerous studies of genre, explains, understanding the new conception requires "releasing old notions of genre as form and text type and embracing new notions of genre as dynamic patterning of human experience, as one of the concepts that enable us to construct our writing world" (573). Genres are not limited to formal features, such as plot structure, meter, and level of diction, but also entail "purposes, participants, and themes" (575–576); they are rhetorical *actions* that respond to but also *construct* recurrent situations. Think of the five-paragraph essay. Implicit in this school-specific genre are not only an introduction-body-conclusion format and a formal writing style but also a deductive pattern of reasoning, a limited range of topics, and a hierarchical relationship between writer and reader.

Genre theory presents a variety of important implications for the writing curriculum. One is that excessive focus on form is bound to constrict the content of students' writing, narrowing its purpose to "filling the container." One September when I asked my new ninth graders what they knew about essay writing, several students brought up the five-paragraph structure they had learned the previous year. After thinking this over for a minute, another student asked earnestly, "What if I have *four* major points instead of three? Should I get rid of one?" *Oh, dear*, I thought. The same problem can occur with "creative" writing, too, such as when composing a poem becomes an exercise in completing a template provided by the teacher. Some explicit teaching of traditional genres is certainly justifiable—a working knowledge of these forms is academic capital essential for school success. But embracing a dynamic view of genre can empower students to establish their own individual purposes within a tradition (as many modern sonnet writers have done, for example). An active conception of genre can also encourage students to think more intentionally about revision. Genre provides "at least part of the writer's notion of ideal text," Devitt states. "In revising, a writer may check the situation and forms of the evolving text against those of the chosen genre" (582), looking for any mismatches.

Perhaps the most promising application of the new thinking about genre is the notion that genres can be stretched and combined in ways that can transfigure the most mundane assignments—even the research paper. The multigenre project, popularized by Tom Romano and embraced by many other English teachers, enables students to develop their topics by mixing genres as diverse as reviews and recipes. Multigenre writing works, writes Nancy Mack in the "Multigenre Teaching" issue of *English Journal* (November 2002), "because students [are] able to use this assignment to write artfully and skillfully about things that matter in their lives" (98).

Delving into some of the now-numerous studies of the composing process and the many pedagogical strategies they have engendered has been inspiring to me— but also overwhelming at times. There are so many factors to keep in mind, it's easy to lose track of important ideas and hard to integrate the best teaching strategies into a practical approach. Several years ago, needing to sort out my beliefs about writing and to focus my efforts with students, I developed a guide for designing a classroom writing program that draws on key concepts from Britton, Moffett, Elbow, and Devitt, as well as on state standards and my own passions and priorities (see Figure 2.2). My goal was to develop a system that incorporated the best practices in composition. I have used this table as a planning tool for all kinds of classes, and I have shared it in workshops with other teachers, who have helped me to refine its contents. Its logic is simple: If students are to become confident, versatile, effective writers, they need a variety of opportunities to practice their craft in a safe, supportive, authentic environment. At the same time, the teacher needs a management strategy that is realistic, flexible, and efficient. The steps I took to create this table still guide my thinking whenever I map out a course or unit.

Integrating Key Composition Theories

I chose the grid format for my writing program model because at the time I developed it, I wanted to accomplish two goals: to provide more frequent opportunities for low-stakes writing, as suggested by Elbow, and to offer a richer blend of modes in my writing assignments, as recommended by Britton. I had embraced these ideas

Modes of Writing	"Low-Stakes" Genres	"Medium-Stakes" Genres	"High-Stakes" Genres
Transactional Writing (writing that conveys information or arguments or conducts "business")	Writing-to-learn activities Note taking Discussion starters Study questions	Analytical essays News articles Open-response/essay tests Business letters	Research projects/papers Formal speeches/presentations Standardized local/state tests School or class publications
Expressive/Poetic Writing (writing that explores the writer's ideas and feelings or that interprets experience for artistic purposes)	Journal entries Freewrites Personal responses to literature Voice exercises on characters Creative writing experiments	Progress reflections Personal experience essays Friendly letters/emails Additions to literary works Poems/short stories/plays	Portfolio self-assessments "Published" books Media productions Multigenre projects Performances of original works
Audience (who reads the writing and for what purposes)	Self (for learning and exploring) and/or peers and teacher (for sharing only)	Peers (for sharing and feedback) and/or teacher (for feedback and assessment)	Peers/larger audience (for presentation and feedback) and/or teacher (for evaluation)
Characteristics (level of polish, amount of revision, type of evaluation)	Informal, exploratory, tentative, unrevised, ungraded (except possibly in totality)	Semiformal, organized, revised (but subject to further revision), graded (in folder?)	Formal and polished, product of considerable revision or preparation, graded/scored
Frequency	Daily or several times per week	Weekly or biweekly	Long-term

Figure 2.2. Creating a balanced writing program in any class.

and pursued them in a variety of ways for many years but had never really developed a coherent system.

I started by focusing on stakes (in the columns of the grid) and soon decided that I wasn't comfortable with just "low" and "high" as levels. It had been my practice for some time not to grade individual papers (I'll explain why and how in Chapter 4), and I always gave students opportunities to revise their work, so I concluded that most of my assignments were "medium" stakes—they "counted" as assessments, but not too heavily, at least not individually. My objective was to add more items to the low-stakes column, but in the process of completing the table I realized that I needed to give more thought to high-stakes writing as well.

Next I turned to modes of writing (in the rows). I knew that most school assignments fit Britton's description of "transactional" writing, and appropriately so. But my aim was to create a better balance in my classes between the transactional assignments (mostly analytical essays) and other kinds of writing—the "expressive" and "poetic" modes. The two "modes" rows and three "stakes" columns in the table created six cells (e.g., "low-stakes transactional" and "high-stakes expressive/poetic"), and I proceeded to list all of my current practices in the appropriate spots. Some boxes were full, and some were nearly empty. I knew what I needed to work on.

Contemplating changes in my writing program led me back to other key concepts in composition theory, such as Moffett's insistence on the importance of authentic peer feedback. So I added a row below the grid for audience, just to make sure that my planning always included provisions for students to write for their peers and other "real" readers, not just for me, the teacher. Other concerns arose as well. How and how often would I incorporate all of this writing into my course calendar? What were my expectations for the various types and levels? How and when would I evaluate students' work? I added more lines to my table to address these important questions. Later, I pondered the implications of genre theory for the classroom writing program. I'll explore these points in more detail later.

Your turn. In Figure 2.2 I have listed, according to their stakes and types, some examples of writing tasks that I frequently assign (though I certainly don't use all of them in every course). I have developed these lists over time, often by borrowing ideas from colleagues and presenters. Figure 2.3 includes a blank grid that you can use to take stock of your own writing program. Concentrate on the "current practices" boxes for now. In each one, list the assignments or tasks that you ask students to do in your classes. Some will probably be the same as mine, but I'm sure you will have others that I have not included. When you have finished, reflect on what this worksheet tells you. What are the strengths of your writing program? Where are the gaps? Are you concentrating on only one type of writing? Do you provide enough low-stakes practice to ensure success on high-stakes assessments? What other patterns do you see?

Linking Stakes with Audience

To clarify further the purposes of the writing program grid, let's look at each dimension separately, starting with the horizontal one, which provides for a variety of stakes.

As noted earlier, when I created the table I was looking for ways to increase the frequency of writing in my classes. I believed that the discipline of writing every day would not only make my students more fluent writers but also enable them to capitalize on the power of writing as a learning tool. But I was already overwhelmed by the sheer volume of writing that students were producing. How could I have them

Modes of Writing	"Low-Stakes" Genres	"Medium-Stakes" Genres	"High-Stakes" Genres
Transactional Writing (writing that conveys information or arguments or conducts "business")	Current practices:	Current practices:	Current practices:
	Future possibilities:	Future possibilities:	Future possibilities:
Expressive/Poetic Writing (writing that explores the writer's ideas and feelings or that interprets experience for artistic purposes)	Current practices:	Current practices:	Current practices:
	Future possibilities:	Future possibilities:	Future possibilities:

Figure 2.3. Writing program worksheet.

write every day without further burdening myself? I also wanted to act on my belief that students should write for audiences other than the teacher, for authentic purposes, and to publish their work. I had included projects of this kind in my courses from time to time, but never systematically because they were so time-consuming. How could I ensure that all of my students would have genuine opportunities to "write for real"?

I worked out solutions to these problems by connecting stakes to *audience*. What makes a study question or a journal entry or a freewrite *low stakes*, besides the fact that it's not graded? I think it's who reads it. Low-stakes writing is mainly for the writer and for trusted peers. It may be shared with the teacher and even serve as a formative assessment (see Chapter 4), but often the teacher doesn't read this writing at all. Low-stakes writing is typically exploratory and expressive, close to the self. To be useful, it has to feel safe.

There are so many good uses for low-stakes writing. Having students write their way into a class is a great way to get them focused and ready to engage in the day's lesson. An open-ended prompt that invites personal response—or just an open invitation to write freely—can help students pack away whatever they brought in the door and orient themselves to the work at hand. One of my favorite strategies for getting students thinking about an assigned reading (this is a technique I learned in a National Writing Project workshop) is to ask them to "take a line for a walk": to choose an evocative quotation and comment on it. When students engage in this kind of activity, they reflect on the text and are thus better prepared to participate in a rich discussion. The discussion can even be conducted in writing: in a process called "inkshedding," which I learned from Peter Elbow, students pass their freewrites around in a circle, with each person adding to or commenting on what already has been written (see Hunt for the origins of this procedure). The end of class is another good opportunity to use low-stakes writing as a tool for processing the day's learning. I may give a specific prompt or just an opportunity for reflection. Sometimes I ask students to hand in this writing as a "ticket to leave" (another technique I learned from a workshop). A quick review of these informal responses lets me know how well students comprehended the lesson and what, if anything, I need to reteach.

Low-stakes activities also work well for creative writing, especially when students are reluctant to try something new. For example, when I teach the sonnet to ninth graders during our Shakespeare unit, I like to have them try writing one or two poems of their own. What better way to develop an understanding of the genre? But they are (understandably) intimidated by the prospect of writing in iambic pentameter and a set rhyme. So, one day in class we undertake the "sonnet challenge." I draw fourteen lines on the board and ask students to call out random words (the more random, the better) for the ends of the lines to create an ABABCDCDEF EFGG rhyme scheme. They copy the words on a worksheet. Then, while I try to construct a sonnet in front of them, they try to create their own at their seats in a friendly competition. The results are never great art, but because the students have had some fun with the sonnet form in a low-stakes, social environment, they are much more willing to take on the challenge of writing a sonnet for real.

Other teachers often ask me whether students will be motivated to do low-stakes writing if it's not graded, and the simple answer is *yes*. I used to wonder about this myself, but I've found that once they understand that this kind of writing is safe and serves their own purposes, they will engage in it willingly and even ask for more. If you want to give "credit" for low-stakes writing, you can include it (in totality) in periodic notebook checks or class participation evaluations. Occasionally I ask students to pick out one or two pieces of notebook writing that they would like me to read and respond to. But I *never* evaluate these pieces individually.

Medium-stakes assignments in my courses are the weekly or biweekly writing tasks typically associated with English class: essays on literature or personal experience, original stories and poems, letters and newspaper articles—assignments that I expect students to revise thoughtfully and to submit well polished. These are assignments that "count." For me these are "medium" stakes because although I do *count* them, I don't *grade* them, at least not separately. Instead I have students collect them in a folder and eventually choose one out of three or four for further revision; I then give a cumulative grade (see Chapter 4). The audience for these pieces is also medium stakes: this kind of writing is not just for the writer, but it's not for intense public scrutiny, either. I try to ensure that students' medium-stakes writing receives a lot of supportive response from peers as well as from me (more on this in Chapter 5).

The *high-stakes* tasks that I assign at least once or twice each term are not just the ones that "count" the most but the ones that have the most public and authentic audiences. These assignments include formal speeches to which parents and friends are invited, major features or investigative reports for the school newspaper, mixed-media productions and Internet sites, and class publications resulting from long-term reading and writing projects. An example of the latter is the immigrant interview assignment I use in American Literature and Society. While students are studying novels, stories, memoirs, and poems written by immigrants, I ask each of them to interview someone in the school or community (possibly a family member) who immigrated to the United States and write a profile like the one in Figure 2.4. After these profiles are revised and polished by the writers, they are carefully proofread and laid out into a booklet with desktop publishing software by a student editorial board, which is also responsible for designing a cover. The project culminates in a publication celebration, including distribution of copies for each author and interviewee and readings from the text. In this and other high-stakes assignments, I insist on perfection (or something close), and the promise of publication—of "writing for real"—makes most students willing to strive for it.

I also classify as high stakes the course-end portfolio that my department requires of all students (and weights as 10 percent of the final grade). The primary audiences for this work are the student and the teacher, though sometimes parents, special education liaisons, or others are included. But because students are expected to pull together and *reflect* on everything they have learned and achieved during the term in the portfolio, it takes on a greater significance than even a similarly weighted final exam. A detailed discussion of portfolios is included in Chapter 4.

Your turn. Return to Figure 2.3 and think about how you use low-, medium-, and high-stakes writing tasks in your classes. Are some parts of the table scanty? What types of writing might you add to vary the stakes? List these under "future possibilities." For example, if most of the writing you assign is *graded* and *read only by you*, consider introducing low-stakes assignments that would spur fluency, promote critical thinking, and generate peer interaction (without adding to

---

Too Big, Too Many, and Too Fast: The Story of a Burundian Political Refugee
(Author's name withheld by request)

Outside the hotel on his first morning in the United States he saw a homeless man, not an uncommon sight in New York City. The homeless man looked up at Léonce and asked if he could spare some change for food. This was, perhaps, the biggest shock of Léonce Ndikumana's life. It wasn't that he had never seen a homeless person before, for he had seen many in Burundi. It wasn't that he didn't expect to see a poor person in America, the "land of prosperity." Rather, it was that this man was a *white* man, and he was begging to a black man. In Burundi, all of the Caucasians Léonce encountered were successful, powerful experts. "Priests, expatriates, people from the ministry of agriculture, Belgian economists, teachers, headmasters, and coaches, they were all sent to Burundi to do something and were treated with the utmost respect. In this homeless white man, I saw for the first time the world in which I would be living. I saw America," he said.

"Too big, too many, and too fast. Huge skyscrapers, runners, cars, hurried English which I had to struggle to understand, and a general chaos met me when I first arrived in the United Sates, and left me completely overwhelmed," says Léonce. At the end of the day, all he felt like doing was sitting in his room, staring blankly at the wall and thinking about nothing. And still, he could hear the English words and the honking cars and the buzzing of thousands upon thousands of engines.

Given a scholarship from the African-American Institute to get his PhD in economics in the U.S., Léonce arrived in New York on August 6, 1990, from Burundi, a country in central Africa. He intended to remain in the U.S. for only four years. Having left his wife and two kids behind, he was extremely lonely at first. He was forced to cook for the first time in his life, was taken aback by the new social conventions he encountered (Americans are much less affectionate), and was struggling to mix and reconcile American culture's high demands on time with the cultural expectations that he had brought with him from Burundi. What hit him most was the small amount of social interaction practiced by Americans in comparison to what he was used to in Africa. "Workdays in Burundi ended when they ended. People did not work after they went home. I would go over to a friend's house, and then we would go to another friend's house, and by the end of the night there would be a huge group of us, laughing and having fun. Here, I go home, eat dinner, and then drive my kids around or do work for the rest of the night."

In October 1993, a civil war broke out in Burundi. In disagreement with the government, Léonce and his family were in great danger in Burundi. His wife and kids joined him, and they were granted political asylum in the U.S. He is still amazed by the way Americans freely criticize their government on the radio or on television. In Burundi, criticizing the government often led to imprisonment. As political refugees, he and his family were unable to return to Burundi until the political situation calmed down many years later. Most immigrants are able to find comfort in the fact that they can go home, whereas political refugees know they can't. Léonce could not go home and look after his mother or siblings; he could only talk to them on the phone. Until he returned to Burundi in August 2005, he had met only four of his older brother's nine children. He had only met three out of the eight of his older sister's children and knew none of those of his younger sister, who was 16 when he left.

"You may be wondering if people ever adjust," says Léonce. "Not fully. Even after fifteen years, there are cultural things which I keep doing differently and will probably do differently for the rest of my life. I can already see the difference in my kids. They like hot dogs and fruit rollups, things which my wife and I would never touch. When they grow up, it will be interesting to see if, culturally, they are more American than Burundian. To a certain extent, I will always feel like a stranger. Amherst is physically my home, but mentally, Burundi will always be my home. If Amherst ever mentally becomes my home, it will not be for a long while."

Figure 2.4. Immigrant profile from class publication.

your paper load). On the other hand, if you rarely include projects that are high-stakes in terms of *audience*—writing for publication beyond the class and other authentic purposes—imagine some new ones that would engage your students and extend your curriculum.

Rethinking Modes and Genres

Now let's consider the vertical dimension of the writing program grid, which represents my goal of diversifying the modes of expression sanctioned and encouraged in my classes. I wanted to incorporate more expressive and poetic writing in my assignments to develop students' awareness of genres and to expand their repertoire of composing skills.

There are plenty of appropriate ways to include expressive writing in English courses. In addition to journals and other low-stakes genres, many teachers assign various kinds of autobiographical pieces in conjunction with "personal experience" literature. For example, reading Sandra Cisneros's *The House on Mango Street* and studying its form provides an opportune moment for students to learn to write vignettes about people and places in their communities. Personal writing of this kind can even become high stakes if published or adapted for performance as in National Public Radio's popular *This I Believe* essay series, a project devoted to engaging people in discussing their core values (see *This I Believe in the Classroom*).

The poetic mode, which includes all forms of imaginative expression, tends to be the most neglected in school assignments. It has always struck me as odd that we English teachers, who devote so much attention to appreciation and study of fiction, poetry, and drama, provide remarkably few opportunities for students to try their hands at these forms. Imagine a culinary arts class with no cooking. Isn't a literature course without imaginative writing just as absurd? This kind of writing is valuable in its own right, but it is also a powerful tool for interpreting texts. When we ask students to intervene in a literary work (by retelling a story from another viewpoint or adding a "missing" scene, for instance) or to mimic the style of a particular writer or genre (as in the assignment in Figure 2.5), we engage them in a process of close reading that goes deeper in some respects than the work they do for an analytical essay. I'm not knocking essays—the skills they foster are important, and I assign them regularly—but the kind of analysis that goes on when students create their own literary works is just as valid and deserves attention.

For example, reading the Bible as literature presents significant challenges for students: unfamiliar contexts, lack of explanatory detail. Some of the best "readings" I receive from students in my Bible and Related Literature course are fictional adap-

Louise Erdrich's novel *Tracks* employs techniques common to much contemporary literature: **multiple narrators** and **magical realism**. These techniques challenge the reader to sort out the story through shifting perspectives and a blending of real and surreal events.

Your assignment will be to **try one (or both) of these techniques** in telling a story of your own. You could continue the story line of *Tracks* (or perhaps *Huckleberry Finn* or the slave narrative you read) **or** you could tell a story of your own—based on your own experience or completely made up. Since the piece will be due on Halloween, you might want to try something scary! The important task will be to try to capture the essence of the technique(s) you choose:

- **Multiple Narrators:** Choose characters that will have different perceptions and interpretations of the events. Perhaps they will come from different backgrounds or have different ages.
- **Magical Realism:** Move back and forth between "real" (i.e., plausible) occurrences and those that seem impossible in everyday circumstances. The trick is to make the "unreal" events connect seamlessly with the "real" ones—to make them *seem* possible.

Your finished story should be two to four pages long (12-point, double spaced). If you wish, you can write it as a poem (like Frost's longer ones). The story will be completed in three stages:

- **Step 1 (due Monday, October 30):** Decide which technique you want to use and brainstorm several topics. Write one or two pages of rough draft and bring it to class for feedback and additional drafting.
- **Step 2 (due Tuesday, October 31):** Complete the story and make a revised "final" copy. Be sure that the progression of events and character development are logical.
- **Step 3 (in November, date to be announced):** After getting peer response and teacher comments, polish your story further and make a third draft for your writing folder.

I hope you have some fun with this! The stories should be interesting to share.

Figure 2.5. American Literature and Nature creative writing assignment.

tations of the original texts. In one memorable piece, a self-described "geek" transformed the God of Genesis 1–2 into a master computer programmer, writing and editing lines of code to create the world. In another extraordinary submission, a student wrote a first-person account of the destruction of Sodom from the viewpoint of Lot's wife, whom she saw as a bewildered and disempowered woman suddenly wrenched away from all she had ever known and ultimately unable to resist looking back in longing. Both of these creative responses provided ample evidence that the students "got" the essential themes of the stories they were analyzing. Similarly, the students studying Louise Erdrich's *Tracks* who completed the assignment in Figure 2.5 were forced to grapple with the possibilities and challenges of multiple narration and magical realism as they created stories using these techniques. In the process of bending the genres to their own purposes, they came to understand and appreciate them. One young man was so intrigued by the problem that he continued revising his piece for a year and eventually used it in a college application.

I have been arguing for greater use of expressive and poetic writing, but even within the transactional mode of writing, there are many possibilities for authentic assignments that break the routine of read-the-book-then-write-the-essay. I mentioned earlier a project that my students have found engaging—an immigrant profile—but that is just the start. Writing persuasive business letters to companies or public officials or articles for the school newspaper on subjects of actual concern to students teaches valuable lessons about audience and purpose, accuracy and clarity. If you don't have a school paper, consider producing one as a class project. The dreaded research paper can also be transformed into an authentic project if the work focuses on real issues and is presented to real audiences. The final outcome of a class research project doesn't have to be a stack of dry reports read only by the teacher; it can just as easily be a series of pamphlets distributed to other students, an informational PowerPoint presented at a public event, a website posted on the Internet, or any number of other products.

And what about the formal analytical essay? Like it or not, it is here to stay in the high school curriculum, and it should be. But it need not be a fossilized form that students approach with fear and loathing. If the essay is approached as a living genre, adaptable to students' styles and purposes, writing one can be a *creative* challenge (see, for example, Deborah Dean's *English Journal* article on mixing genres in the five-paragraph theme). Chapters 5 and 6 of this volume include some specific recommendations for teaching the analytical essay with gusto.

Speaking of mixing genres, the multigenre project is the most stimulating approach I know of to help students learn—and break—genre conventions. At the suggestion of my colleague Malia Hwang-Carlos, I added a multigenre autobiography to my ninth-grade course as the culminating assignment (in lieu of a final exam). The students spend days and days looking back on their lives (and ahead as well), drafting memory pieces and descriptions, selecting from a wide range of genres (including several not usually associated with schoolwork, such as advertisements and obituaries), and producing beautiful booklets representing who they have been, are, and hope to be. The contents speak of both pleasure and pain. One student writes of his passion for hip-hop dancing; another reflects on her exclusion from the clique of popular girls. On the last day of class, we celebrate the completion of the projects with readings from the students' work. In a course devoted in large measure to learning how authors use and modify genres (epic, drama, sonnet, memoir, etc.), this project seems like a fitting way to show students that they, as members of the circle of writers, have the same kind of artistic control.

Your turn. Return one more time to Figure 2.3 to look for gaps in modes of writing. If you currently assign low-stakes writing for *expressive* purposes only—such as starting each class with private freewriting—think about the possibilities for using *transactional* low-stakes writing that would help you teach your content. Or if the reverse is true—if all of the low-stakes writing your students do consists of note taking and answering questions—consider how you could open things

---

up. What about graded writing assignments? Do you focus on analytical essays? What other kinds of writing (expressive, poetic, transactional, multigenre) could you assign that would serve as valid assessments? Ideally, when you finish revising your grid, you will have viable choices in all six boxes—and thus be prepared to plan a varied writing program in any course.

Planning with Writing

Putting the focus on student writing helps with course planning. Consistent with the principles of "backwards design" outlined in Chapter 1, developing writing assignments early in the planning process is a good way to determine acceptable evidence of students' achieving the desired results of the course. When I start planning a course, I use my writing grid to help me decide what assessments to include. First, I think about high-stakes work: the course portfolio and at least one other project that includes publication or performance. For example, in the Bible and Related Literature course, one of the high-stakes assignments is a research project and teaching presentation on a book of the Bible not read by the class as a whole. Next I develop a regular schedule of medium-stakes assignments in a variety of modes. In the Bible course, that means students write expressive, analytical, and creative papers (with a wide choice of topics) in the first half and again in the second half. Later, as I map out units and individual lessons, I decide what kinds of low-stakes writing to incorporate (see Figure 2.6).

Doing this planning deliberately helps me to stay true to my desire to provide a rich, authentic, varied writing program in which students learn to write by writing to learn. Working out my writing goals and assessments in advance also helps me to keep my own workload manageable. Building in time to read and respond to student work has to be part of the process.

High Stakes	Medium Stakes	Low Stakes
Bible reference project (with analytical annotations)	Personal response papers (2)	Notebook prompts
	Analytical essays (2)	Open-ended response
Independent research project on selected book of the Bible (with PowerPoint presentation)	Creative pieces (2)	Voice exercises
Course portfolio	Open-response quizzes/tests and final exam (4)	Carousel brainstorms and other group work

Figure 2.6. Writing plan for Bible and Related Literature.

> **Your turn.** Refer back to the plans you developed in Chapter 1: the course out-line, the "big picture" planning sheet, and the unit plans. Rework a set of course plans with writing in mind, using your completed grid from Figure 2.3 as a guide. Does the course outline specify the kinds of writing you will assign? How much it will "count"? Are the course and unit plans built around writing assessments that constitute "acceptable evidence" of whether students have met course goals? Have you planned an appropriate mix of stakes, audiences, modes, and genres?

One Step at a Time

This chapter has thrown a lot of ideas at you, and it may take you a while to sort through them. It certainly took me a long time to figure out how to develop a pro-gram that was both authentic for students and manageable for me. Don't try to change everything at once. Focus on one dimension of writing at a time, and, if pos-sible, get a few colleagues to work with you. Two important factors to keep in mind are *frequency* and *variety*. Students need lots of opportunities to write, using writing to learn as well as to demonstrate learning, sometimes within the safety of "evalua-tion-free zones." They also need chances to exercise all of their writing muscles, in assignments that call for passion and creativity as well as analytical skills. This writ-ing should occur in the context of a supportive *process*. More on that in Chapter 5.

Recommended Reading

Dean, Deborah. *Genre Theory: Teaching, Writing, and Being.* Urbana, IL: NCTE, 2008. Print.
>   This Theory and Research Into Practice book provides a thorough explanation of cur-rent genre theory and its implications for teaching along with helpful suggestions for classroom activities.

Elbow, Peter. *Everyone Can Write: Essays toward a Hopeful Theory of Writing and Teaching Writing.* New York: Oxford UP, 2000. Print.
>   The title says it all. In this provocative collection of essays on topics ranging from free-writing to grading, Elbow presents ideas and strategies to make success and satisfaction in writing accessible to all.

National Writing Project and Carl Nagin. *Because Writing Matters: Improving Student Writing in Our Schools.* San Francisco: Jossey-Bass, 2003. Print.
>   This book surveys key research on writing and identifies best practices, distinguishing *teaching* writing from merely *assigning* it.

Romano, Tom. *Clearing the Way: Working with Teenage Writers*. Portsmouth, NH: Heinemann, 1987. Print.

> Romano emphasizes teaching compassionately and giving students room to "cut loose with language" (ix). Topics include writing to learn and writing "amid" literature.

Spandel, Vicki. *The 9 Rights of Every Writer: A Guide for Teachers*. Portsmouth, NH: Heinemann, 2005. Print.

> In nine brief chapters, Spandel outlines a "bill of rights" for student writers that could serve as the guiding principles of a writing curriculum in any course or program.

3

Developing a Literature Curriculum

I've always enjoyed reading, and when it occurred to me during my senior year of high school that I could actually make a career of studying and teaching literature, my future as an English major was sealed. Every so often, even now, when I'm reading new titles or reviewing old favorites while planning a course, I stop and think, *I can't believe I get paid for this! Part of my job is to read stories and talk about them with students!* Sharing the riches of literature with young people is great work.

This is not to say that it's easy work. Teaching literature at the secondary level raises a host of curricular questions, starting with *what* we teach and *why* we teach it.

One of the quirks of our field is that we never get rid of anything. Biology classes learn about evolution, but they don't read Darwin's *On the Origin of Species*. In English class, though, we continue to study works by Darwin's contemporaries, and much older ones, too—and for good reasons. But we constantly add new selections and new literatures to our repertoires—also for good reasons. As a result, we (as individuals and as departments) face tough choices when we create courses and units for our classes. How do we balance tradition and innovation, consistency and diversity in the literature curriculum? How do we decide which authors and titles are appropriate and beneficial? The choices we make are political as well as pedagogical, so they are prone to controversy. No decisions we make as educators more clearly represent our values than the texts we put before our students and the ways we teach them.

Putting texts before students doesn't guarantee that they will read or appreciate them. What English teacher hasn't heard this complaint: "Why do I have to read this stuff? What good is it going to do me in life?" Although we may be tempted to dismiss such questions as adolescent whining, the students who ask them are actually probing the reasons for literature's place in the high school curriculum—so we ought to have some good answers. Why *do* we consider literature so important? What do we get out of it ourselves? What do we believe students can gain from reading great works of the past and present? And how can we organize literature instruction to facilitate those goals?

The object of this chapter is to address the problems of selection and purpose by offering strategies for developing an *intentional* literature curriculum: one that takes students on a varied and challenging interpretive journey driven by big ideas and essential questions, rather than on an aimless stroll through unrelated titles or a forced march through literary history. Whether we teach from required anthologies or prescribed lists of individual titles or book rooms full of choices, we face the challenge of arranging the study of literature to help students find relevance in great works—classic and contemporary—and to expose them to the diversity of experience they represent. This chapter presents a variety of approaches to assembling a syllabus; methods of changing the pace of literary study throughout the term; and tips for coping with the limitations imposed by textbooks, curriculum mandates, and censorship. It also makes a special plea for the teaching of poetry, the genre most often neglected in the high school curriculum.

The Pilgrim's Progress toward Intentional Literature Instruction

When I entered graduate school at the University of Massachusetts in the early 1970s, I received a handout outlining the requirements for the MA-qualifying exam in English. The test was a public, two-hour oral conducted by five professors who could ask questions about any title on the reading list: three single-spaced pages of titles and authors ranging from *Beowulf* to Baldwin, including such perennial favorites as Carlyle's *Sartor Resartus*. Needless to say, I was terrified, and I wasn't the only one. English graduate students seemed to talk about nothing else. Luckily, before I finished my program, the department decided that students who weren't going on for the PhD could opt out of the test if they took two additional courses. I jumped at the chance. (And I still haven't read *Sartor Resartus*.)

About ten years later, I was visiting the book exhibit at an English conference and noticed Heinemann's display of its African Writers and Caribbean Writers series. I had been thinking about broadening the horizons of my courses, so I figured I might get some ideas. There must have been fifty or sixty different books on the table. Looking them over, I realized, to my shame, that not only had I never read any of them, I had never even heard of most of them. I do know quite a few of those books now, and I have even taught some of them. But the list keeps growing, and I'll never get through it. Not to mention the comparable lists of titles from Asia, Latin America, and other parts of the world.

These two vignettes highlight a major challenge for any teacher of literature: there is just so darn much of it. As daunting as the MA-qualifying exam list was at the time, it wouldn't be considered comprehensive today; it consisted almost entirely of works by dead, white, British men. American literature was poorly represented, and the titles written by women and people of color could be counted on two hands. The rest of the world didn't even exist. By now most English teachers—and most textbook publishers—have embraced the idea that the literature curriculum should be multicultural and gender-balanced. Scores of previously neglected writers from the past have been resurrected, and hundreds of contemporary authors from across the globe have entered the classroom. Then, too, the term *literary text* has expanded to include films, graphic novels, and a host of other genres. If there were still an MA-qualifying exam at the University of Massachusetts, the reading list would have to be thirty pages long to even partially represent the diversity in the field of literature today. Can anyone keep up?

My answer is simple: No. I will never finish all of the books I already own, much less the myriad new ones published every year. But that doesn't stop me from constantly trying to broaden my knowledge and deepen my understanding of the world of literature, both by making more stops along the well-worn path of the traditional canon and by exploring the many enticing trails that lead away from it. And I can always use diversity as a lens for scrutinizing the content of my courses, making sure that I'm pursuing my own and my school district's multicultural goals. There's no way that I can "cover" everything that I think my students should read, but I can at least ensure that their literary experience is rich and diverse, representing the experiences of people of many backgrounds, not just those of the dominant culture. (For a full discussion of the ongoing debate over teaching canonical and noncanonical literature and the application of multicultural teaching principles in English, see Chapter 9.)

Exposure to diversity is one of my answers to the *why* of teaching literature. Even in multicultural communities, such as Amherst, students' opportunities for in-depth learning about people different from themselves are limited. Literature offers an insider's view of a foreign culture that no textbook can match and that only living abroad can exceed. Books also provide windows into the past and glimpses of how the world appears to a person of a different race, ethnicity, age, gender, or sexual orientation. Reading books builds empathy for others, and empathy usually leads to tolerance. The vicarious experience that literature presents also spurs growth in *self*-knowledge, humanizing the reader (that's why English is considered one of the humanities, I guess). I don't think it's making too great a claim to say that reading literature is not just an enjoyable pastime but also makes the world a better place.

People can and do read on their own, of course, so what is the value added by literature *instruction*? I've thought about that question quite a bit over the years. Systematic knowledge about authors and texts and genres and traditions certainly has some worth as cultural capital, and we do promote that kind of knowledge to some extent, but the main purpose of literature courses seems to be to teach *interpretation*—at least that's the main activity of literature courses. It's a worthwhile activity, too—a life skill, really. Most human endeavors, including careers and relationships, involve interpretation of documents and data, symbols and signs, mannerisms and motives. The study of literature provides invaluable opportunities to practice.

But it's in teaching interpretation that literature class sometimes goes terribly wrong, and some students learn to hate reading. Author Julius Lester explains the problem this way:

> I was fortunate throughout my education to have English teachers who didn't think that ferreting out and analyzing the symbolism in a novel or poem was what was most important. And I wonder if this is one of the reasons why fewer and fewer Americans read. In English classes they have been taught that they must understand symbolism if they are to be considered good readers. They have been taught that a novel cannot be appreciated unless its structure and characters have been critically analyzed. Students graduate from high school and college without the confidence that they can sit down and read a book. And, in the worst cases, they graduate vowing never to read a book because the experience was made so unpleasant. (31)

Ouch. I tremble at the thought that my teaching of interpretive skills might have turned any of my students into nonreaders, but I know that I have overdone it at times. It's a clue that I need to lighten up when someone complains, "Why do we have to analyze everything to death?"

The kind of interpretation that Lester is complaining about is the New Critical approach, the dominant form of literary criticism in the middle of the twentieth century and still the basis of most high school literature instruction—because it's the way that most teachers were taught. New Criticism introduced the practice of "close reading" (attention to formal elements such as images, symbols, metaphors, point of view, plot structure, meter, rhyme, etc.) of "the text itself," with no concern for the author, reader, or social context, which were all considered irrelevant (Tyson 117–119). New Critics "called their approach *objective criticism* because their focus on each text's own formal elements insured, they claimed, that each text—each object being interpreted—would itself dictate how it would be interpreted" (132; emphasis original). Thus the goal of New Critical analysis was the "single best reading" of each work. This method has given us valuable tools and procedures, including a critical vocabulary and the habit of finding evidence in the text, but it's easy to see how it turned problematic in the classroom. If each work has only one "best" interpretation, students are bound to be wrong most of the time. No wonder so many of them come to believe that literature is written in secret code, and only English teachers have been given the key.

Contemporary critical theory has departed from New Criticism in every imaginable way, from focusing on the aspects of the reading situation that the New Critics thought unimportant (author, reader, and context) to insisting that there can be no stable reading of a text, much less a "single best" one. The writing of many influential theorists is nearly impenetrable, baffling even to literature professors and graduate students, but as interest in teaching critical theory at the undergraduate and high school levels has grown, a number of readable guides have become available. My favorite is Lois Tyson's *Critical Theory Today: A User-Friendly Guide*, which not only explains all the leading theories (psychoanalytic, Marxist, feminist, New Critical, reader-response, structuralist, deconstructive, new historical, cultural, lesbian/gay/queer, postcolonial, and African American) but also demonstrates them by interpreting *The Great Gatsby* from each perspective.

Why should high school English teachers be concerned with this cascade of critical approaches? Because teaching students how to interpret literary texts from multiple perspectives (or even a few) gives them strategies for understanding the larger "texts" of their everyday lives. "Critical lenses provide students with a way of reading their world; the lenses provide a way of 'seeing' differently and analytically that can help them read the culture of school as well as popular culture" (Appleman 3). Introducing critical theories also changes the dynamics of literature instruction, moving the teacher off center stage and widening the range of possibilities for "valid" interpretations (for more on this aspect of teaching critical theory, see Chapter 6). Moreover, the multiple-lens approach dovetails nicely with student-centered writing pedagogy. As I stated in Chapter 2, I have come to believe that student writing should be at the center of the English curriculum, even in literature courses. Like my mentor Charles Moran, I once taught

> literature as "art," the work standing essentially free of the culture and the reader, an object to be contemplated and interpreted. The student was an apprentice; the teacher was the master-contemplator and master-interpreter. . . . Writing in these classes was a marginal activity, valuable only as a field in which students practiced the interpretation of literature in the form of the critical essay. (44)

Broadening the scope of writing in my classes and using it as a learning tool along with critical lenses has democratized response to literature, making even challenging texts more accessible to readers of diverse abilities. Students may not be experts on theory, but they are experts on their own multifaceted lives, and writing helps them to connect their reading and their experience and perhaps to understand the world a little better. What Moran observes about the transformation of his teaching goes for me, too: "We turn to literature for its energy, its forms, its history, but at the center of the class is our own writing. As an English teacher, this is the kind of classroom, whether its title be writing or literature, that I try to establish. This is English at its best" (46).

"English at its best" occurs only when students are engaged in the work. In an increasingly visual, technological world, building enthusiasm for books can be a real challenge, especially with adolescent boys who don't see literacy as central to their future lives. Ironically, while the literary contributions of women are still underrepresented in the English curriculum, there is growing evidence that the culture of English classes alienates many young men. Michael W. Smith and Jeffrey D. Wilhelm explore this problem extensively in their landmark study, *"Reading Don't Fix No Chevys": Literacy in the Lives of Young Men*. Among their findings: to engage successfully in literate activities, their subjects needed a sense of "competence, control, and challenge" (96). Don't we all. To answer these needs, Smith and Wilhelm advocate a student-centered, inquiry-based approach based in part on the theories of Lev Vygotsky: "Vygotskian instruction goes through a process of modeling (Show Me), of assistance in which expertise is gradually handed over to the student (Help Me), and then observation as the student independently uses the learned strategies in a meaningful context (Let Me)" (130). They also make several recommendations about the curriculum: balancing literature with informational texts, using shorter and more humorous texts, providing more choices; and about classroom practices: frontloading activities that activate background knowledge and build procedural knowledge before students read, making reading more social (194–200). Above all, they emphasize the importance of fulfilling an implicit "social contract" that requires teachers to get to know students personally, care about them as individuals, attend to their interests, help them learn, and demonstrate passion and commitment (99).

Smith and Wilhelm's conclusions seem wholly in line with desires I've heard expressed by many high school students and not just disaffected young men. Even the most successful often feel disconnected from their schoolwork. Our challenge as literature teachers is not only to develop a curriculum that responsibly balances classic and contemporary works, that represents the diversity of human experience, and that democratizes interpretation and response, but also to make it relevant to students' lives. A tall order, for sure—but not impossible.

Assembling a Syllabus

Contemplating new texts and teaching methods is the exciting part of developing a literature curriculum, but innovation meets reality when it comes to fitting everything you want to do and everything you need to do into the school calendar. Time is always too short, so it's essential to plan the syllabus carefully before the term begins. Better to make the hard choices in advance than on the fly. You have to build in some flexibility, too; conditions change, and you need to be able to adjust (I often write "Tentative Syllabus" on my course outlines). To help you reflect on your process of course construction, I will give some examples of the ways I have selected and sequenced readings in my classes and explain the reasoning behind these choices. I know that the degree of control teachers have over their teaching schedules varies from school to school, so some of my suggestions may apply more than others.

There are several basic principles I try to follow when designing a course, and they can be divided into external and internal imperatives. The external ones have to do with obligations outside of my classroom: being mindful of state standards, considering district mandates, and especially respecting agreements with my English colleagues. We have worked out what I think is an effective system of balancing consistency and autonomy in our department. As a group we have decided that all courses will include certain features such as portfolios and Honors or AP options, and as grade-level teams we have determined overall objectives and a few core texts for each course. These accords leave plenty of room for teacher choices of readings and the order and manner of presentation. With funding for resources perennially short, we usually have to negotiate with each other about who will use what books when.

The internal mandates that guide my process of syllabus construction reflect long-held and still-developing beliefs about teaching. One is that every course should allow for some choice of readings. Another is that students should be exposed to the full range of literary genres. We all do a great job of teaching fiction and drama, and even narrative nonfiction, but many of us seem to be afraid to teach poetry. Recognizing that fear in myself, I have made it a priority to feature poetry in every class (I'll say more on this point in a later section). Most important, I believe that courses should be built around big ideas and vital questions, the bigger and more vital the better, and that these should be discussed early and often, not to arrive at settled answers but to foster a spirit of inquiry. Controversy should be welcome. I sometimes tell my classes that our goal for the term is to seek "the meaning of life." They laugh, but they don't think this is a corny quest. Teenagers of all backgrounds and abilities are interested in philosophical, psychological, and social questions. This point was driven home to me by a twenty-year-old, in-and-out-of-jail, unwed father with limited reading skills who was placed (not by choice, I'm sure) in my Renaissance and Modern Literature class. He looked pretty glum most of the time, and he never did any homework, but his ears perked up one day when we were discussing an excerpt from *Paradise Lost*. "This reminds me of stories my grandmother used to tell me," he said, and then proceeded to offer his thoughts on women and men, good and evil, freedom of the will and original sin. I smiled at the end of the year when I saw next to his name on the list of unreturned library books *The Complete Works of John Milton*. I hope he still has it.

As I see it, there are at least three valid ways to organize a literature course: chronology, genre, and theme. Each has its advantages, and I've sometimes changed from one to another in the same course. All three approaches should probably play some role in every class.

Chronology is probably the most common method, at least in upper-level survey courses, because that's the way many anthologies are constructed. Studying works by historical era does offer rich possibilities for exploring cultural contexts and tracing philosophical or artistic trends, but there are drawbacks, too. Chances are, students don't have a fully developed narrative of history in their heads onto which they can map the course readings. Textbooks chunk selections into periods, but the divisions tend to be arbitrary and usually serve to reinforce conventional views. Then, too, the sheer number of potential authors and texts to be included in a survey course raises the danger of sacrificing deep understanding to broad but superficial coverage. The main idea in a chronological course has to be bigger than the march of time.

Teaching British literature exemplifies these challenges. To make room for more global offerings, we decided to reduce our Brit Lit course to one trimester and simultaneously changed its title to British and Irish Literature, thereby adding Celtic myths and several modern writers. The new course "covers" more than a thousand years in about twelve weeks; comprehensive treatment of the literary tradition is clearly impossible. My approach to organizing this course (aided by my colleagues Danae Marr and Ellen Reich) has been to focus on what makes British and Irish works relevant to contemporary American students. The evolution of the English language is certainly one of the big ideas, but many of the texts also explore social issues, such as oppression and class conflict that are all too current. Another key question is the influence of British and Irish ideas on American consciousness. I don't try to apportion the too-little time available equally. In my syllabus the first third of the term spans the Middle Ages through the early Renaissance. The middle third runs from the late Renaissance to the Victorian Era. That means I can devote the final third of the course to the twentieth century, including highlights of the Irish Renaissance and at least some attention to the diversity of contemporary postcolonial England.

I incorporate at least one complete work in each part of the course—*Beowulf*, a choice of *Pride and Prejudice* and *Jane Eyre*, and *Pygmalion*—but I have to rely on anthologies for most of the shorter readings. These textbooks are helpful in many ways: having a single volume that collects a wide variety of texts, plus illustrations and background material, is a real time saver. But there are also drawbacks, some of which I'll discuss later in this chapter.

Genre isn't my favorite method of organization, but I do use it in our ninth-grade course, which is functionally titled Writing and Literature. The course is divided into two parts, A and B, and to maximize book usage, some classes start with A, some B. Each term has a set of core writing expectations and a set of required readings. In most cases, the teacher has some choice: one of two Shakespeare plays, one of four novels, and so on. The overall theme for the year is "the writer as conscious artist"; the goal is that students develop an understanding of the author's craft, both as readers and as writers. To ensure that I give writing all of the attention it deserves, I develop my A term syllabus around *writing assignment genres*, using the readings as models and as springboards for thought. For example, the course sometimes follows the sequence listed in Figure 3.1. The primary focus in the A term is the students' writing, but a "conversation" develops among the literary works on family relationships. In the B term, I organize the readings according to *literary genres*, often as outlined in Figure 3.1. This term's syllabus is usually supplemented by several films (*Smoke Signals, Shakespeare in Love,* and *Life Is Beautiful*) and poetry (Native American, sonnets, Holocaust). Exploring the conventions and possibilities of the various forms of literary expression is the focus of many discussions as well as analytical and creative papers. And the conversation on families among the texts continues.

I've found organization by *theme* to be effective—as long as I don't try to push the theme too hard. Our tenth-grade program includes a wonderful course called Literature as Social Criticism. The concept is great, but it's easy to fall into the pattern of asking, "Okay, kids, what kind of social criticism do we have in this book?" That's a sure way to kill any enthusiasm for the readings. Better to let the connections evolve naturally from discussion and reflection.

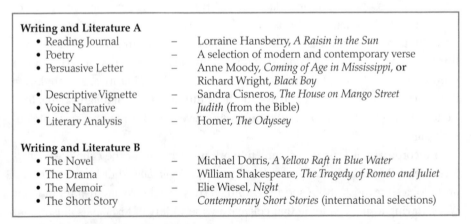

Writing and Literature A
- Reading Journal — Lorraine Hansberry, *A Raisin in the Sun*
- Poetry — A selection of modern and contemporary verse
- Persuasive Letter — Anne Moody, *Coming of Age in Mississippi,* **or** Richard Wright, *Black Boy*
- Descriptive Vignette — Sandra Cisneros, *The House on Mango Street*
- Voice Narrative — *Judith* (from the Bible)
- Literary Analysis — Homer, *The Odyssey*

Writing and Literature B
- The Novel — Michael Dorris, *A Yellow Raft in Blue Water*
- The Drama — William Shakespeare, *The Tragedy of Romeo and Juliet*
- The Memoir — Elie Wiesel, *Night*
- The Short Story — *Contemporary Short Stories* (international selections)

Figure 3.1. Sample ninth-grade syllabus.

I've used the thematic approach most often in American literature. The first course I created myself was called Toward a Definition of America. The guidance office hated that title because it wouldn't fit neatly on the transcript, but it did capture the essential question of the course. I even asked each student to write his or her "definition of America" for the final exam. Over the years the department has revised the general American literature offerings many times, sometimes veering toward chronological surveys but recently settling on two thematic courses: American Literature and Nature and American Literature and Society. Both provide powerful lenses for studying canonical and multicultural texts. I've related some of my thinking about the former in Chapter 1; here I will explain one of the ways I've organized the latter.

American Literature and Society typically draws a diverse crowd, so it's especially important that the course have a big idea that everyone can relate to (see syllabus, Figure 3.2). One obvious choice is the so-called "American dream," always a pervasive theme in politics and the popular media. The most persistent and problematic myth in American culture, the rags-to-riches, luck-and-pluck success story was invented by Benjamin Franklin and popularized by Horatio Alger. At one time I taught both of those authors in American Literature and Society, but I had to drop them to make room for more diversity. *The Great Gatsby* always seems like a good place to start. Its New York setting embodies the success myth, which the novel both celebrates and critiques. Racist remarks by two of the characters (Tom and Nick) provide a natural entrée to the contemporaneous Harlem Renaissance, where students experience a different New York. The city also symbolizes the promise and perils of immigration, so that's the focus of the next unit, which includes a choice of three books (discussed in literature circles) and the immigrant interview assignment explained in Chapter 2. *Avalon*, a bittersweet film about a successful immigrant family, pulls together many of the threads in the first two units.

The next three units combine the thematic and genre approaches. All of them extend the conversation on the concept of the American dream, but they also provide opportunities for performance: acting out cuttings from the plays and reciting assigned or original poems. The poetry collections, like the texts for the earlier immigration unit, represent the cultural backgrounds of significant groups of students in our school. Since much of the work of the drama and poetry units happens in class, students have a chance to get a head start on their chosen readings for the fiction unit, in which they study in small groups. This unit also moves the course outside the Northeast for a sustained period. That's important because some of our students don't know much about other parts of the country.

The culmination of the course is the final unit on Ralph Ellison's extraordinary novel *Invisible Man*. Now, before you think, *There's no way to teach that book in high school—it's hard, and it's over five hundred pages long,* let me say this: I don't assign

The "American Dream." F. Scott Fitzgerald, *The Great Gatsby*, the classic novel about the glitzy but empty lives of the rich and glamorous in the "Roaring Twenties." **Supplement:** a selection of poems from the Harlem Renaissance, which was taking place in the same time period and the same city as *The Great Gatsby*.

Immigration. One of the following: Anzia Yezierska, *Bread Givers*, a turn-of-the-century novel about the lives of Jewish immigrants on the Lower East Side; Maxine Hong Kingston, *China Men*, a collection of sketches, stories, and historical/cultural information about the experiences of several generations of Chinese immigrants; Richard Rodriguez, *Hunger of Memory*, a controversial autobiography by a second-generation Mexican American left unsatisfied with his success. **Supplement:** Barry Levinson's *Avalon*, a film about an immigrant family that "made it."

Family Drama. Arthur Miller, *Death of a Salesman*, the classic dramatic portrayal of an ordinary man's American dream and the forces that conspired to defeat it. **Supplement:** One of the following plays about American families—their dreams, their secrets and lies, their successes and failures: Edward Albee, *Who's Afraid of Virginia Woolf?*; Lorraine Hansberry, *A Raisin in the Sun*; Eugene O'Neill, *A Long Day's Journey into Night*; Tennessee Williams, *A Cat on a Hot Tin Roof*.

Personal Poetry. Selections from the following: Gwendolyn Brooks, selected poems, portraits of ordinary African Americans trying to make meaning of their lives in the city; Faythe Turner, ed., *Puerto Rican Writers at Home in the USA*, a collection of short works (mostly poems) by a variety of Nuyorican writers; George Chigas, ed., *Cambodia's Lament*, poems by refugees from the war and genocide in Cambodia.

Regional Fiction. One of the following: Kate Chopin, *The Awakening*, a groundbreaking novel about a woman's new consciousness set in turn-of-the-century Louisiana; selections from Malcolm Cowley, ed., *The Portable Faulkner*, a collection of stories by a master storyteller set in mythical Yoknapatawpha County, Mississippi; Louise Erdrich, *Tracks*, a recent novel about the struggle to survive and forge an identity amid changing circumstances on a North Dakota reservation early in the twentieth century.

The "American Dream" Revisited. Ralph Ellison, *Invisible Man*, a major novel about a young African American's attempt to live the American dream—and an all-inclusive story about individualism and invisibility in the modern world. **Supplement:** Michael Moore's *Roger & Me*: a wacky documentary film with a serious message.

Figure 3.2. Sample American Literature and Society syllabus.

the whole novel, and I differentiate the assignments according to students' abilities. If possible, I sandwich the reading around a school vacation so those who want to read it all will have time. I used to believe that teaching just part of a text was sacrilege, but I've gotten over that. Sticking to the whole-work rule would exclude too many titles that are too good to be missed. *Invisible Man* is such a book. It speaks to all students, especially those who would typically be grouped in lower-level classes. They may not be able to read more than a few chapters in the time we have available, but they know what invisibility means. This novel recapitulates most of the questions and problems examined throughout the course, but it also concludes with an alternative vision of America:

Whence all this passion toward conformity anyway?—diversity is the word. . . .
America is woven of many strands; I would recognize them and let it so remain.
It's "winner take nothing" that is the great truth of our country or any country.
Life is to be lived, not controlled; and humanity is won by continuing to play in
the face of certain defeat. Our fate is to become one, and yet many—This is not
prophecy, but description. (577)

It may seem odd to pair *Invisible Man* with *Roger & Me*, but that film explores the
theme of invisibility in complementary ways. Both works encourage students to
"shake off the old skin," as the invisible man puts it, and develop a new consciousness about the American dream.

> **Your turn.** Think about how you arrange the curriculum in your courses. Is your
> basic organizing principle chronology, genre, theme, or something else? What
> are the advantages and disadvantages of the approach(es) you are using? Are
> there other possibilities? Experiment: Create the syllabus for a particular course
> three different ways. What happens to the conversation among the texts when
> the groupings are changed? Would combining methods be beneficial?

Changing the Pace

Since I began teaching untracked classes (see Chapter 9), I've become more and
more aware of the differences in experience, capacity, and attitude students bring to
the study of literature. In truth, students in tracked classes are heterogeneous, too,
but labels such as "college prep" and "honors" tend to blind us to their real variety.
Now I try hard to make sure my classes have something for everyone, that they are
accessible to all kinds of learners. I'll explain my strategies for working with students
who have special needs in Chapter 10; here I'm referring to features of a course that
can help students like Smith and Wilhelm's resistant boys to feel that they have
the "competence, control, and challenge" they need (96). Variety is essential. I have
already alluded briefly to some approaches I use to change the pace of my classes, to
alter the look and feel of literature study. I'd like to reiterate those here and mention
a couple of others.

One way to achieve variety and accessibility is to assign *short* works. As you can
see from the syllabi I've included, I like to use plays, poems, and stories—pieces
that can be read or reread in class to build confidence and capacity. I tend to choose
relatively short novels and autobiographies as well: *The Great Gatsby, The House on
Mango Street, Night.* Short does not mean *easy,* but a challenging text seems much

more manageable to reluctant readers when they know that it won't take weeks to wade through. When short isn't possible, I often go for *partial* works, for excerpts that can stand on their own or with a little help from transitional summaries. For example, when I teach *The Odyssey*, I usually omit about half of the narrative, concentrating on Odysseus's adventures and homecoming. To shorten *The Joy Luck Club*, I may assign the whole first section but then ask each student to follow just one of the four families for the remainder of the novel. Reading the entire text would be better, and I certainly encourage that, but if the choice is some or none of a great book, it's an easy decision.

On the other hand, I do think it's important at times to slow down for in-depth study of a *major* work. In most classes I include one multiweek unit focused on a single text. Many of my colleagues do this, too. Typically this is a book that anchors the entire course, as *Invisible Man* does in American Literature and Society or *Crime and Punishment* does in Renaissance and Modern Literature. Other examples from my department: Margaret Atwood's *The Handmaid's Tale* in Women in Literature and Toni Morrison's *Song of Solomon* in African American Literature. Students need strong scaffolding, frequent pep talks, and lots of individual support to complete and comprehend lengthy novels such as these. Some need substantial cuts in assignments to keep up, and a few require rescue operations after bogging down early on. But reading and discussing a bonafide "classic" gives them tremendous pride.

I mentioned earlier that I try to offer a *choice* of readings at least once in every course. Students appreciate having some control over their work, but that's not the only reason I employ this strategy. Having students read different texts requires setting up study groups, ensuring that I am off the stage for part of the term. Working together in literature circles and other group configurations gives students the opportunity to apply what they have learned from whole-class lessons. Another benefit is that small-group and independent readings expand the knowledge base in the room. Presentations and jigsaw activities enable students to share their expertise. I'll come back to this topic in Chapter 6, which focuses on encouraging response to literature.

Finally, I think it's invaluable to vary the media in our courses. Yes, we should focus primarily on print, but for many students, such as visual learners, other art forms open windows onto the literary concepts we teach. Film is increasingly important in my classes, but I don't mean "now that we've read the book (or not), let's watch the movie" (see Chapter 7). Visual art and music are also natural complements to literature, both as texts to "read" and as modes of response (see Chapter 6). Drawing examples from popular culture helps students connect their worlds with the classroom, but English class is also a great venue for introducing them to forms that they may not encounter on their own: films with subtitles, sculpture, classical music, etc.

> **Your turn.** Reflect on the strategies you use to change the pace of your litera-
> ture classes. What is the proportion of short and long works? Do students have
> choices of readings? Do they meet in study groups to discuss texts on their own?
> Do you incorporate film, visual art, and/or music in your courses? For what pur-
> poses? After answering these questions, choose one aspect of your practice that
> you would like to modify and develop an action plan. If it's feasible, connect
> this work to the syllabus exercise you completed for the previous section of this
> chapter.

Coping with Textbooks, Curriculum Mandates, and Censorship

I know what some of you are thinking: *Your talk of diversifying the course texts and
rearranging the syllabus and changing the pace is all well and good, but I'm required to
teach from a textbook.* Or *I have to follow a district-mandated curriculum.* Or *I can't
include the books I want to use because of censorship.* I hear you, and I sympathize. I
have friends who constantly deal with these problems, which have only occasionally been impediments to my teaching. I feel blessed to work in a district and community that generally respects teacher knowledge and creativity and for the most
part lets us do our jobs. I can't offer any panaceas for those of you facing such academic restrictions—the solutions, ultimately, are political—but I would like to offer
some observations that might help you to rethink how to cope with them.

First, the textbooks. There's nothing inherently wrong with the idea of teaching
from anthologies, but the thick, heavy tomes created for high school English classes
are problematic for several reasons. Their physical appearance alone is a deterrent
to reading: their bulkiness, their rigid covers, and their long columns of text do not
say, "Curl up in your favorite chair for a cozy read." Then, too, the order of presentation always seems idiosyncratic. I figure that the editors must have reasons for
juxtaposing apparently unrelated titles and separating similar ones, but they're just
not evident to me. Some texts are organized by chronology, some by theme, and
some by genre. Ginn's *American Literature*, which I've used intermittently since the
1980s (we don't replace textbooks very often), employs all three methods. It begins
with "Major Themes in American Literature" (e.g., "The Individual"), which, it says,
"have grown naturally out of our experience of living in this land" (Porter, Terrie, and
Bennett 4). Hmm. *Whose* experience? The next major chunk of the book is arranged
chronologically, in units entitled "A New Land," "A New Nation," and so on, but
the newness eventually wears off, and the twentieth-century titles are grouped by
genre. Something for everyone, I guess. A growing problem in newer anthologies

is the apparatus that accompanies the selections. What used to be a handful of questions and vocabulary after each piece has become in some cases several pages of standards-based lessons, which, if followed faithfully, would kill any interest in literature the reading might generate.

I'm mindful that the contents of high school anthologies are determined largely by economics: what will sell to the broadest audience. With the growth of statewide adoption, publishers have become cautious, sticking to the most widely accepted choices. So I constantly ask myself who and what has been left out and go looking for alternative sources. I've also grown wary of the versions of canonical works that appear in textbooks. Over the years I've found numerous examples of bowdlerizing. For example, our Brit Lit anthology, *Adventures in English Literature*, skips a big chunk of the drunken porter's speech in *Macbeth*—when he says that drink provokes nose-painting, sleep, and urine; and that it "provokes and unprovokes" lechery. This passage has been removed without ellipsis marks or any other indication that the play has been edited. Similarly, the witches' incantation omits an ingredient from their concoction: "liver of blaspheming Jew"—presumably because its inclusion would be offensive to many readers. In contrast, the line about "Nose of Turk and Tartar's lips" has not been cut (Damrosch et al. 191). What does that say? My discovery of these changes to *Macbeth* has provided great openings for discussions on censorship, anti-Semitism, and "socially acceptable" biases, but I often wonder how many other instances of bowdlerizing I have missed.

Despite all of these shortcomings, I find the literature textbooks I use helpful, though not always in the ways the publishers intend. Besides conveniently collecting what might otherwise be hard-to-access works and providing useful background information, they prod me to revisit authors I wouldn't otherwise think about very often (Washington Irving and Amy Lowell, for example) and introduce me to others I don't know (this is how I first met Leslie Marmon Silko, Mari Evans, and Cathy Song). There is hardly ever enough of an author's work in an anthology to give an adequate feel for its range—many are represented by a single poem or a one-page excerpt, often on a "safe" topic—but it's enough to get me (or, better, my students) started on some research that will turn up other selections that can be shared with the class. Even the sins of omission in textbooks can be turned to advantage. Made aware of the bowdlerized texts, sanitized author biographies, and one-sided historical accounts that many textbooks include to avoid offending potential purchasers, students learn to question what they read and to seek other authorities. I keep a variety of sources (including sample copies of competing textbooks that I've collected over the years) on my bookshelf for cross-checking and sleuthing.

Whenever possible, I avoid sending anthologies home with students. They thank me for this, since their backpacks are already overloaded with mammoth history, math, and science books. I generally use individual titles and handouts for homework and reserve the textbooks for in-class readings of background material and literature selections. There are several advantages to this approach. First, I'm available immediately to answer students' inevitable questions about the typically dense articles on political and literary history. Second, setting aside class time for readings gives me a window into students' reading strategies. Third, it ensures that I will use the textbook selectively, not try to march through its entire contents. Finally, on a practical note, keeping the textbooks in school means that I need only one set, and that it will last a long time, leaving more of the department's meager supply budget for other book purchases.

One reason that schools buy textbooks is that they provide well-researched, prepackaged resources for teachers who don't have the experience or the time to assemble their own materials. Fair enough. But amid concerns about test scores and pressures to reform, some districts have taken the extreme step of developing mandated curricula, sometimes including detailed lessons. The intentions behind such decisions are probably good, but what they say to teachers is, in effect, "We don't think you're smart enough to do your job, so we're doing it for you." For teachers I know who are working in such conditions, that implicit message is a morale killer.

All schools impose some curriculum mandates, and rightly so. There are state standards to be met, district priorities to be implemented, and a general need for some consistency from classroom to classroom. Mandates work best when teachers, working in groups, are given the opportunity to understand the purposes behind the directives and to develop their own collective means of implementation. That way, teachers become responsible to each other as well as to the school administration or central office. A few years ago, my department was required to come up with a separate AP literature course, as opposed to the AP option we were offering within our heterogeneous classes. Most of us were strongly opposed. When we probed the reasons for the mandate, we learned that its main purpose was to ensure that AP students could have a cohort of peers rather than just a few classmates pursuing independent projects. After much deliberation, we came up with a team-teaching plan that paired an AP section with a "regular" section of the same course. This model provided the "critical mass" of AP students the administration wanted but honored our commitment to untracked classes—and created peer mentoring opportunities in the process. I suspect that a similar approach might also work for more specific curriculum mandates. If teachers in a department worked together to examine what's really behind them—what the bottom line is—they might find ways to implement the requirements that would satisfy the district's needs while preserving a measure of professionalism and academic freedom.

A perennial threat to academic integrity in the English classroom is censorship. In some communities readings are challenged all the time, and in others rarely, but no school is immune. The sources of and the reasons for objections to particular books are not always predictable. Some time ago, a member of my department proposed adding two books with gay protagonists to the curriculum, arguing that these titles would support our district's multicultural goals. Our obviously nervous principal approved one, a young adult novel, but rejected the other, a teenage autobiography, even though the content was similar. Why? "GAY" was printed in big red letters on the autobiography's cover. His comment: "What's going to happen when a student plunks this book down on the coffee table?" The novel had a more "discreet" cover, and its title, *Counter Play*, didn't announce its subject overtly. The principal feared that conservative parents would object to the inclusion of literature about homosexuality. Indeed, most challenges do come from parents who don't want their children to read books with sexual content, obscene language, or "depressing" themes. But those are not the only reasons for parental objections. I've witnessed or been a part of censorship cases involving race, religion, and politics as well.

When responding to parents and others who question our reading lists, we would do well to remember that they are generally not wild-eyed radicals itching to burn all heterodox books. More likely they have sincere concerns that the curriculum is incompatible with their values. Suzanne M. Kauer writes of a parent that she worked with who "felt that so much of high school literature took people to a dark place. Even if one puts a positive spin on the themes, they are still heavy and dark. She wanted happy endings, inspirational stories that left one feeling good at the end. She wanted books that showed people experiencing punishment and remorse for bad behavior" (58). Kauer was "shocked and even a bit offended at the extent of her rejection of high school literature," as most English teachers would be, but the episode caused her to reflect on *why* we choose what we teach in our classrooms. I have experienced similar disquieting moments after parental challenges to books I have assigned, including Ken Kesey's *One Flew over the Cuckoo's Nest*. In that case the student's mother was struggling with mental illness, and her father thought that the book would be too upsetting. I gladly provided a substitute reading, but the episode made me cognizant of my responsibility to "thoroughly interrogate" the curriculum, as Kauer recommends (59), and consider its potential unintended consequences.

I don't mean to suggest that parents' objections to controversial books are always valid. For one thing, there's a big difference between asking for alternative reading materials for one's child and trying to ban titles from the curriculum altogether. We need to know our districts' censorship policies, and we need to be prepared to fight, if necessary, to protect students' right to read. But we also must be prepared to engage in dialogue, with parents, administrators, and each other, to explore our rationales for teaching potentially divisive titles, and to develop reasonable processes for handling disagreements. ReLeah Cossett Lent, a national authority on censorship, recommends organizing community forums on reading and intellectual freedom to develop mutual understanding and respect. "Communities and school districts have an obligation to support students' reading choices, teachers' instructional practices, and family standards; it will be much easier for that to happen if the groundwork is laid prior to a censorship threat" (66).

> **Your turn.** To what extent is your teaching affected by required textbooks, curriculum mandates, censorship of reading materials, or other impediments to academic freedom? Research your district's policies on these matters. Are there procedures in place for adopting instructional materials, establishing course content, and handling complaints? What role(s) do teachers have in these processes? Initiate a discussion with your colleagues about how you could collectively address or forestall limitations on academic freedom in the English program.

Acknowledging the Poets

Percy Bysshe Shelley famously remarked in his 1819 essay "A Defence of Poetry" that "Poets are the unacknowledged legislators of the world" (90). I'm sure that most poets concur with at least part of this statement—the "unacknowledged" part, which applies, I'm afraid, even to high school English classrooms, where poetry is often neglected in favor of novels and other narratives. "Many of us avoid poetry entirely or teach it without enjoying it or modeling love of it," writes Katherine Keil, who admits having been "one of those frightened, uncomfortable teachers" who liked poetry but "didn't know quite what to do with it" (97). I've been one of those teachers, too, but like Keil I've overcome most of my discomfort, so I'd like to conclude this chapter on developing a literature curriculum with my own brief "defense" of poetry as an essential and potentially joyful element of literature study.

I think that our anxiety about poetry, which we unwittingly pass on to students, stems from fear of getting the interpretation wrong, or not getting it at all. For example, I've always loved Emily Dickinson's poems, but until recently I haven't had the courage to "teach" the ones I don't fully understand. This is one of the unfortunate legacies of New Criticism: the need to get the analysis "right" by developing a "reading" that accounts for all elements of the poem. Failing that, we sometimes retreat to the opposite extreme, implying that all interpretations are equally valid or, as students put it, "It's all your own opinion." That position is a trap, too, because it leaves us with nothing to teach except, perhaps, terminology. As H. R. Swardson points out, we do have something important to offer students: our experience as critical readers. Experience, he notes, "tells me how to arrive at the sort of fun . . . arranged for readers in a poem, how to stay on rather than wander (*errare*) off the path to the fun" (162). But contemporary critical theory has taught us that there are many paths "to the fun" in a poem, and by learning to use critical lenses, students can also see them and even lead the way.

Fun is a word that we ought to use more often when thinking about teaching poetry. The toddler who asks to have *The Cat in the Hat* read aloud repeatedly knows intuitively that poetry is fun. So do the enthusiastic audiences at poetry slams. Why isn't it always fun in the classroom? Probably because we tend to focus on interpretation first or even exclusively. Before we can get to the kind of intellectual fun Swardson describes, we have to rediscover the simple joys of poetry through play, performance, and writing, as Keil and many others suggest. Despite the dearth of poetry in many English classes, there is no shortage of creative ideas for teaching it in the field. The September 2006 issue of *English Journal* includes ten valuable articles on classroom strategies plus a survey of the journal's contributors' suggestions on poetry instruction going back almost a hundred years. As long ago as 1917, teachers were calling for new methods that would help students relate to poetry and take pleasure in reading it: including modern and contemporary texts, making connections to social context, emphasizing performance and group work, and so on (Dressman and Faust 76–78). It's evident that English teachers have had problems with poetry for a long time; it's equally clear that there are plenty of solutions.

Over time I've learned practices that help me feel more confident teaching poetry. As I noted earlier, I now have a self-imposed rule that requires me to include poetry in every course. Sometimes individual poems provide thematic counterpoint to longer texts students are reading. William Butler Yeats's "The Second Coming" is an obvious choice to accompany Chinua Achebe's *Things Fall Apart* since the title of the novel was taken from the poem. Robert Frost's "Design" pairs well with the chapter "The Whiteness of the Whale" in Herman Melville's *Moby-Dick* because both treat the frightening blankness of natural objects that have no color. Cathy Song's "Lost Sister" complements Amy Tan's *The Joy Luck Club* in its exploration of the duality of being a Chinese American woman. Another approach I use is author study: mini-units on individual poets such as Anne Bradstreet, Walt Whitman, Emily Dickinson, Charles Baudelaire, and Gwendolyn Brooks; or on groups of poets, as in the American Literature and Society syllabus in Figure 3.2. A third method is genre study, ranging from short takes on particular forms, such as the sonnet or the haiku, to major undertakings, such as the oral interpretation of poetry unit outlined in Figure 3.3, a major segment of our tenth-grade oral communication course.

No matter how I incorporate poetry into a course, I try to make sure that three core elements are included in my lessons. The first is performance, both mine and students'. Poetry is meant to be read aloud, so it's important that students hear it read well and have opportunities to practice feeling the words and lines of poems in their mouths and to present their own oral interpretations to safe audiences.

1. **Original poem:** Experiment freely and save all drafts; revise one to improve word choice, rhythm, and imagery; use a large sticky note to reflect on the process of writing the poem.

2. **Memorized poem:** Learn a poem of eight lines or more (more credit for more challenge!) and deliver it to the class with appropriate feeling; preface the recitation with an introduction.

3. **Poetry presentation:** Select an established classic or modern poet, study a collection of his or her poems, research his or her biography, and prepare a five-minute presentation that includes background information, an effective reading of one to three poems (depending on length), and introduction(s) analyzing themes and style (in other words, a mini-lesson on the poet). For example, you could read James Weldon Johnson's "The Creation" *or* two or three poems by Emily Dickinson. The poems need not be memorized, but they should be well practiced. Obviously the aim is to do more than merely read the poems; oral interpretation means acting them out. To do an effective job, you'll have to take some risks. Your introduction(s), which must be thoughtfully written and word processed, should address the following points:

   a. What is the subject or theme of your presentation?
   b. Who is the author of the poem(s)? (not just the name)
   c. What should we listen for as you are reading the poem(s)?
   d. If you are reading more than one poem, how are they connected?

   NOTE: It is possible for two people to work together on this presentation—to make use of different voices in interpreting the poetry. See me if you have a joint performance idea.

4. **Poetry analysis essay:** Write a three- to four-page analysis of your poems incorporating material from your presentation and your library research. The essay must include the poem(s) as well as appropriate textual citations and a bibliography in MLA format.

Steps in preparing the poetry presentation and analysis:

a. Consider several poets and browse through collections of their poetry.

b. Select a substantial collection of poems by one author and read widely in the collection to develop a sense of the poet's style and themes. Write a notebook response to your reading.

c. Find at least two in-depth, reputable biographical sources on your poet, prepare a bibliography, and take detailed notes (keeping track of sources and page numbers).

d. Select and study in depth one to three poems, practice reading them aloud with appropriate expression, and prepare appropriate introductions. We will videotape your performance.

e. Draft and then revise thoroughly your poetry analysis essay, using the materials you wrote for your presentation but going deeper into the poem(s) using appropriate terminology.

Figure 3.3. Oral interpretation of poetry unit requirements.

Another element is low-stakes writing about poems. Writing-to-learn activities help students deepen their understanding of poetry through risk-free exercises in meaning-making; this kind of writing also prepares them to participate more confidently in discussions. The third element is composing original verse. There is no better way to develop appreciation for the poet's art than to try it—in a playful, low-risk environment. In major poetry units, I sometimes also include formal analytical writing, but this comes only after students have had the chance to get comfortable with poetry through the other three strategies. Above all, I want them to feel confident and in control when they read and discuss poems. I want them to know that this ancient and contemporary, public and personal form of literature can be just as accessible and relevant to them as the popular music they listen to and share.

> **Your turn.** How would you rate your comfort level with poetry? What positive experiences have you had in school or elsewhere with reading and interpreting and/or writing poetry? Have you been able to replicate those experiences or develop similar ones for your students? What about negative experiences? What made these encounters unpleasant? How can you avoid creating the same conditions in your classroom? Looking more specifically at the courses you teach, where and for what purposes is poetry included? How do students respond? Are there places where you could add poetry? Are there ways you could make your teaching more playful? More performance-based? Less focused on getting the "right" interpretation?

The Happy Ending

The field of literature has become both dauntingly complex and electrifyingly broad in recent years. The globalization of literary culture has made it impossible for anyone to feel truly "well-read" nowadays, but it has also opened wide the possibilities for literature study. At the same time, tech-savvy teens question the relevance of "ancient" (read: before they were born) ink-on-paper texts, and career-oriented students wonder what they have to gain from reading. Amid these challenges, we would do well to remember what attracted most of us to the profession we're in: the transformative power of literature. As Emily Dickinson expressed it,

> There is no Frigate like a Book
> To take us Lands away,
> Nor any Coursers like a Page
> Of prancing Poetry— (501)

Literature takes us outside of ourselves, builds empathy for other people, fires our imagination, and makes us more human. It can do the same for our students if we help them get ready to travel. Our job is to be readers ourselves and to model and share the excitement of literary exploration. It is also to create a literature curriculum that includes many voices and much variety and that invites students to participate. This is difficult, important, and rewarding work.

Recommended Reading

Appleman, Deborah. *Critical Encounters in High School English: Teaching Literary Theory to Adolescents*. New York and Urbana, IL: Teachers College Press and NCTE, 2000. Print.

> Appleman makes a convincing case for teaching critical theory in high school and demonstrates her approach using several lenses. The appendix includes more than twenty adaptable classroom activities.

Moon, Brian. *Studying Poetry: Activities, Resources, and Texts*. Urbana, IL: NCTE, 2001. Print.

> This lively volume from the NCTE Chalkface Series is a treasure trove of information, ideas, and activities for teaching poetry. It includes chapters on performance, language, form, critique writing, and critical theory, as well as one exploring the question, "What is poetry?"

Smith, Michael W., and Jeffrey D. Wilhelm. *"Reading Don't Fix No Chevys": Literacy in the Lives of Young Men*. Portsmouth, NH: Heinemann, 2002. Print.

> An investigation of the literacy practices and preferences of adolescent boys, this book offers insights into the causes of reading resistance and strategies for connecting alienated students with texts.

Tyson, Lois. *Critical Theory Today: A User-Friendly Guide*. New York: Garland, 1999. Print.

> Tyson presents the panoply of contemporary critical theory in readable language, explaining key concepts and terms and providing clear illustrations. Each chapter includes a new interpretation of *The Great Gatsby*, as well as brief commentaries on other works and helpful study questions.

4

Creating an Assessment System

Every time I travel to the NCTE Annual Convention, I play a little game on the airplane called "spot the English teachers." It's easy, really—they're the ones who pile stacks of papers on their tray tables and gulp coffee in hopes of staying alert enough to get them all read. They know in their hearts that it's not going to happen, that most of these essays (and the others in the bag under the seat) are going to return from the trip ungraded. But hope—or perhaps guilt—springs eternal, so these teachers, who feel lucky to have finagled a day off from school to attend the conference, have brought their work with them, against all reason. They do the same after school each day, stuffing their briefcases with far more papers than they can read in a night. It's the English teacher's burden, and I, too, have been carrying it my entire adult life.

I used to think that with experience I would gain speed. It didn't turn out that way. The better I understood student writing, the longer the grading seemed to take. About fifteen years ago, desperate to change my work habits, I decided to do a "time and motion study" of myself in the act of assessing student work. What I learned astonished me: I was spending almost half of my time agonizing over grades. *Is this paper a B+ or an A-? How does it compare to that other B+? Maybe I'd better go back and check that one again.* And so on. I'm sure you have been there. Worse, I realized that many of the comments I was writing were designed more to justify the grades than to respond helpfully to the students' work. I concluded that I was spending hours each week engaged in a painful process that probably wasn't doing much good.

That epiphany led to a momentous decision: to stop putting grades on papers, period. I'll say more about how I did that later. More important, I began to reflect more deeply on school assessment practices and on why students often experience them as arbitrary and unfair. I started paying more attention to how I was responding to student work and looking for effective ways to bring the students into the assessment process. I'm still working on how to balance providing humane, effective feedback to my students and fulfilling my reporting obligations to the school.

The aim of this chapter is to suggest ways to minimize the role of grading in assessment and to maximize student reflection and growth. I'll argue that we should proceed with caution when using rubrics to assess student work. I'll also suggest that we give at least as much attention to assessment *for* learning (formative assessment) as we do to assessment *of* learning (summative assessment). The chapter includes ideas for managing writing folders and portfolios, using student- and teacher-generated evaluation criteria, and creating meaningful projects and tests. I can't promise that these strategies will drastically reduce the time that you spend on assessment, but I do think that they will help you feel that your time is being well spent.

Forty Years in the Wilderness

Well, forty years is an exaggeration, and it wasn't exactly a wilderness, but I did spend a long time wandering around without much of a theory of assessment—and I still haven't reached the promised land of totally effective evaluation methods. I did get some early help. My student teaching mentor, the late Larry Crouse, taught me that writing assignments should always include criteria for evaluation, and that astute advice encouraged me to clarify my expectations to students and helped me to be consistent in my focus while grading. But the process by which I arrived at an A or a B or a C on a paper was a bit of a mystery, and I always wondered if I was being too hard or too soft. Many of my colleagues felt the same way, and we often talked about exchanging papers to compare grading standards—but we rarely had time to do this.

Late in the 1970s I attended a workshop on holistic scoring at the Educational Testing Service in Princeton. Under pressure from leaders in the emerging field of composition studies to make its achievement test in writing more valid, ETS had added an on-demand essay to the multiple-choice items on sentence structure and mechanics. To achieve reliability, test makers had applied the procedures developed for the AP exams: writing prompts, anchor papers and scoring guides, and methods of achieving acceptable agreement (Yancey 490). I still remember the workshop leader's explanation of how holistic scoring works: he said that while experienced teachers of writing may never agree on a definition of effective writing, they can be remarkably consistent in recognizing it. After they have been "calibrated" by the training process, that is.

Back at school, I replicated the workshop for my colleagues, and for many years after that we conducted large-scale writing assessments using the ETS methods. I'm not sure how valid or valuable the *scores* we produced were, but the *conversations* that happened around the process of producing them were extraordinary. Teachers from different schools and grades shared their values and strategies. Together we analyzed what was strong about the papers we had given high scores and what was weak in the papers we had given low scores, and on the basis of what we learned, we established priorities for our writing program. The collaborative scoring sessions actually provided rich professional development. Learning holistic scoring didn't reduce my paper load, though. From time to time I tried just rating students' papers on a four-point scale to save time, but a bare number never seemed like sufficient feedback.

Many years later, several of my colleagues and I became interested in a promising new trend in writing assessment: portfolios. Portfolio assessment had been introduced by some university writing programs as an authentic alternative to holistically scored writing samples, which were increasingly seen as inconsistent with the writing process taught in composition classes. Portfolios allow students to submit a variety of work written in natural circumstances, and they proceed from a fundamentally different premise than proficiency exams, which yield a bell curve of scores: "the ideal end product," wrote Peter Elbow and Pat Belanoff, who started a portfolio system at Stony Brook, "is a population of students who have *all* finally passed because they have been given enough time and help to do what we ask of them" ("Portfolios" 98–99; emphasis original).

Through workshops and articles, I learned that teachers were using portfolios effectively for classroom assessment also, replacing one-shot grading of individual papers with cumulative evaluation of a body of work. It was this revelation that gave me the courage to stop putting grades on writing assignments, and so began my long series of experiments with writing folder systems, culminating in the one explained later in this chapter. Others in my department were experimenting, too, so we arranged for a workshop on the portfolio process by a local teacher. The seeds planted at that session grew beyond our expectations. As a first step, three of us decided to try portfolios as a means of assessing whether students who had elected the Honors option in our heterogeneous classes had met the expectations. At the end of the year the department held a retreat to review our results and decide whether all Honors students should create portfolios. Seeing the value of the process, the department went even further, adopting it for *all* students. Our course portfolios have undergone many changes since then, but they are still in use.

A basic question that we had to wrestle with comes up often in the assessment literature: what, exactly, is a portfolio? The answer, we learned, is "it depends." Context is everything. What is the purpose of the portfolio? Who decides what goes in it? How is it to be evaluated? Decisions on these and other points have to be made locally. Dixie Dellinger of the National Writing Project outlines four common types of portfolios:

- **"How I'm Growing"** (shows the student's growth over time by including works of all types from the beginning to the present, not all the best quality)

- **"How I Function"** (shows the student's writing and perhaps reading process by including drafts, notes, journals, and/or other artifacts leading to finished pieces)

- **"What I Can Do"** (shows the student's learning of concepts and skills taught in a course by including products that exhibit his or her level of mastery)

- **"What I Have Done"** (showcases the student's achievements and talents by including the best work he or she has produced in a course) (20–23)

These purposes are not mutually exclusive, and a portfolio may serve more than one. My department's course portfolios include all four to some extent. At first we focused on the "What I Can Do" function, but we found that the "What I Have Done" approach fostered more student ownership. Whatever the aim of a portfolio, however, there are three essential elements to the process, as Liz Hamp-Lyons and William Condon point out in their theory of portfolio assessment: collection, reflection, and selection (118–120). *Collection* of a variety of pieces (differing in genre, purpose, circumstances of composition, etc.), including information about the instructional context, is what distinguishes a portfolio from a writing test. *Reflection*, usually in the form of one or more cover letters, encourages the writer to learn from the work. *Selection* allows the writer to fashion an exhibit that tells his or her individual writing story.

The rub in portfolio assessment is the assessment part. Student reflection and reader responses (from teacher, parent, and/or peers) are natural and beneficial phases of the process, but for institutional purposes (within a particular course or in a larger proficiency program) grades or scores, usually determined by a rubric, are required. Robert L. Broad argues, however, that "portfolio scoring" is a contradiction in terms. Because "the construction of textual meaning depends upon social context," textual value *"also depends upon social context,"* and we can therefore *"establish no single, fixed meaning or value for any text"* ("Portfolio Scoring" 303; emphasis original). In other words, the value assigned to a portfolio will depend on who is reading it and the circumstances in which it is produced. That's true in my experience—and appropriate, given the ongoing collaboration between student and teacher that a course portfolio represents. Even so, in our department we wanted to establish a measure of consistency in our evaluation of portfolios. Our lengthy discussions eventually focused on several key dimensions of the process and product, similar to the ones that Hamp-Lyons provided to teachers at the University of Colorado–Denver as a "heuristic for developing criteria" for portfolios:

1. Range of writing
2. Development of writer's abilities
3. Engagement with ideas and issues
4. Textual excellence
5. Self-reflection (Hamp-Lyons and Condon 143)

Addressing these elements ensured that our assessments would honor all aspects of our program: range as well as depth, progress as well as polish, consciousness as well as conscientiousness.

The assessment guide we developed (presented later in this chapter) is, of course, a kind of rubric. Rubrics represent "the state of the art" in assessment today, as Carol Jago explains:

> In the bad old days teachers simply assigned and evaluated writing, giving grades according to an inner sense that students were expected to intuit and accept without question. Rubrics help to clarify the grading process. While there will always be discrepancies among teachers however well "normed" they might be, adherence to a common scoring guide across a department—and ideally throughout a school—can bring consistency to what from a student's perspective is a somewhat idiosyncratic process. (*Papers* 15)

Developed originally for large-scale writing assessments, scoring guides are everywhere now. Every state and national testing program has its own set of scales, and many schools have adopted or created general writing rubrics for teachers to follow. One of the most popular and highly regarded is the 6+1 Trait model developed by the Northwest Regional Educational Laboratory, which provides scoring guides and exemplars for six aspects of writing—ideas, organization, voice, word choice, sentence fluency, and conventions—plus one: presentation. The strengths of the 6+1 approach are that it applies to all kinds of writing and to students of all ages and abilities and that it can be used selectively to focus on different skills at different times. (For a detailed presentation of the 6+1 model, see Culham.) In addition to using such published rubrics, teachers are now often expected to (or choose to) supply specific scoring guides for each assignment they give. The Internet offers abundant resources to assist the process, including rubric-generating tools such as RubiStar (www.4Teachers.org).

Besides clarity and consistency, rubrics also promise efficiency. Time spent creating and explaining rubrics, finding and sharing exemplar papers, and having students rate their own work "should reduce the amount of time you need with red pen in hand later" (Jago, *Papers* 15). Well, maybe. I have often found that the opposite is true—that my struggles with grading are *multiplied* by the number of criteria in the rubric. Another problem I have encountered is that the whole is not always equal to the sum of the parts. The first time I used a detailed scoring guide was in oral communication, a tenth-grade requirement in Amherst. Using a colleague's public speaking rubric, I carefully rated the speeches on all of the specified standards. But when I added up the points, they just didn't jibe with my gut sense of the students' achievement. Some of the most powerful presentations were scoring 70 or 75. Something intangible was missing.

I am not alone in my ambivalence about rubrics. I recently taught the 6+1 Trait model to a group of college students, all prospective teachers. They applauded some aspects of this set of guides (especially its inclusion of voice), but most of them struggled when trying to apply it to student writing. Some felt that at seven pages the 6+1 model was overwhelming; others thought that it *reduced* the complexities of writing too much, not accounting for individual differences.

My students' reservations are quite similar to some recently published critiques of rubrics. Bob Broad argues that while rubrics played an important role in legitimizing writing assessment, they no longer represent the values and practices of the field. Rubrics send the wrong message to students by limiting evaluation criteria and by overemphasizing surface traits in the interests of brevity and clarity, and they "prevent us from telling the truth about what we believe, what we teach, and what we value in composition courses and programs" (*What We Really Value* 2). Building on Broad's work, Maja Wilson makes the case that teachers' use of rubrics damages students, both those who "refuse to fit into our molds" and those who comply.

> Those who conform to our molds may receive high grades, but we do not encourage them to develop the ideas and ways of thinking through writing that they may need to deal with the complex issues presented by today's society. Rubrics encourage us to read and our students to write on autopilot. (39)

Broad and Wilson suggest that differences in reactions to pieces of writing, which scoring guides tend to minimize, should be *embraced* as opportunities to make visible "the internal standards, assumptions, and experience that readers bring to their readings and assessments" (Wilson 65). Contextualizing readers' dissenting responses can help writers clarify their rhetorical intentions.

I've made my peace with rubrics by employing them—a wide variety of them, including student-generated ones—flexibly and as teaching tools, not just as grading tools. Amid frequent self-reflection and genuine peer and teacher response, rubrics can serve usefully as one type of formative assessment. Assessment *for* learning, as this kind of in-process measurement is also known, is designed to help students *progress* toward established goals, in contrast to summative assessment, or assessment *of* learning, which is designed to *test* whether they have met them.

Formative assessment can take place "on the fly," as in listening in on a small-group discussion; in planned interactions, as in asking comprehension questions about an assigned reading; or in curriculum-embedded evaluations, as in reviewing the mid-process draft of an analytical essay (see Heritage for an explanation of the elements of formative assessment). Teachers use formative assessment all the time, but most of us could be more deliberate about incorporating it into our planning. "Teachers must view formative assessment and the teaching process as inseparable and must recognize that one cannot happen without the other" (Heritage). Providing regular opportunities for students to reflect on their progress, to hear authentic responses from their peers, and to receive thoughtful feedback from us are more important than filling our record books with grades.

That's the real lesson of my forty years in the assessment wilderness: to be of any lasting value, an assessment system has to involve the students in meaningful ways. Students learn to place value on grades, but what they crave are *connections*—to mentors who believe that they can succeed and who want to help them grow.

Developing an Assessment Philosophy

The first step in establishing a student-centered evaluation system is to articulate a philosophy of assessment, first to yourself and then to your classes. My creed keeps evolving, as I've explained earlier, but it now includes several core principles:

- **Clear expectations.** Students should understand what is expected of them—the kinds of work they are required to do, the criteria and methods by which it will be assessed, and the degree of flexibility they have in meeting these standards.

- **Genuine feedback.** Students have a right to expect authentic reactions and helpful advice in response to their work, not just criticism and judgment. This feedback should come from peers as well as the teacher.

- **Frequent reflection.** Self-assessment is essential to progress, so students should have regular occasions to reflect on their learning. Many need encouragement and coaching to realize the benefits of this kind of self-examination.

- **Progress focus.** Products are certainly important in school, but they should be looked at as measures of growth, not as ends in themselves. Consequently, most assignments should not be graded individually. The evaluation process should reward risk-taking and progress rather than safe, static performances.

- **Second chances.** Students who fail to meet expectations for any reason should have ample opportunity to recover and improve. Confusion, misdirection, and even lapses in judgment or effort should not be fatal.

Enacting these principles in the classroom requires frequent repetition and explanation. Some are embodied in my course outlines and assignment sheets, some are the subjects of whole-class presentations, and all are reinforced in student conferences.

For example, the "Course Requirements" section of every course outline I write includes expectations on class participation, reading assignments, notebook writing, papers, projects, tests, and the course portfolio (see Chapter 1, Figure 1.1). These explanations are designed to give students a clear sense of what matters in the course—active involvement in class; regular low-stakes writing; a rich composing process, including peer review, reflection, and revision. The course outline also includes an explanation of my grading policy and process, as in this example from a second-trimester ninth-grade section:

> **EVALUATION AND GRADES:** Most assignments **will not be graded individually.** Instead, I will assess most of your work over a period of several weeks. This process will include *self*-evaluation. *Progress* counts as much as *products.* Final grades will be calculated as follows:
>
> | | |
> |---|---|
> | Class Participation/Notebook Evaluation #1 (January) | 10% |
> | Class Participation/Notebook Evaluation #2 (March) | 10% |
> | Writing Folder Evaluation #1 (January) | 15% |
> | Writing Folder Evaluation #2 (February) | 15% |
> | Writing Folder Evaluation #3 (March) | 15% |
> | Quizzes and Tests (ongoing) | 15% |
> | Final Exam and Course Portfolio (March) | 20% |

The goal of this listing is to clarify for students what counts and how much, forestalling any surprises at report card time, but it also helps me with my planning. Having decided what the major assessments will be, I can map out a schedule for the term that spaces assignments and evaluations reasonably, avoiding a paper pile-up or a last-minute rush.

For many students (and parents), my practice of not grading individual assignments is new and a little bit scary, so I always take time to explain in depth the rationale for this approach, like this:

> In this course I will be asking you to try many new things, to stretch yourselves as writers and thinkers. Some of this work may be hard at the beginning, and your first attempts may not always be successful. I don't want to discourage you from

taking risks by giving you low grades when this happens. Instead, I will give you lots of feedback and lots of opportunities to revise. We'll see how your work progresses over time and base your grade on your overall performance rather than on individual pieces. That doesn't mean that individual assignments don't count. They do, but only as parts of a larger whole. I hope and believe that you will get *better* grades using this approach. But if you ever have doubts about where you stand, just ask—and don't worry, if you're in any danger of earning less than a B, you'll be hearing from me.

This speech usually allays most students' fears, at least for the moment. But when I hand back the first set of papers, someone usually asks where the grade is, so I remind the class of my policy and the rationale for it. I also preview my overall approach to assigning *folder* grades:

B means that you have completed your writing assignments on schedule, reflected thoughtfully on the subjects, organized your thoughts, expressed yourself clearly, and supported your ideas with evidence from the texts, when appropriate. You must also have demonstrated progress in writing skills.

A means that, in addition to the criteria listed for a B grade, you have demonstrated exceptional insight in your interpretations of literature, unusual depth and creativity in your personal and imaginative writing, and/or substantial progress in writing skills.

C means that you have met most of the requirements for the writing folder but that you have lost some credit due to persistent lateness, superficial analysis, skimpy development, inadequate revision and proofreading, etc.

INC means that your writing folder is unfinished and will receive a D or F if not completed.

This general rubric, coupled with supportive feedback on the papers, reassures the students that they will do well if they make a decent effort. I also remind them that they have many chances to recover when things don't go well. I encourage them to revise any pieces that they are not satisfied with, and I tell them that I almost always accept late work—even very late work—for reduced credit. At the same time, I implement procedures (explained later) to prompt ongoing self-reflection. As a result, students hardly ever seem to fret about grades in my classes.

There are always a few students who don't fret *enough* about their grades. You know who I mean—the ones who rarely manage to complete assignments thoroughly or on time. Like most teachers, I spend a lot of time working one-on-one with these students, cajoling them, boosting their confidence, scaffolding assign-ments to enable them to succeed (see Chapter 10). I suppose it could be argued that my policy of not grading individual papers lulls these students into a false sense of security, but I maintain that the opposite is true: Long-term assessment makes them less likely to give up. Since I started using a folder system, I have had far fewer failing grades in my classes; given the chance to improve, most students eventually come through.

> **Your turn.** Reflect on your philosophy of assessment. What are your core beliefs about evaluation? List several principles that embody these beliefs. Then look at your current assessment practices. Do they reflect your principles, or are there discrepancies between what you believe in and what you do to accommodate school policies or the day-to-day pressures of the job? If so, how might these tensions be resolved? Also think about how you communicate with students about assessment and include them in the process. Do class documents (course outlines, assignment sheets, rubrics, tests, etc.) convey your expectations clearly? Do your presentations focus students' attention on progress rather than grades? Do your policies allow for meaningful opportunities for recovery if students fall behind?

Managing Writing Folders

First, a clarification: I use the term *writing folder* to refer to the right-hand side of the pocket folder that each of my students keeps in a special box in the classroom. This pocket collects nearly all of the written work that students do in the course: rough and final drafts of papers, quizzes and tests, and projects, if they fit. Only the stu-dents' class notebooks are omitted. The left-hand pocket is reserved for the course portfolio. More on that later.

Students set up their writing folders on the day that I return the first set of papers, usually about a week into the course. The first assignment is generally a short piece of personal writing, often related to the subject matter of the course, something that allows students to draw on their experiences and prior knowledge and that allows me to get to know them as people and as writers. For instance, in my American Literature and Nature course, I ask students to write about their percep-tions of nature and some of their experiences in nature. It's the kind of assignment that allows for a range of responses, from the concrete to the philosophical. I don't write many evaluative comments on these early pieces; I just respond to the stu-dents' ideas. Here's an example. Tim, a junior, wrote a two-page essay that explored his views of humans' impact on nature and his scientific and recreational interests in it, then concluded with this paragraph:

> I do believe nature could be symbolic of something or even spiritual, but I don't [know] of what. Nature is peculiar, because of the way it behaves, the things that happen for [a] reason, but nobody knows that reason is strange to me. Nature could be a spiritual force that we don't know about or a symbol that is supposed to tell us something about why we are [here], or it could be giving us clues to unknown answers, like the cure for aids. Whatever it is it is a very powerful and unknown phenomenon.

Tim's essay showed that he needed to work on several writing skills, but at this stage in the course I was more interested in the quality of his thinking and his evident curiosity. Besides a few positive marginal notations, I limited myself to this response: "Trying to figure out what nature means has been the project of many writers and philosophers—and I think you're one of them. Very interesting and thoughtful essay!" I wanted him to know that he was engaged in the same kind of work as Emerson and Thoreau and other authors we would be reading.

Along with the papers, I hand out a writing folder cover sheet, the first of two that students will use during the term to keep track of and reflect on their work—not only their writing but also their class participation—and that I will use to evaluate their progress. I have tried out several variations of these forms, but I have found that they work best if I customize them to each course, including a list of the required papers and a worksheet itemizing how the grade will be computed. Figure 4.1 shows the version that I used for the first half of Tim's class, and the shaded row includes the reflection he wrote on his first paper. The reflection is crucial. If students are to improve as writers and contributors, they need to examine what is working well and what needs fixing. In this case, given a few days' separation from the writing and a chance to reread his work, Tim recognized—without my telling him—that his paper wasn't cohesive.

Timeliness and *time* are key factors in making student reflection successful. If we want students to see each writing assignment as part of a continuous growth process, we need to make sure they get prompt feedback. An easy and authentic way to ensure immediate response is to schedule a fifteen- or twenty-minute peer sharing session on the day a paper is due. My students love having the opportunity to hear and discuss each other's work. After that, it's my job to read the papers and get them back before the students have forgotten them. My goal is a two- or three-day turnaround, and I can usually make it if I plan my due dates carefully (as explained in Chapter 1) and focus my responses (as explained in Chapter 5). When I hand back the papers, I ask students to review them carefully, not only to digest my feedback

American Literature and Nature			Name ___Tim R.___	
			Writing Folder—First Half	

#	Date	Title/Type of Paper	Comments on Process/Product/Progress
1	9/5	*My Perception of Nature* **Perceptions Paper**	*Good points, but scattered ideas/thoughts throughout paper. Not very transitional from one idea to another between paragraphs.*
2	9/19	*My Song of Myself* **Creative Piece**	*Very good I think, shows varied stanzas, different sides of myself. Doesn't have examples though. Show my inner feelings/views on life.*
3	10/3	*America's Representation within Huck Finn* **Analytical Essay**	*I think I had all the symbols, but the paragraphs could have included more examples from the book. I could have also organized the symbols better into paragraphs, but it's still my best paper so far.*
R	10/13	*The Representation of America with Huck Finn* **Revision**	*I went more in depth about each of the key points, and symbols, and why they are related to America. I also added lots of related quotes and examples from the book.*
	10/15	**Teacher Comments:** *You've done a nice job of revising your paper, Tim. I see big improvements in several parts —especially more evidence. You had one late assignment, but you're making good progress.* <div align="right">**Writing Folder Grade:** *B+*</div>	

				Class Participation—First Half

#	Date	A	T	Reflections on Preparation for Class/Contributions to Discussion/Notebook
1	9/22	0	0	*Rarely volunteers, but gives insight when called upon. Always prepared with material, except once for a paper, and carefully does notebook writing and keeps it organized.*
2	10/11	2	0	*Volunteering a lot more. Was able to give more detail about Douglass and volunteered a lot in Reading Groups. Has been participating a lot more and still coming prepared to class and staying organized.*

Midterm Grade Worksheet
Writing Folder Evaluation #1:   __88__ (x 3)
Class Participation Evaluation #1:   __88__ (x 2)
Nature Journal Evaluation #1:   B+88
Quiz Grade Total: __88__

Midterm Average: __88__ (Total ÷ 7)

Teacher Comments:
The book group work was a good opportunity for you to make your voice heard, which you are other- wise shy about doing. As noted above, your contributions have increased somewhat. More please!

Class Participation Grade: *B+*

Figure 4.1. Writing folder cover sheet.

but also to make their own judgments about the strengths and weaknesses of their writing. Then I distribute their pocket folders and ask them to record the date and title of the paper and to write comments about the process of composing it, the quality of the product, and/or their progress as writers. I follow a similar procedure every two or three weeks to invite students to assess their own class participation (including their attendance, preparation for class, and notebook writing). Each of these reflections takes about ten to fifteen minutes, and I think it's time well spent. Of course, while some students engage in the process readily, others need encouragement. Unaccustomed to self-assessment, they tend to see the teacher as the only reliable authority when it comes to valuing their work. For these students especially, *regular* practice in reflection is essential.

The reflections that students write on their cover sheets, like the comments that I write on their ungraded papers, are formative rather than summative; the goal is to foster improvement in their habits and skills and to spur revision of their writing. Students have many chances to revise their papers in my classes. First, they have the option of redoing any assignment they are not satisfied with at any time. When I evaluate their writing folders, I "count" only the best version. Second, before each writing folder review, I ask everyone to choose one paper to rewrite—not necessarily the one that needs the most work, but the one that the writer feels most motivated to revisit and most capable of improving. Giving students a choice about which papers to revise—and permission to be "done" with assignments that just didn't click for some reason—allows them to take ownership of their writing and responsibility for their progress. The pieces revised for writing folder reviews are usually among those selected for end-of-term course portfolios, which offer students yet another chance to refine and polish their work.

A few weeks before midterm grades are due, I start preparing my students for their first writing folder and class participation evaluations. By then they have reflected on their work at least a couple of times, and they are ready to begin thinking about how it is adding up. My usual procedure is to ask the class first to review the goals and expectations enumerated in the course outline and the various assignments they have completed and then to work collaboratively to develop guides that they (and I) can use to assess their achievement and progress. The examples in Figure 4.2 are tidied-up versions of two student-generated rubrics. The process of creating them starts with brainstorming the general criteria. When the class has reached a consensus on these (with some input from me), I draw the grids on the chalkboard and ask the students to suggest performance descriptors, starting with the B level (which to me denotes "meets expectations"). When those are complete, we extrapolate up and down to fill in the other grade levels. A volunteer copies down the finished rubrics, and I take them home to type up. In the process I clarify the wording here and there and add spaces at the bottom for students to make

WRITING FOLDER EVALUATION RUBRIC

Grade	Completeness/ Deadlines	Interpretation of Literature	Relevance and Originality	Quality of Written Work	Progress in Writing
A	All papers and drafts completed fully, on time	Unusual insight and in-depth idea development	Papers always include original approaches	Writing shows clear strengths in most traits	Substantial improvement or error reduction
B	All papers and drafts completed but with one submitted late	Develops topics fully and supports ideas with details and evidence	One or more papers include original ideas or approaches	Writing shows moderate strength in most traits or is a mixed bag	Some signs of organizational improvement or error reduction
C	All papers completed with missing draft or more than one late	Develops ideas partially or with limited supporting detail or evidence	Papers fulfill assignments but without originality or flair	Writing shows weaknesses in several traits or has major flaws	Few signs of improvement and/or repetition of errors
D	All papers completed but with minimal effort or progress or well after deadlines				
F	One or more papers missing from writing folder or minimal work completed well after deadlines				
Midterm Review Student Notes					

CLASS PARTICIPATION RUBRIC

Grade	Attendance and Use of Passes	Preparation for Class	Notebook Writing	Contributions to Discussions	Attentiveness, Respect for All
A	Few absences or tardies (excused), limited pass use	Usually ready with topics and questions to raise	Thoughtful, thorough notes and comments	Shows leadership in small- and large-group work	"B" criteria plus makes frequent use of the text
B	In class on time almost all days and occasional use of hall pass	Homework completed and materials in class almost all days	Regular note-taking and honest effort to respond to prompts	Poses questions and responds to others regularly (or increasingly)	Pays attention to others, avoids side interactions, respects all ideas
C	One unexcused absence and/or regular tardiness and/or frequent use of hall pass	Homework often incomplete and/or work materials often missing during class	Infrequent note-taking and/or limited effort to respond to writing prompts	Rarely responds or contributes and/or makes negative or rude comments	Frequently inattentive, distracting, and/or listless during class
D	Significant cutting or tardiness, limited preparation for class, little effort to participate or listen				
F	Frequent cutting or tardiness, poor preparation for class, lack of cooperation or respect for others				
Midterm Review Student Notes					

Figure 4.2. Student self-assessment guides.

notes. This rubric sheet then becomes part of the writing folder, and students refer to it in subsequent reflections. Taking part in the development of these rubrics is in itself an exercise in formative assessment, and the process is probably more important than the products.

Full disclosure: creating rubrics with a class is a labor-intensive enterprise, and some classes take to it better than others. When I'm really pressed for time, I streamline the procedure by preselecting some of the criteria or by completing one or two of the columns ahead of time as examples. Sometimes the finished document isn't quite as formal as the one in Figure 4.2. But even limited opportunities to engage in conversations about what constitutes quality work are beneficial, I think. When students help to set the standards, they generally aim high.

Midterm arrives, and it's time for me to do some summative assessment. (In Amherst Regional High School's trimester schedule, progress report grades are due about six weeks into the term.) By now my students have written several papers and revised at least one, but I don't have many grades in my record book—a couple of quizzes and a small project, perhaps. I do have a lot of check marks and other symbols indicating which assignments have been completed, which were most and least successful, which were revised, and so on. Of course these notations are only a supplement to the students' writing folders, which include the real evidence of their achievement. If everything has gone according to plan, their papers are assembled in reverse-chronological order and their cover sheets are completely filled in, with reflections on each piece of writing and two or more on class participation.

Figure 4.1 shows what Tim's reflection sheet looked like at midterm. Besides the initial essay on nature, he had written a creative piece modeled after Whitman's "Song of Myself" and an analytical essay on *Huckleberry Finn*. Thus, in keeping with my plan for a balanced writing program (see Chapter 2), he had completed expressive, poetic, and transactional pieces. He had chosen to revise the formal essay because it was a challenging assignment, and he was proud of what he had accomplished—and he wanted to make it even better. His brief reflections show that he understood how he was progressing in writing and class participation.

Grading at this point is actually pretty easy. I've already read and commented on all of the papers, and I'm quite familiar with the students' strengths and weaknesses, so I can devote most of my attention to assessing how much they have grown. I look carefully at their revisions and at whether they have addressed in later pieces the problems that were identified in earlier ones. I use the class rubrics to guide my evaluations, but I don't attempt to assign a specific number of points to each category. Instead, I check or circle the descriptors that best represent the student's work, and then I look for the overall trends and choose the appropriate grades, usually without much agonizing. In truth, the students have already done most of the heavy lifting in writing their reflections, which I have found to be almost universally candid and realistic. (If anything, they tend to be too hard on themselves.) My comments frequently underscore points that students have already made, but I also try to identify specific gains I have noticed or to point out the next steps to improvement. My final task is to complete the grade worksheet: I want students to know their grades before they get their reports cards. If the student hasn't completed enough quality work to earn at least a C, I mark the folder incomplete and specify a date by which it must be remediated. As noted earlier, giving students another chance to recover dramatically reduces the number of failing grades.

Soon the process starts all over again with a new cover sheet for the second half of the trimester. (In my ninth-grade classes, I usually do three writing folder reviews so the evaluation cycles are shorter.) The process is similar the second time around except that students typically have more choices of writing assignments and/or are engaged in long-term projects in the latter part of a course, so I make the cover sheets "customizable" to the work they are doing. Toward the end of the term, the students focus on selecting and revising work for the course portfolio (the left-hand side of the pocket folder), as explained in the next section.

Your turn. Think about the procedures you currently use to manage the ongoing task of responding to students' work. Do you use a folder system (paper or digital) to collect their papers and projects? How does it work? Do your students regularly reflect on their achievement and progress? How and when? Are they involved in establishing the criteria for evaluation? Do you grade assignments individually or collectively? On what basis? Are you keeping up with the paper load? Is your feedback helpful to students? If you are dissatisfied with your answers to any of these questions, experiment with a new process—starting with *one* of your classes. First, revisit the philosophy of assessment you outlined earlier. What principles do you want your new approach to embody? What kind of infrastructure do you need to build to enact your new vision of assessment? Think of the examples shared in this section (cover sheet, reflection process, student-generated rubrics, grading policy, etc.) as starting points rather than as models; develop forms and procedures that will answer the needs of your teaching context. And don't forget to consult your students. Tell them what you hope to accomplish and solicit their input throughout the experiment. They will appreciate being asked to contribute, and their ideas will be valuable. Then reflect on the results of your efforts. What's working? What else needs to change? Make needed modifications and implement the new strategy in other classes.

Taking Stock with Portfolios

As I explained earlier, my department has adopted portfolios as a required form of summative assessment in all courses. Since students take two trimester-long classes each year, they complete eight of these collections in their high school careers. The current guidelines for these portfolios are that they include at least three thoroughly revised pieces of writing from the course (plus an Honors/AP project if the student has opted for that challenge) and a substantial reflective essay on what the student has learned and what the selected pieces show about his or her writing (see Figure 4.3). Portfolio construction goes on throughout the term, but it occurs most intensively in the last two weeks. The school's computer labs are booked solid with English classes as students put finishing touches on their papers and draft their reflective introductions.

Each of you is a writer. To be a writer involves two important acts: writing as often as possible and revising your written work. In each English class, you will spend much time writing and revising, all with the purpose of learning to be a strong writer.

The English portfolio is designed with these ideas in mind. During each class, you will collect all of your work in a writing folder. At the end of the term, you will select three (or more) pieces of writing that represent your best work or work that you are particularly proud of for your course portfolio.

Your portfolio is first and foremost for you, in that you will choose your writing and revise it to the best of your ability. The only entirely new piece of writing in your portfolio will be the final reflection on your learning experience in the class. The course portfolio provides an opportunity to gather your writing, improve your writing, and reflect on your writing.

At the end of each trimester, after the teacher has evaluated your portfolio, each of you will put that trimester's portfolio into your cumulative English folder. You will be able to see your work from previous classes and to remember and reflect on who you were as a writer then. At the end of your time at ARHS, the cumulative folder will be yours to keep.

Selection
- Choose three pieces of writing from the class that make you proud.
- Vary your selections to show the range of your skills, abilities, and talents.
- Include all parts of your writing process for each piece, such as invention strategies (brainstorming, freewriting, outlining, etc.), drafts with peer comments and teacher comments, and final revised draft.
- In addition, include revised Honors/AP project(s) if applicable.

Reflection
- Write approximately two pages about what has been meaningful in your learning process.
- Write about what you learned from the texts, assignments, and class activities.
- Explain and reflect on your strengths and challenges in the class, exploring how you have progressed in your language arts skills.
- Explain your portfolio selections and what they show about you as a writer.
- If the course marks the end of tenth-grade or twelfth-grade English, you should review your cumulative folder and reflect on your progress since you entered high school.

The course portfolio is worth 10% of your trimester grade.

Figure 4.3. Amherst Regional High School English portfolio.

This system has been in place for several years, but it has undergone several revisions—mostly simplifications. Early on, we asked students to demonstrate growth in communication skills as well as mastery of course goals even as they documented their writing processes and showcased their best products. I was particularly keen on this comprehensive approach: if the portfolio guidelines represented our shared expectations and values, I reasoned, they would drive our instruction toward our departmental goals. The assignment sheets for these first portfolios were quite elaborate, listing ten or twelve requirements ranging from research projects to class participation evaluations. At one point we even developed separate guidelines for each course. Assembling these portfolios was hard work for students and teachers, and no one was enjoying it very much. Fortunately, several of my colleagues were wise enough to see that, however well-intentioned, the constraints we had placed on the portfolios had taken away student ownership of the process. By emphasizing the *collection* of such a wide range of artifacts, we had essentially precluded any *selection* and discouraged *reflection*, two key elements of portfolio assessment. Now that we are less directive about the contents, students are more engaged in the process.

Another challenge in building a departmental portfolio system was coming to agreement on evaluation criteria and procedures. We all seemed to feel that the real worth of the portfolios was in the "value added" through self-assessment and revision, but some teachers wanted a detailed rubric with scales while others preferred a holistic approach. We compromised on a scoring guide that includes a set list of criteria but gives teachers the option of choosing a rating for each item or making a collective judgment about each broad category (see Figure 4.4). Either way, the grade is based primarily on the portfolio work, not on past success or failure. Even strong writers can get low marks on this project if they don't rework their pieces and reflect on their learning; conversely, struggling and reluctant writers can get high marks if they do.

Since I use writing folders as well as portfolios in my classroom assessment system, I make it a point to explain the difference early and often: "The writing folder (on the right-hand side of the pocket folder) is the ongoing repository of all your coursework; the course portfolio (on the left-hand side) is the final showcase of your best work." Students begin moving pieces into their portfolios after the first writing folder evaluation. Most choose the papers they have just revised, but some decide on others that they feel particularly proud of. Students have the option of replacing their selections later, but getting one or two pieces in shape before the end of the term makes the job of completing the portfolio much easier.

Whenever possible, I take my classes to the computer lab to write their reflective essays. Most students do a much better job in the company of their peers. They ask each other about the assigned books and projects and in the process spark recollections of class discussions and activities. They review their folders repeatedly and

AMHERST REGIONAL HIGH SCHOOL ENGLISH DEPARTMENT **PORTFOLIO ASSESSMENT GUIDE**	Name_____ Year_____ Term_____	
ASSESSMENT CRITERIA COURSE:		
The Portfolio Selections:	_____/25	Notes
1. Show a range of skills, abilities, and talents.	1 2 3 4 5	
2. Demonstrate achievement and progress in language arts skills.	1 2 3 4 5	
3. Demonstrate that the student has strived to reach his or her writing potential.	1 2 3 4 5	
4. Include evidence of thoughtful revision (not just editing).	1 2 3 4 5	
5. Demonstrate creativity, flair, craft, and pride of authorship.	1 2 3 4 5	
The Portfolio Reflection:	_____/20	Notes
6. Includes thoughtful attention to texts, assignments, and class activities.	1 2 3 4 5	
7. Considers the student's personal strengths and challenges in the class.	1 2 3 4 5	
8. Explores the student's progress in language arts skills.	1 2 3 4 5	
9. Explains the portfolio selections and what they show about the student as a writer.	1 2 3 4 5	
Portfolio Presentation	_____/5	Notes
10. Displays pieces that are word-processed (or neatly handwritten), carefully edited, organized, and clean.	1 2 3 4 5	
TOTAL POINTS / PORTFOLIO GRADE (10% of course grade)		
GENERAL COMMENTS: TEACHER_____	**KEY** **5 = Thoroughly or deeply** **4 = Essentially or mostly** **3 = Partially or basically** **2 = Barely or minimally** **1 = Poorly or not at all** **GRADING RUBRIC** **43–50 = A** **35–42 = B** **27–34 = C** **19–26 = D** **10–18 = F**	

Honors/AP credit ____approved ____not approved. Signature_____ Date_____

AP Project: _____ AP Level: 1 2

Figure 4.4. ARHS English portfolio assessment guide.

check in with me when they have questions. They think, and they write. Some are able to finish in an extended class period, but many ask for more time, which I am happy to grant. I can almost see them becoming smarter as they compose these

This class has been an extensive learning experience. I have seen different views of nature, and have gained a new perspective of nature, different from the one I wrote about at the beginning of the trimester. The books range differently in my interest level, but they all had one thing in common. The fact that they were all related to nature is something that sparked my interest, because I'm a kind of person who loves nature. I thoroughly enjoyed this class, and would take it again if I could. I also liked the nature journal entries, and like I said in my last entry, I wouldn't have seen all the observations I saw throughout the trimester, if I wasn't required to do the journal entries.

I included in my portfolio three pieces, each of which displays various types of writing styles. I think these pieces of writing best represents my best writing that I have done in this class. One of the papers I wrote was called, "The Representation of America within *The Adventures of Huckleberry Finn*." This paper is about how the book represents America at that time, and how Huck Finn is a symbol of America. Another paper I wrote was called, "The Race for Popularity." This was a creative writing assignment that could be about any topic, as long as it included multiple perspectives. I wrote about a kid who spent his whole high school career trying to be popular, and lost that popularity to a kid who never wanted to be popular. It wasn't what he did that made him popular, but his father's wealth. The last paper that I included in my portfolio was called, "Whaling in the 19th Century." This was a research paper about whaling in the 19th century. But instead of just writing a typical research paper I also included information about *Moby-Dick* relating to whaling. My goal was to connect *Moby-Dick*, which was the book we were reading, to whaling. I picked three different papers to show my range of writing abilities. I had a research paper, a creative story, and an analysis paper.

In the paper "The Representation of America within *The Adventures of Huckleberry Finn*," I had to do a lot of symbolism. That was the main purpose of the paper, to connect different things symbolically. I think that was one of my challenges when I started the class, but I strengthened that skill, that is why I chose to include this piece of writing. I chose this paper also, because I believe it was the best one that I done for the whole trimester. I believe I accurately explain quotes, examples, and symbols. I also believe that this is one of the best analytical papers I have ever done.

The paper "The Race for Popularity" was a struggle for me to do. I had never done a multiple perspective story. Also, because the topic was open-ended, I had trouble thinking of a topic, and then coming up with a way to show two perspectives, but at the end I think I did a good job. It wasn't the best creative stories that I have done, but it was up with the top five. I also liked this story, because I mentioned two of my favorite kinds of cars, and I'm a car fiend.

"Whaling in the 19th Century" was also another paper I had trouble writing, because there's so much information about whaling, that I had to cut a lot of things out of my paper. Also, the paper could only be one page long and also include information from *Moby-Dick*, which made it very difficult for me to decide what to keep and what to leave out. I wasn't able to go in depth about the information I was providing, so I kept things very vague in order to provide as much information about whaling as I could. Research papers were never a challenge for me due to the amount of papers I had to write in my previous history classes, but trying to fit a lot of information in one page was very challenging for me.

This class helped me gain new views on nature and life in general. I've found a whole new respect for nature. Before this class living in Wendell was sometimes great, but I also got annoyed, but now I see the opportunity to live in a place full of wildlife differently. I feel really privileged to be able to see different kinds of plants and animals, and different stages of seasons, something I wouldn't have been able to see if I lived in the city. Also when I started reading *Walden*, I thought he was boring, but now I'm start to see things his way, and I have actually changed my future plans to move to the northwest and own some land, and maybe do some farming, after my career. I have new values and beliefs on what life should be like and am glad to have been able to learn from the authors of whose books I read.

Figure 4.5. Tim's American Literature and Nature portfolio reflection.

reflections, and I certainly get smarter as I read them. They learn what they have learned in the course, and I learn what I have taught—explicitly and implicitly. I think I gain more insight about my effectiveness as a teacher from these reflections than from course evaluations.

Tim's portfolio essay (Figure 4.5) demonstrates the kind of thoughtfulness students usually bring to the reflection process. His overall achievement in the course had been average or a little better—he had tried hard on the papers, but some had been quite challenging for him. I found it interesting that he focused on the challenges in his reflection: overcoming them and learning new skills was clearly what made him most proud. He still had work to do, including getting better at editing, but his portfolio highlighted his progress as a writer and thinker.

The strongest students' portfolio reflections are always gratifying to read. Insightful and articulate, though sometimes hyperbolic ("I learned more in this course than in all my other high school classes combined . . ."), these essays tend to mirror my best images of my teaching self. But the least successful students' reflections are the most instructive. I often wince when I read them, not because they place blame on me (on the contrary, they are usually self-critical) but because they remind me that I haven't figured out how to support the students adequately. Even these essays have pleasant surprises, though. Here's an excerpt from a reflection by a student with learning disabilities, a last-term senior who had struggled throughout high school:

> The English language is hard enough for me, and then to add taking a course in Bible and [Related] Lit I thought I was going to die. But I learned a great deal more than I ever thought I would have. The bible is very interesting. It is full of exciting stories that you have to look deeper into to interpret and compare to life. The history of the ancient people and the Israelites was fascinating. The history of mankind and the bible is more than I knew. The reading was very hard but with support from [special education] teachers and Mr. Penniman I was able to slog through and even write about it. At first this was very intimidating but in the end I really felt it was all worth it because I felt like I knew so much more about one of the most important books there are.

Not exactly the makings of a transformative Hollywood teacher-hero movie, but I'll take it. These comments put some flesh and bones on the student's barely passing final grade.

> **Your turn.** If you have never used portfolios as summative assessments, pick one course in which to try them out. Try to enlist several colleagues to work with you. Start by deciding what you want to learn: a portfolio is a collection with a

purpose. Do you want to assess growth? Examine process? Measure mastery of basic skills? Showcase success? How you answer this question will determine what kind of portfolio you develop. But remember, less is more. Leave room for students to find and fulfill their own purposes in this project. Also remember that the portfolio process includes three essential elements: collection, reflection, and selection. Plan and schedule activities throughout the course that move the work along, and be sure to save adequate time at the end, not just for students to assemble their portfolios, but for you to read and reflect on them. Finally, think through the knotty problem of evaluation. In the best of all possible worlds, portfolios wouldn't be graded at all, but in school, grades are hard to avoid on major assessments. What criteria and methods will you use to place a value on each student's work? If you have tried portfolios before, use the questions posed in this paragraph to review your goals and procedures. What aspects of the process are you satisfied with? What elements need to be revised? If possible, initiate a departmental (or interdepartmental) discussion of portfolios. Developing a *culture* of portfolio assessment within a school promotes acceptance of this alternative to testing among students and parents and provides a support network for teachers.

Diversifying Assessment with Projects and Tests

Like most other English teachers, I rely primarily on writing assignments and class participation to monitor students' learning. Composition and discussion are natural means of formative and summative assessment in our field. Nonetheless, there are appropriate roles for other forms of evaluation—hands-on projects and quizzes or tests. Even these tend to be writing intensive, but they have a different feel to students from ordinary papers. The nature journal that Tim mentioned in his portfolio reflection required a lot of writing; however, this project also encouraged drawing, and it happened outdoors, far away from computers and desks. The multigenre autobiographies that my ninth graders create are collections of writings, but they often include nonacademic genres and elements of graphic design. Though the tests I give are mostly writing, too, the focus isn't on processing but rather on producing on the spot.

Projects tend to be time-consuming, so to be worthwhile they must be carefully aligned with course goals (a "cool" project does not necessarily make a valid assessment). For example, a major objective of my Bible and Related Literature course is that students understand the Bible's influence on the arts and popular culture. The principal means of achieving that objective is an annotated collection of fifty Bible references. Spotting, researching, and analyzing biblical allusions over a long period of time enables students to make connections in ways that writing an essay would not. Similarly, preparing individual or group presentations may engage students in research and literary analysis more deeply than doing a paper for the teacher because the work has a clear, authentic purpose. I try to ensure that each of my students makes at least one formal oral presentation every term (see Chapter 8). Some projects are high stakes, such as teaching a lesson (complete with PowerPoint slide show) on a book of the Bible that the student has read and researched independently. Some have more moderate stakes, such as a group performance of a cutting from a play or a recitation of a memorized sonnet.

Many teachers say they have trouble evaluating projects—perhaps they're uncomfortable analyzing creativity, or they find, as I do, that it's hard to judge a performance by breaking it down into its component parts—but core principles of assessment still apply: clear expectations, genuine response, ongoing reflection, progress focus. Because some projects don't really allow for second chances, formative feedback is especially important. I learned this the hard way with the Bible reference collection. Despite regular reminders and excellent exemplars, some students just didn't get the idea and came up short at the end. So the next time I instituted a series of checkpoints, starting with five allusions, to monitor progress and clear up any confusion. Staging the work this way can't guarantee success, but it helps. I still find it hard to put grades on students' finished projects, especially when they have put a lot of hours into them. I like to start by publicly celebrating their collective achievements. Then, to ensure consistency of focus, I use guides like the one in Figure 4.6—developed, such as the ones presented earlier, with student input. Most of these rubrics have descriptors rather than rating scales. If a project has many steps, process work also counts in the final evaluation. Most important, students' creations and oral presentations always get responses from their peers, sometimes in personal letters of commendation and recommendation, sometimes in informal discussions.

Though tests aren't nearly as much fun as projects, especially for students, they can be efficient tools for assessing learning. I don't include that many quizzes and tests in my courses, and I don't usually count them too heavily, but I do find them useful for gauging how well students comprehend the readings and grasp the concepts I have taught. Besides, in the current atmosphere of high-stakes assessments, I would feel irresponsible if I didn't give students some practice responding to on-demand, open-response questions. I don't believe in "gotcha" tests, though. I even promise my classes that I won't give pop reading quizzes unless they absolutely force me to do so (the threat of a quiz isn't a good motivator anyway). My core belief about tests is that students should *learn* by taking them. That's right: not just show what they have learned, but actually gain new insights and make new connections.

Sonnet Memorization	Sonnet_____	Name_____

Sonnet Memorization   Sonnet_____   Name_____

1. **Introduction** (stating author and title, topic, and interesting facets of sonnet):

    Incomplete   Needs prompting to finish   Complete and practiced   Thoughtful and fluent

2. **Memorization** (number of lines learned by heart):   0 2 4 6 8 10 12 14

3. **Recitation** (smoothness of presentation): Labored   Halting   Rushed   Clear and well paced

4. **Expression** (interpretation of sonnet): Just says words   Conveys meaning   Develops emotions

5. **Comment:**   **Grade:**

Figure 4.6. Sonnet performance evaluation form.

To meet this standard, tests have to be scaffolded for success. Review sessions and practice with equivalent items should be part of the scaffolding, but the tests themselves should be constructed so that students can capitalize on what they do know and understand rather than get stymied by what they can't recall.

Here's a simple example. When I teach *The Odyssey* in ninth grade, I include several mini-lessons on the characteristics of the classical epic. Students are expected to learn terms such as *archetype* and *in medias res*. When I quiz the students on these concepts, I don't use multiple-choice items or ask for memorized definitions. I get a more realistic picture of students' understanding when I create a *context* for the terms that allows them to *apply* their knowledge, as in Figure 4.7, which shows the first part of a quiz on *The Odyssey*. Even scaffolded fill-in-the-blank items can only show so much about students' learning. The other parts of this quiz (not shown) include open-response questions on characters and themes in the epic, such as "How does Telemakhos prove he has 'come of age'?" These too are designed to allow students to apply their knowledge: each has more than one possible answer.

Mixing modes is important in testing. Students bring different strengths and learning styles to the classroom, so we need to offer some variety in the ways that we ask them to show what they know and can do. I'm especially cognizant of this obligation during final exam week, when the stakes are high and students are on edge. I'm always looking for unusual approaches that will make the two-hour exam period as relaxing as possible and a good learning experience. It's the last meeting of the term, and I want students to leave with a sense of accomplishment.

Three of my favorite test-design strategies are group work, art, and humor. My Bible and Related Literature final exam incorporates all of them. During the first half hour of the period, students participate in small-group discussions of the course's "big ideas." Their goal: to come up with three *questions* that would be suitable for a final exam. They don't have to answer the questions, but they do have to provide

1. **Epic Characteristics** (20). Fill in the blank with the correct term or explanation (see **word bank**):

a. An epic is a long _____ poem in a _____ style telling the story of a _____ important to a people. _____'s *The Iliad* and *The Odyssey*, the national epics of _____, depict the events of the _____ and its aftermath.

b. At the beginning of most classic epics, the poet calls on one of the nine _____ for _____. The opening lines of the epic often include a brief _____ of the entire story. This didn't spoil the suspense for the poet's audience because _____*.
Another convention is to begin the story _____, at one of the most exciting parts. Like most hero stories, the epic typically follows a pattern of separation, initiation, and return known as the hero _____.

c. Epics include a variety of descriptive language. One common device is the _____, a short descriptive phrase such as "gray-eyed Athena." Two other examples of this device are _____* and _____*.
Another descriptive device is the _____, a long _____ that often uses "so" or "just so" as a connector, as in the following example from *The Odyssey*:

> Think of a catch that fishermen haul in to a half moon bay
> In a fine-meshed net from the white-caps of the sea:
> How all are poured on the sand, in throes for the salt sea,
> Twitching their cold lives away in Helios' fiery air:
> <u>So</u> lay the suitors heaped on one another.

d. In classical epics the gods play important roles, and sometimes they are needed to resolve the action at the end. A story ending involving such divine intervention is called a _____ ending. An example of this kind of ending occurs in *The Odyssey*, when _____ _____*.

Word Bank for Part 1 (answers are not provided for items marked *):

epic simile	Muses	deus ex machina	Trojan War	formal
epithet	hero	in medias res	comparison	Greece
archetype	summary	narrative	inspiration	Homer

Figure 4.7. Terminology section of quiz on *The Odyssey*.

a justification for each one (see Figure 4.8). My rationale for this exercise is that it helps students pull together the threads of the course better than merely responding to an essay question that I gave them would. Their discussions are always lively. Another portion of the exam includes a slide show of artwork based on biblical stories and a list of open-ended sentences, such as "These people will spend the next forty years . . ." Students use visual cues in the slides (in this case, a large crowd of people crossing through parted waters) to activate their knowledge and fill in the blanks (". . . wandering in the wilderness"). I run through the slides as many times as necessary for all students to feel satisfied that they have done their best. This portion of the exam has the atmosphere of a game, but it's effective at capturing

> **Part A. Essay Questions (50 points—15 per question plus 5 for the overall range of questions)**
>
> After participating in a group discussion of "big ideas" in Bible and Related Literature, create **three essay questions** that you feel would be suitable for a final exam in this course. Each question should cover a major theme in the Bible, and taken together, the questions should cover a substantial portion of the course's content (**be sure to cover all major parts of the course**). Each question should be accompanied by a **rationale** for asking it. Follow the example below. Do not answer the questions. The group may develop questions and rationales together, but **each student must write his or her own paper**.
>
> Example: Water is associated with cleansing and beginning again in many parts of the Bible. Choose four stories from different parts of the Hebrew and Christian Bibles in which water plays a symbolic role. Explain the importance of water in each one and make connections between them.
>
> Rationale: From the Flood story to the Exodus to Joshua's crossing of the Jordan to Jonah to Jesus' baptism, crossing or being immersed in water signifies the start of a new life for an individual or a people. This symbolism may be associated with the primeval waters and the waters of the womb.

Figure 4.8. Essay portion of Bible and Related Literature final exam.

students' understanding of the biblical texts. So is the last segment of the test, which I created from one of those funny emails that circulate on the Internet (in this case, derived from a piece by Richard Lederer in *National Review*). Entitled "From the Mouths of Babes," it is purported to be composed of unretouched statements about the Bible written by children:

> In the first book of the Bible, Guinessis, God got tired of creating the world, so he took the Sabbath off. Adam and Eve were created from an apple tree. Noah's wife was called Joan of Ark. Noah built an ark, which the animals came on to in pears. Lot's wife was a pillar of salt by day, but a ball of fire by night.
>
> The Jews were a proud people and throughout history they had trouble with the unsympathetic Genitals. Samson was a strongman who let himself be led astray by a Jezebel like Delilah. Samson slayed the Philistines with the axe of the apostles. (Lederer 38)

The passage continues for several more paragraphs. By the time they finish reading it, students are practically falling out of their chairs—because they have enough knowledge of the Bible to get the humor. I ask them to find and correct twenty mistakes; most of them end up doing more.

There are many valid strategies for creating quizzes and tests in English: completing plot diagrams, analyzing quotations, and comparing texts are a few others. What's important, finally, is that the tasks are relevant to the goals of the unit and that students have a fair chance to demonstrate what they know. Sometimes they demonstrate that they are not as well prepared as they should be. Whenever it's feasible, I give students another opportunity to show that they have mastered the material—but only if they prove they are in earnest by coming after school for help or producing notes from independent study. Another possibility is that overall test results demonstrate that I botched something—the test itself or the lessons leading up to it. In that case I try to be honest enough to admit my mistakes and try again.

> **Your turn.** Do an inventory of the assessments you include in your courses. Besides writing papers and participating in discussions, how do your students show they are fulfilling course objectives? Are you satisfied with the array of assessments you are using? If not, what changes would you like to make? If you decide to design or modify a hands-on project, be sure to consider, besides the requirements, the audience and purpose of the activity. Build in regular process steps to scaffold the work, and plan (preferably with your students) the celebration and evaluation of the finished products. As you review your quizzes and tests, take a close look at what they assess. Do items rely on simple recall of facts, or do they also demand higher-order skills such as application and analysis? Do your tests include a variety of modes, and are they structured for success? That is, do they maximize students' chances to show what they know?

A Formative Summation

Of all the elements of classroom organization teachers have to manage, assessment is among the most challenging. There are so many principles to keep in mind: linking assignments and tests to course goals, fostering the habit of reflection, providing supportive feedback, scaffolding for growth, and more. Then there's the problem of finding adequate time to work through those bottomless piles of papers—and making sure that your efforts are doing some good. My best advice is to adopt an inquiry stance toward assessment: to ask yourself constantly what you are learning from students' work, what they are learning from your responses, and what you could do to make the process more effective and efficient. Desperation drove me to self-examination, but you don't have to wait until you're in such dire straits. By questioning your assessment practices, you will learn, as I did, that although there is no way to slough off the English teacher's burden, there are ways to make it easier to bear, and chief among them is to let your students help carry the load. Learner-centered (as opposed to grade-centered) assessment is more beneficial and more satisfying for everyone, and well worth striving to achieve.

Recommended Reading

Calfee, Robert, and Pam Perfumo, eds. *Writing Portfolios in the Classroom: Policy and Practice, Promise and Peril*. Mahwah, NJ: Lawrence Erlbaum, 1996. Print.

> The fifteen essays in this volume present research on portfolio assessment and explore issues related to its implementation. The book would be valuable to a department/school considering adoption of a portfolio system.

Golub, Jeffrey N., ed. *More Ways to Handle the Paper Load: On Paper and Online*. Urbana, IL: NCTE, 2005. Print.

> This helpful collection updates and extends NCTE's 1979 classic *How to Handle the Paper Load* by offering strategies for portfolio assessment, peer review, and especially electronic evaluation. The contributors advocate more writing and less grading.

Smith, Jane Bowman, and Kathleen Blake Yancey. *Self-Assessment and Development in Writing*. Cresskill, NJ: Hampton, 2000. Print.

> Though grounded in the college writing classroom, this collection of essays raises theoretical and practical questions of interest to the secondary teacher. Smith and Yancey's concluding essay is especially helpful in explaining the nature of self-assessment and identifying issues related to implementing it.

Wilson, Maja. *Rethinking Rubrics in Writing Assessment*. Portsmouth, NH: Heinemann, 2006. Print.

> This thoughtful critique of rubrics raises important questions about the values we bring to writing evaluation and advocates seeking and learning from divergent responses.

2

Raising the Structure

Teaching Writing as a Process

I n Chapter 2 I offered some ideas for designing a manageable and authentic classroom writing program, one that includes frequent opportunities for writing in a variety of modes for a variety of audiences, and for low, medium, and high stakes. That chapter dealt with the "big picture" of writing instruction. Chapter 4 focused in large part on writing assessment, including tools, such as writing folders and portfolios, that promote student reflection and growth. In this chapter I focus on day-to-day aspects of teaching the writing workshop—on some approaches to putting student-centered and strategy-oriented writing instruction into practice.

By now the "process model" of writing instruction is well established in most high school English classrooms, at least in theory, but there are some tensions in the field over the ways it has been implemented. Some versions of "the" writing process currently being taught are just as inflexible and artificial as the outdated "product model" of writing instruction. Every textbook now includes an apparatus for teaching process skills, and off-the-shelf writing programs supply graphic organizers and rubrics for every "stage" of the process. However, if writing process research has shown us anything, it's that the act of composing doesn't follow a lockstep, linear path, so requiring students to follow a rigid sequence of steps is an oversimplification at best. On the other hand, some educators have argued that the "writing-as-natural-process" approach is too unstructured and open-ended, good for students who come to school with plenty of academic capital, perhaps, but not for those who need to gain access to the discourses of power. Students may learn to write by writing, but they need some explicit instruction to guide their development. Without it, they may needlessly persist in using ineffectual forms that will damage their chances. These tensions create a dilemma for teachers: how can we teach writing so that students acquire necessary skills without reducing the process to a step-by-step procedure devoid of authenticity?

The answer is to teach the truth about writing: that it is a set of strategies that writers draw on selectively depending on the purpose and situation. Our goal should be for students to develop control over their writing by building a rich repetoire of flexible strategies, rather than slavishly following a set of rigid rules. Assembling some insights from writing process research, this chapter will present several approaches to structuring classroom writing workshops to encourage strategic thinking. Invention (idea development) strategies, peer and teacher feedback, revision, and publication are key topics in the chapter.

More Insights from Research about Writing Process

If the 1960s and 1970s were about overthrowing the traditional paradigm of writing instruction (as discussed in Chapter 2), the 1980s were devoted to learning how writing process works and how the habits of effective writers could be taught. Research revealed the complexity of composing, and subsequent studies have complicated the picture even more, but some of its lessons have yet to be fully absorbed in the secondary writing curriculum, which, for a variety of practical reasons, still often follows a straightforward brainstorming-to-editing model.

Several important papers were published in *College Composition and Communication* in 1980, including three much-anthologized pieces in a single issue (December). The one that has affected my thinking the most is Sondra Perl's "Understanding Composing," which was my introduction to the concept of *recursiveness*, the idea

> that throughout the process of writing, writers return to substrands of the overall process, or subroutines (short successions of steps that yield results on which the writer draws in taking the next set of steps); writers use these to keep the process moving forward. In other words, recursiveness in writing implies that there is a forward-moving action that exists by virtue of a backward-moving action. (364)

I remember how relieved I was when I first read that passage, realizing for the first time that my writing behavior was normal, not the product of disorganization. Writers move back to move forward in several ways: reading parts of what they have written, repeating key words, and especially returning "to feelings or non-verbalized perceptions that *surround* the words, or to what the words already present *evoke* in the writer" (365; emphasis original). Perl likens these feelings, which she terms *felt sense*, to inspiration, and she argues that skilled writers draw on them more readily than unskilled writers. She calls the process of attending to felt sense *retrospective structuring*. "It is retrospective in that it begins with what is already there, inchoately, and brings whatever is there forward by using language in structured form" (367). This process works hand in hand with another that she calls *projective structuring*, "the ability to craft what one intends to say so that it is intelligible to others" (368). One process is internal, the other external, and the writer shuttles back and forth between them. Attempting to reduce the writing process to a linear plan-write-revise sequence obstructs this movement and is likely to cause frustration.

Nancy Sommers's article on revision strategies sounds similar themes. She critiques the linear model of writing because it diverts attention from the aspect of writing that distinguishes it from speech: the opportunity to revise, not just at the end but also throughout the composing process. Sommers's case studies of students' and experienced writers' revising strategies showed that the former concentrated mainly on changing words, while the latter focused on "finding the form and shape of their argument" (384) as well as on audience concerns. For them, revision was integral to the process of discovering meaning. "Here we can see the importance of dissonance; at the heart of revision is the process by which writers recognize and resolve the dissonance they sense in their writing" (385), which arises, perhaps, from what Perl calls felt sense. Sommers argues that students should be taught to seek "the dissonance of discovery" (387) to capitalize on the key advantage of writing—the possibility of revising (ideas as well as vocabulary).

Writer's block is the subject of another well-known study by Mike Rose. Drawing on problem-solving theory, he studied two groups of college writers: blockers and nonblockers. He found that the blockers were "stymied by possessing rigid or inappropriate rules, or inflexible or confused plans" (393). Ironically, these blocking mechanisms often originated with teachers or textbooks. They included precise rules used as if they were mathematical algorithms: always grab your reader's attention immediately; always make three or more points in an essay (394). Another trap was inflexible plans, such as detailed outlines from which the writers would not stray. In contrast, nonblockers employed flexible rules, or *heuristics*, to guide their work (e.g., use as many ideas as needed in the thesis paragraph and develop body paragraphs for each one) and abandoned them if they didn't help (396–397); they also made effective use of feedback.

Cognitive processes are also at the center of Linda Flower and John R. Hayes's work. In one study they compared experts' and novices' approaches to developing ideas and found that "writers themselves create the problem they solve" by the ways they represent the writing task as they work through it. Expert writers consider all aspects of the rhetorical problem, including both the rhetorical situation—assignment and audience—and the writer's goals regarding influence on the reader, the writer's persona or presentation of self, the meaning to be conveyed, and the features of the text. In contrast, the novice writers focused on a few aspects, primarily textual conventions (29–30). Flower and Hayes conclude that the ability to explore rhetorical problems is teachable and learnable, not some kind of mystery or magic. "If we can teach students to explore and define their own problems, even within the constraints of an assignment, we can help them to create inspiration instead of wait for it" (32).

Teaching students how to "create inspiration" was the focus of my dissertation research in the early 1980s. It's one thing to know what strategies skillful writers use; it's quite another to design instruction that will enable students to learn those strategies. I was especially interested in students who got stuck at the beginning or in the midst of the composing process, feeling they had little or nothing to say on a given topic. My study focused on *invention,* the aspect of writing concerned with developing ideas, which was receiving a lot of attention at the time. I looked at the effects of teaching a range of heuristic strategies to ninth graders. I'll discuss some of what I learned and how I still make use of those insights in the next section.

The field of composition studies has taken several turns, some of them into heated disputes, since the foundational papers discussed earlier were published. One controversy of special importance to secondary teachers is the so-called skills versus process debate. Critics of writing process pedagogy, such as Lisa Delpit, argue that a student-centered workshop approach may deny essential instruction to those who lack cultural capital, typically students of color:

> Many liberal educators hold that the primary goal for education is for children to become autonomous, to develop fully who they are in the classroom setting without having arbitrary, outside standards forced upon them. This is a very reasonable goal for people whose children are already participants in the culture of power and who have already internalized its codes.
>
> But parents who don't function within that culture often want something else. It's not that they disagree with the former aim, it's just that they want something more. They want to ensure that the school provides their children with discourse patterns, interactional styles, and spoken and written language codes that will allow them success in the larger society. (28–29)

Delpit argues that these patterns, styles, and codes need to be taught explicitly, not left to a "natural" process of development. She does not advocate that students "attend to hollow, inane, decontextualized subskills" through worksheets or endless drills, but rather learn the language of power through meaningful communication. She also insists that students "be helped to learn about the arbitrariness of those codes and about the power relationships they represent" (45).

As Delpit herself points out, the skills/process debate is really a false dichotomy. Explicit instruction is not incompatible with the goals of the process approach, but the writing workshop needs to have more focus. Jeffrey D. Wilhelm, author of several influential books on adolescent literacy, makes a similar argument: "I think that there is a widespread notion that if you just get kids reading or get them writing a lot, they'll become better readers and writers. I've become convinced that this is absolutely not the case. They'll get better at reading and writing the kinds of things they already know how to read and write" (11). To learn advanced intellectual tools, such as argument, classification, and extended definition, students need to practice them in exploratory writing and use them in real contexts. "We need to help students get to the heart of the matter for any convention we teach," he continues. Once students know the rules and how they work and for what purposes, they have creative control of them.

> With understanding comes the capacity to extend, apply, transform, and revise the tools you have learned. In general, I don't think we do a very good job of that in school. Kids learn a lot of *what* and not very much *how, why, when* or *where*. Information isn't very exciting or important until you start to purposefully use it in real situations. So in effect, our teaching misses the point because we don't teach how what is learned really matters in the kids' lives, in the here and now and in the real world beyond school. (12; emphasis original)

But if, on the other hand, we can teach sophisticated writing skills explicitly *and* give students opportunities to use them authentically, we can promote real progress.

Two recent books address the criticisms of process pedagogy by looking at the writing process as a strategy. James L. Collins's *Strategies for Struggling Writers* sensibly suggests "rejecting notions of incompatible extremes in the teaching of writing in favor of a view that integrates seemingly discrete alternatives," such as skills and process, tradition and innovation, creativity and conformity (21). Collins seeks to create a common ground in the teaching of writing by fostering "self-regulated, culturally responsive strategic writing":

> Writing strategies stand midway between process and skill. A strategy is a sequence of cognitive steps designed to accomplish a particular outcome, and therefore we can think of strategies as controls over inward processes which result in outward manifestations of skills. Writing strategies, accordingly, are cognitive controls or procedures that transform the intention to write into marks on paper. Strategies, furthermore, are acquired or learned in social contexts. Some strategies are acquired intuitively from experience in situational contexts, and others are learned deliberately, usually in education contexts, but the acquisition or learning is always accomplished through social interaction with people or texts or both. (21–22)

Collins suggests that strategic writing instruction should focus on three kinds of knowledge: *declarative*, which gives us knowledge, or the *what* of writing; *procedur-*

al, which gives us strategies, or the *how*; and *conditional*, which gives us deliberate intention and design in specific contexts, or the *why, when,* and *where* (53). He further recommends that development of new writing strategies be facilitated by drawing on struggling students' "default" strategies—the ones that they bring to school: copying, visualizing, and narrating. Straight copying is usually seen as cheating, of course, but emulation of professional writers' texts helps students generate content and gain control over structural patterns. Creating visual representations of ideas and structures helps them develop and organize their material. And using narrative forms to achieve expository purposes helps them to clarify and communicate what they have to say (140–183).

Deborah Dean's *Strategic Writing: The Writing Process and Beyond in the Secondary English Classroom* aims to get writing process instruction out of the rut that it has fallen into in many English classrooms: Monday for prewriting, Tuesday for drafting, Wednesday for revision, Thursday for editing, and Friday for publishing (3). Instead of elements in a recursive act of creation, isolated "process steps" have become ends in themselves, often graded separately. What writing should be, Dean argues, is "a process of using strategies to accomplish a *goal*. And in order to be strategic, students need to stop thinking of prewriting, drafting, revising, and editing as *products* the teacher requires, as products they create after the paper is done in some cases—just to get the points the teacher would give for the 'process'" (4; emphasis added). To reorient writing instruction, Dean advocates teaching a variety of strategies for inquiry, drafting, and product. *Inquiry* strategies comprise activities involving experience, art/drawing, talking/listening, reading/viewing, and writing (26). *Drafting* strategies focus on investigating genre, considering audience, and responding to purpose. *Product* strategies include revising "globally" (organization), revising "locally" (sentence fluency and word choice), editing (mechanics), and evaluative reading (peer response). Dean's categories and terms are certainly familiar to writing teachers, but her emphasis on treating them as reusable strategies rather than items to be ticked off on a checklist gives them heuristic power.

I think it's evident that the writing process researchers, who published influential studies in the 1980s on how novice and expert writers' methods differ, and writing process critics, who have more recently called for explicit instruction in writing skills, are really after the same thing: students who can use writing strategically not only to meet academic and workplace expectations but also to fulfill their own desires and purposes—to work from a place of confidence and control. Where writing process instruction has gone wrong in some instances is in assuming that students will become competent writers without much teacher intervention—just by writing frequently. Most of the secondary English teachers I know already strive for the kind of balance Delpit and Collins call for, shunning ideology in favor of "what works." As I see it, teaching the writing workshop effectively requires keeping four imperatives in mind when planning instruction:

- **Allowing adequate time for thinking and writing.** Ideas germinate slowly, and texts develop recursively. If we want students to truly revise (that is, resee) their ideas and texts, we need to schedule ample class and home-work time.

- **Providing opportunities for student interaction.** Knowledge and skills are socially constructed. Students need opportunities and techniques for solving problems together, sharing ideas, and responding helpfully to one anothers' work.

- **Preparing strategy lessons and activities.** Teachers have experience and expertise in all aspects of the writing process. Designing mini-lessons and longer activities to help students develop their own experience and expertise (as opposed to assigning lockstep procedures) helps them to become strate-gic writers.

- **Conducting individual conferences.** Every student comes to class with a different set of cultural, cognitive, and creative tools and resources, and each will respond to class instruction in his or her own way. Conferring with students individually personalizes the curriculum and facilitates targeted teaching.

These writing workshop essentials underlie the recommendations I offer in the following sections, each of which focuses on one aspect of writing process. These suggestions for teaching writing strategies are not intended as "stages" to be completed for each assignment. A particular writing unit might include lessons on all of these elements or only one or two. What's important is that all students have the chance to build repertoires of strategies over time.

Teaching Invention Strategies

As I noted earlier, when I was in graduate school I was interested in learning how students developed ideas for writing—or rather, why some of them seemed to have so much trouble with this aspect of the process. I always felt for the student who stared at a blank sheet for a whole class period or generated text a few words at a time and then hated the result; I had experienced the same frustrations myself many times. I was also concerned about the more fluent writers who didn't seem to probe their topics deeply, just recording whatever came to mind. Fortunately, lots of composition theorists and researchers were thinking about the same questions at the time, and there had been a great revival of interest in invention, the rhetorical art of discovery. Early writing process models used the word *prewriting* to refer to generative activities, such as brainstorming and planning, but *invention* seemed the more accurate term because it described idea development as a *strategy* rather than a *stage*. Given the recursiveness of writing, there might be a need to develop new ideas or insights at any time in the process. There were plenty of strategies to choose from, ancient and modern. I found that they could be sorted into two broad categories: intuitive ones, which draw on the writer's natural creativity, and systematic ones, which rely on heuristic routines to discipline the mind (Penniman 24).

Each type of invention had its partisans and supporting research, but since I was a teacher rather than an academic, I took the pragmatic approach: why not expose students to several kinds of strategies and let them choose the ones that help them the most? So I created a booklet with eight invention techniques drawn from current theory and research—everything from freewriting to diagramming—explained and adapted for a high school audience. Another teacher introduced these strategies to his three ninth-grade classes while I examined the effects on students' writing processes, written products, and attitudes toward writing. Not surprisingly, I found that students' preferences and results varied a great deal. Some found freewriting helpful, some didn't, and so on for all of the other strategies. However, blind-scored writing samples showed that those who engaged in any kind of process of invention produced better writing (232–235). Perhaps the most interesting finding was that working with invention strategies increased students' metacognitive awareness and control. One of the case study students, a basic writer I called Don, was able to describe his preferred heuristic, a visualizing strategy, in more and more detail as he learned about and experimented with other heuristic strategies. In fact, I liked his technique so much that I substituted it for my own description of visualizing in subsequent editions of my booklet.

I still teach invention strategies in my classes, though generally just one at a time now. I'm careful to introduce them as *potentially* useful aids to planning, drafting, or revising, not as required steps in writing assignments. Usually I launch a new strategy through a class activity with a social component; working in pairs or groups encourages participation and boosts students' chances of success. Often students ask for a reprise of a particular strategy lesson ("Can we do that 'close your eyes' thing again?"), but even if they don't, I make sure to point out—in class and in conference—situations that might be ripe for particular heuristics. What follows is a brief overview of how I integrate invention strategies in my classes. I'll focus on ninth grade for these examples, but the approaches are easily adapted to other grades.

Freewriting is a perennial favorite with my ninth graders. I think its emphasis on writing "without rules" makes them feel like they're getting away with something. Also, they seem to find ten or fifteen minutes of silence and reflection to be an oasis of calm in their frenetic school days. The hardest part about teaching freewriting as an invention strategy isn't getting students to write—with few exceptions, they participate quite willingly—it's helping them figure out what to do with the texts they generate. Freewriting often yields provocative passages or kernels of promising ideas, but they're usually embedded in a lot of not-so-useful stuff. Reviewing the text with a highlighter in hand is a useful next step, and so is group-talk. After a freewriting session, students are usually brimming with enthusiasm, and sharing helps them to clarify their thoughts.

Freewriting works especially well as a follow-up to a visualizing exercise, the invention strategy my ninth graders relish the most. I often introduce visualizing as a way to prepare for writing a personal narrative. I begin the visualizing exercise by turning off the lights and pulling the shades and asking the students to get comfortable and close their eyes. After the requisite amount of giggling and squirming, they settle in, and I lead them through some simple relaxation techniques. If this is the first round of visualizing, I take them through a series of questions to probe their memories, starting with pleasant ones ("Think of a place you love to go . . .") and leading eventually to harder ones ("Think of a time you felt betrayed . . . or you betrayed someone else . . ."). If students already have their topics, I ask them questions (inspired by Don's visualizing strategy) that help them to conjure up the scene, "zoom in" on various parts, "listen" to the dialogue, use all of their other senses, and examine their feelings about what's happening. I leave a lot of silence between prompts. At the end, I tell them that when they open their eyes, they should pick up their pencils and, without speaking, freewrite for ten minutes, recording everything they can remember. I keep the lights low. When the writing time is over, most of them are eager to share, and I get them into groups and let them go. I'm always on the lookout, though, for anyone who might have become upset by reliving a sad or troubling experience and try to offer whatever that student needs—a sympathetic ear, a few minutes alone, or a walk down the hall with a friend. I'm always a little nervous when I introduce the visualizing strategy, but it works every time. The students' thinking about their topics goes deeper than just the events.

Another kind of visual strategy that many students find beneficial is diagramming. As Collins points out (160), primary students always begin their stories by drawing pictures, and the technique still works well in high school, especially for analyzing stories. Rendering a key scene or even a quotation as art helps to clarify events and relationships, making overt, perhaps, the visualizing that good readers do in their heads (I'll say more about this in Chapter 6). But I'm also referring to more "mechanical" forms of diagramming: tables, graphs, flowcharts, etc. Writing teachers make frequent use of these tools as graphic organizers, but I want to make an important distinction here. I don't generally use diagrams as *templates* for writing assignments. Rather, I present them as *strategies* for collecting and analyzing information. Venn diagrams show relationships between sets of data; flowcharts outline sequences of steps; tables compare and contrast (see Chapter 7 for a student example). Diagramming usually *leads* to organization, but its real purpose is to stimulate thinking, as in the example in Figure 5.1. I ask students to complete this exercise before drafting persuasive letters to businesses or government officials to help them examine the issues they are writing about more carefully than they otherwise might.

I'd like to recommend reconsideration of two systematic invention strategies that were the rage for a while but then fell out of favor. Or I'd like to recommend my much-simplified versions of them; part of the reason for their decline was that their original designs were opaque to most students and teachers. One is the unfortunately named "tagmemic heuristic," which came from a branch of linguistics and used terminology from physics (Young, Becker, and Pike 127). The original heuristic was much too complicated for high school use, but its most salient feature was thoroughly usable—the idea that any topic could be viewed from three perspectives:

- **Particle**, which I call the "contrast view": looking at the distinguishing features of a subject and contrasting it with similar subjects;
- **Wave**, which I call the "process view": looking at the subject's development over time; its origins, the changes it has undergone, and its future; and
- **Field**, which I call the "system view": looking at the subject as a system composed of many parts or as one part of a larger system.

Thesis:		
	Supporting Arguments:	**Opposing Arguments:**
1		
2		
3		

Figure 5.1. Persuasive letter worksheet.

The beauty of this technique is that it can produce a thorough investigation of just about any topic. One particularly effective application is literary character analysis. Using the "changing perspectives" heuristic moves students beyond merely recounting the character's actions to a systematic examination of his or her physical and psychological features, development over time, moral composition, relationships, etc. My students have also used the heuristic to explore a particular spot in nature, the effects of computers on society, and many other subjects. The strategy can easily be presented in columns on the blackboard or in a diagram on a handout. It's important to remember, though, that it is a means to an end, not an end in itself. The three perspectives will not be equally generative for all subjects, nor do they all need to be included in a student's finished product. Heuristics should produce abundance and give the writer choices.

Another strategy that merits revival is Kenneth Burke's "dramatistic method," set forth in *A Grammar of Motives*. Developed originally for theater criticism, the method was adapted for use as a heuristic for writing. In elemental terms, it is based on the idea that anything in life can be examined as a drama with five elements: act, scene, agent, agency, and purpose (Burke xv). This "pentad" is like the reporter's basic questions, except that Burke emphasizes the "ratios" or connections between the various elements. I call the strategy "dramatizing" and usually present it the form of the star diagram in Figure 5.2. My ninth graders use it as a starter for composing original short stories (sometimes in combination with a visualizing exercise). I encourage them to start at whatever point of the star they have the clearest ideas about and then work from there. For example, a student might have a particular setting in mind. He or she could describe that setting in detail, then move to another point. Who would be in the setting? What would that character's history, relationships, and current situation be? What critical act might that character perform? And so on through all the other points. The idea is to push each question deeper and deeper throughout the writing process. Doing this kind of analysis of story elements, a student is much less likely to write the dreaded "and then . . ." narrative—the rambling, disconnected series of events that English teachers know all too well. The dramatizing strategy can also be a useful tool for analyzing stories, historical or current events, and many other topics. Like the changing perspectives heuristic, it ensures that the writer considers a variety of viewpoints.

The possibilities for invention strategies are almost endless. Other heuristics I teach are extended definitions ("What is a hero? What kinds of heroes are there? How do you know when someone is heroic?") and metaphors ("Is the route to success a ladder? A spiral staircase? A roller coaster? An obstacle course?"—see Elbow [*Writing with Power* 78–93] for more examples). The goal is that students be familiar with a range of strategies and know how and when to use them.

Your turn. Think about the strategies you use to develop your ideas when writing. Do they tend to be intuitive or systematic? Do they vary according to the task and situation? How effective are they? What strategies do you teach your students? Are they flexible heuristics, usable at any phase of any writing task, or staged procedures linked to particular assignments? Try introducing one or two new invention strategies to your classes (after trying them yourself). Ask students to share their results and reflect on what worked and what didn't. As a result, they should become more aware of—and thus more in control of—their own thinking processes.

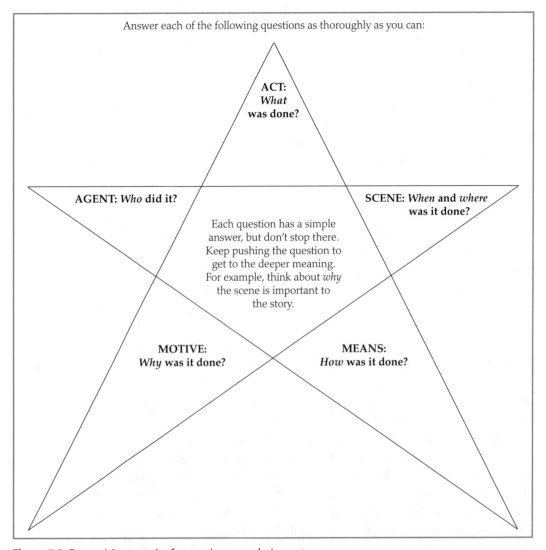

Answer each of the following questions as thoroughly as you can:

ACT:
What
was done?

AGENT: *Who did it?*

SCENE: *When* and *where*
was it done?

Each question has a simple answer, but don't stop there. Keep pushing the question to get to the deeper meaning. For example, think about *why* the scene is important to the story.

MOTIVE:
Why was it done?

MEANS:
How was it done?

Figure 5.2. Dramatizing exercise for creating or analyzing a story.

Strategizing Peer and Teacher Response

Since the early days of my teaching career, I've embraced the notion that students should receive feedback on their writing from their peers as well as the teacher. But for many years I struggled to make peer response work effectively. Although students seemed to take the activity seriously, their comments on each other's work were often superficial or judgmental or just plain wrong. Rubrics helped a little but seemed to take all the joy out of sharing papers. Through my work in the Western Massachusetts Writing Project, I figured out where I was going astray. First, I wasn't giving students enough practice, so their responding skills didn't progress. Second, I was asking them to do some things that they weren't very good at, such as identifying mechanical errors. Third and most important, I wasn't teaching them *strategies* for response. As a result, they often resorted to "playing teacher," pointing out minor problems and making vague suggestions such as "wrap everything up with a strong conclusion" or "watch the transitions."

My current approach to peer response puts a lot of emphasis on sharing and discussion and not so much on written feedback. "What writers need," say Peter Elbow and Pat Belanoff, ". . . is *an audience*: a thoughtful, interested audience rather than evaluators or editors or advice-givers" (*Sharing* 5; emphasis original). I try to make sure that there are opportunities for students to share and respond naturally throughout the writing process, from when they begin generating ideas for pieces up to the day they turn them in. Much of this response occurs spontaneously during workshop time as a student seeks feedback from a neighbor or gathers a small group to share drafts in a corner of the room. But there are also "formal" response group meetings—at least one for each writing assignment—in which each student presents his or her work and receives comments from the other group members. I don't schedule "peer editing" sessions too often now; I find that the editors tend to add as many mechanical errors as they correct. However, in the process of sharing pieces, students pick up many of *their own* mistakes.

I usually preface each response group meeting by introducing or reviewing one or two feedback strategies, many of which I draw from Elbow and Belanoff's *Sharing and Responding* booklet, which includes simple and effective techniques such as the following:

- *Sharing: no response.* Students just listen to and enjoy one anothers' work. I encourage them to say "thank you" at the end of each piece. This strategy is especially helpful at the beginning of a term or when new response groups form.

- *Pointing.* "Which words or phrases or passages somehow strike you? Stick in the mind? *Get through?*" (8; emphasis original). This nonjudgmental form of response helps writers see what portions of their drafts make an impression on readers or listeners.

- *Center of gravity.* "Which sections somehow seem important or resonant?" (8). This technique helps writers identify aspects of their topics that might be worth further exploration—minor points that could become major focus areas.

- *Sayback.* "Say back to me in your own words what you hear me getting at in my piece" (9). Responses to this prompt tell writers what they are communicating.

- *What is almost said? What do you want to hear more about?* Replies to these questions help writers to develop and enrich their pieces (9).

These strategies are nonthreatening, easily learned, and applicable to any kind of writing. As students become more skillful at giving and receiving responses, they may be able to move on to Elbow and Belanoff's more sophisticated exercises, such as "believing and doubting" (11), in which readers first try to support and extend a writer's argument and then try to challenge it.

I always remind students of a few basic ground rules at the start of a peer response session: everyone gets an equal chance to share his or her work and receive feedback; hurtful or destructive comments are not allowed (though that's rarely a problem); and no one can say "it's good" or "nice job" in response to a shared piece. The last rule is especially important. I tell students that while such affirmative feedback may *seem* supportive, what it really says to a writer is, "I don't care enough about you or your paper to bother being specific." In general, I prefer to have students read their papers aloud to each other whenever possible. Sharing in this way puts the writing and the writer's voice in the room, and it reduces the chances that the responders will engage in error-hunting. I also stress that the writer should decide what kind of response he or she wants and state that preference before reading. Later, longer drafts may be shared on paper, typically by passing them around the circle, but the writer still determines the type of feedback.

Good things happen in the response groups. Students who are making solid progress have the chance to deepen their thinking by engaging in lively discussions of their ideas. Students who are blocked or behind benefit from these discussions, too. They feel comfortable opening up to their peers about their struggles, and they get lots of helpful suggestions.

Giving students the opportunity to provide the kinds of feedback that they're good at allows me to concentrate on the kinds that I'm good at: idea development, organization, sentence structure, word choice, and mechanics. When students submit drafts for comments, I ask them to tell me what kinds of feedback they need. I focus my responses on their specific questions and one or two other aspects of their papers that I think need attention. I don't always follow the writing process creed of postponing attention to mechanical problems until the last stage. I see no point in allowing writers to rehearse their misunderstandings again and again. I don't mark obvious typos on early drafts, but if someone makes the same mistake repeatedly (such as misspelling a name or splicing sentences with commas instead of semicolons), I'll note the errors, add an explanation as needed, and try to find an instance where the student got it right.

Many students need what Elbow and Belanoff call "skeleton feedback" (*Sharing* 11): help with sorting out the main points, subpoints, and supporting evidence in their essays. For example, for her analytical essay on *Huckleberry Finn*, Yiting, an English language learner in my American Literature in Nature class, chose a prompt based on this quotation: "Mark Twain may be credited with inventing the master-symbol of nineteenth-century America in the image of a small boy floating down the Mississippi on a raft, uncertain of his destination, but confident of meeting any emergency with pluck and ingenuity" (Whicher 308). Figure 5.3 includes the plan and draft Yiting submitted. She understood the prompt and grasped the novel's main ideas, but she was having some trouble presenting a coherent analysis of Huck as a symbol of America.

I made several marginal notations on her draft, praising the strong points, pointing out aspects of the novel she hadn't addressed, and indicating passages that needed clarification. But my final comments sprang from her question to me on organization:

> This draft is coming along pretty well, Yiting. I think the organization could be improved by looking at some key parts of your thesis:
>
> 1. First, why is the main character a *young boy*, an *orphan* in fact? Why is that like America in the 1800s?
>
> 2. Why does Twain focus on an *interracial relationship*? How is that like America?
>
> 3. Why are they floating on a raft? (You partially answer this one.)
>
> 4. What do they learn about *society* as they travel?
>
> You might find it best to put the part about breaking the rules closer to the end—that's really the *climax*.

My goal was to help her fulfill her plan by considering each aspect of the Huck-on-a-raft-with-a-runaway-slave-fleeing-society symbol as representative of some

Thesis: Huck and the way he chose to live in *The Adventures of Huckleberry Finn* by Mark Twain is the symbol of America. Huck represents America as a newborn baby, trying to figure out what is right and what is wrong.

Huck represents America as a young child, trying to understand society and the real world, and he got together with a runaway slave, and helped each other, which was the right thing to do, but against the society. America was like Huck, on a floating raft, wandering around, to find the best way to live. The "wrong thing," which against the rules is really the right thing.

Huckleberry Finn Essay

In Mark Twain's book *The Adventures of Huckleberry Finn*, the main character Huck was a young white boy who ran away from society. He ran away, and got together with a runaway slave, and they made decisions by following their hearts, never really thought about the rules for society, which represents America. America was just like a young kid by the time Twain wrote the book.

Huck was adopted by Ms. Watson, who always teaches him about society rules, tells him how to behave, and respect others. However, Huck didn't think most of the rules of society were right, that is why he chose to run away from Ms. Watson, from the society. He went on to live his life the way he thinks is right, which was kind of against the society by then. Huck chose not to turn Jim in when he found out that Jim ran away from Ms. Watson. Instead, Huck helped Jim to hide, and get freedom. "I said I wouldn't tell, and I'll stick to it." (55) Huck promised Jim. Help a runaway slave was totally against the laws, but Huck thought it was right because he followed his heart, and not the rules. Rules can be changed when something is not right, but following the heart, love is always the right move. It is just like America years ago, it has rules, but nobody was 100% sure that they were right. People were trying to figure out and change the laws by experiencing more and more. America had to have more experiences to know what was right, just like Huck, because nobody was there to help them make decisions, and there were no sources and examples to follow. They would realize some rules are not helpful sooner or later.

On Huck and Jim's way hiding from others, most of the time, they were on a floating raft, which was the symbol of another side of America. When America was trying to make their rules and people's lives better and better, they were like a raft floating around, there were no specific directions for them to go, they had to face and learn how to solve problems when they floated to the wrong places. They needed to find a way to survive on their own. "Jim said if we had the canoe hid in a good place, and had all the traps in the cavern, we could rush there if anybody was to come to the island, and they would never found us without dogs." (59) Huck and Jim were finding ways to protect themselves, and survive.

When Jim got caught, and Huck was trying to rescue him, he said "I will go to hell!" It sounded like so wrong to go to hell for a slave and Huck knew it was against the rules that Ms. Watson taught him. However he chose to do it. One of the reasons was that he didn't know that much about society, so he did what his heart tells him to do, Jim was a friend of his by then, and he thought helping a friend is more important than breaking the laws, so he would do it no matter what. At the end of the book, almost everybody changed their mind; they figured out that sometimes, rules of society might be wrong too.

P. S. I didn't write all of the specific evidence here. I'll add it for final draft. Sorry

Question—Is my essay well organized?

Figure 5.3. Yiting's essay plan and draft.

aspect of nineteenth-century America. In her next draft, which was completely reorganized and 50 percent longer, she made the topic her own by focusing on what Huck learns during the novel. The following is her revised introduction:

In Mark Twain's book *The Adventures of Huckleberry Finn*, the main character Huck was a young boy who seeks to be free, so he didn't have to live with his drunk father, or being civilized. Also, on Huck's way to freedom, he helped a runaway slave Jim, instead of turning him in. The setting of the book was in South of America, black people had no legal rights, and were being descriminated. At first, Huck was debating with society, helped Jim because he had mercy on Jim, but eventually, they became best friends, treated each other with their hearts. Huck was representing America as a young child, trying to figure out what is right and what is wrong about the society, and finally found the way to live with love.

The second draft was far from perfect; she hadn't always chosen the strongest examples from the book, and many sentences still revealed her ongoing struggles with English syntax. But each paragraph made a clear connection between Huck and Jim's story and American society.

My comments alone don't account for the changes in Yiting's essay, of course. She received feedback from her response group, sought help from her ELL tutor, and met with me individually to review her draft. I think I do some of my best teaching in writing conferences, but quite indirectly. My strategy is to get the student talking about his or her paper, to listen for explicit or implicit ideas and goals, and to reflect back what I think I've heard. I often take notes while the student is speaking, so he or she will have a record of our conversation, but I don't usually make any changes on the student's paper. My aim is to help the writer identify a range of options for moving forward, not to determine exactly what must be done.

> **Your turn.** Reflect on how you manage peer response in your classes. What kinds of feedback do your students give each other? Under what circumstances? What response strategies do you teach them? Are you satisfied with the results? What improvements would you like to see? What changes could you make to bring them about? Also think about your strategies for responding to student work. How does your role differ from the peer responders'? How do you decide what aspects of a paper to address in your comments? How do you conduct conferences? How do you ensure that the writer maintains control of his or her work?

Approaching Revision Strategically

I wish that all students were as committed to rewriting their papers as Yiting. As much as we talk about revision as *re-vision*, the truth is that many students don't get the point of making wholesale changes to their work. They go through the motions of doing another draft, changing a word here or adding a detail there and fixing mechanical errors, otherwise leaving the text undisturbed. They don't seem to use revision as a strategy for developing meaning. I think that oversimplified school models of writing process are partly to blame. Presenting revision as the third of four stages or the fifth of seven makes it another chore to check off the list and suggests, perhaps, that a writer can avoid it by getting things right in the first place. In reality, revision happens throughout the process, driven by felt sense, as discussed earlier. Barry Lane jokes that his seven-step writing process is revise, revise, revise, revise, revise, revise, revise (3). Student writers undoubtedly do a lot more revising than they realize in the course of composing their pieces—word processors hide most evidence of rewriting done in the midst of drafting—but the idea of undertaking major restructuring and rewording of "finished" drafts stops many of them cold. To encourage my students to embrace this aspect of writing as a necessary, even joyous, meaning-making activity, I stress the following points in class:

- Revision is a normal part of writing, not a punishment for doing a bad job.
- Revision happens repeatedly throughout the writing process, not just at the end.
- Revision is not synonymous with editing, which *does* typically happen at the end.
- Revision harnesses the power of language and strengthens the writer's voice.

These ideas are easiest to sell when students are working on papers in which they feel they have a personal stake and creative control, such as personal narratives, poems, and short stories. Getting them motivated to revise analytical essays is generally a lot tougher. Length is a factor, too: it's one thing to rewrite a two-page response, quite another to reconstruct a five-page essay.

As I explained in Chapter 4, one of my strategies for encouraging deep revision is to give students time and choice. I expect all compositions to be developed to at least a semipolished state, and I always ask students to reflect on how they could be improved before placing them in their writing folders. But I don't require that they thoroughly revise every paper. After they have collected several pieces, I ask them each to pick one to rewrite. They reread their selections with their response groups and develop specific plans for improving content, organization, and expression. Some ask for conferences with me to refine these plans. I can't say that this strategy always results in transformative revision, but it does seem to get students engaged in the process. I think that coming back to their papers after a little separation enables them to bring new energy to the work, and having some choice in the matter gives them a feeling of control.

I developed another effective revision strategy quite by accident: the partial draft. I had assigned an analytical essay to one of my literature classes, and I was planning to collect and return the students' drafts before the upcoming school vacation so they would have plenty of time to think about revisions. But for one reason or another we fell behind schedule, so students didn't start work on the papers until three days before the break. I really wanted to give them some kind of feedback before the long hiatus, so I said, "I'll tell you what: why don't you write *one page* of your essay for tomorrow, and I'll take a look at what you've done tomorrow night and try to give you some guidance for continuing the paper." This brainstorm turned out to be a stroke of genius. I was able to review the whole set of drafts in a little over an hour and make three kinds of comments: (1) "You clearly have a sense of direction—carry on with your plan"; (2) "Your purpose is still a little unclear, but you seem to be saying *x*, and you might consider *y*"; and (3) "Let's talk." During the next day's writing workshop, I met with the latter group at the beginning of class to help them get a better sense of how to approach the task and develop plans. Then I worked with students in the middle group to make sure each of them was finding a focus. Finally I checked in with the on-track group to see if they had any questions. By the end of class, I was satisfied that everyone knew what to do next. All of the students seemed appreciative of the opportunity to receive my feedback before committing the time required to develop a full first draft. When the papers came in, I was surprised by how many had started their second drafts from scratch—something I hadn't previously found most students willing to do. But it made perfect sense: since they hadn't spent hours struggling to grind out essays they didn't feel good about, dumping the partial first drafts didn't feel like losing a huge investment.

Now I schedule a partial draft review as part of every major writing assignment. I ask students to come up with one or two pages of text—not outline—and a tentative plan for the rest. Yiting went a bit overboard, composing almost six hundred words for her first take on the topic. Her classmate Jeremy's start was more typical (see Figure 5.4). He was writing about the controversial ending of *Huckleberry Finn*, and he was clearly ambivalent about the topic.

In my comments I tried to offer him some suggestions for making the essay more focused. By the time he completed his final draft, he had clarified his position, as indicated by his title, "The Disappointing Ending to Huckleberry Finn," and written the following new introduction:

> The ending to *Huckleberry Finn* by Mark Twain has caused many different reactions and readers have shown many different opinions. Some readers were very pleased with the ending and thought Mark Twain couldn't have ended such a "great American classic" any other way than he did. Others didn't think too much of the ending and might have thought of it as boring and not satisfying. Some

The book Huckleberry Finn, by Mark Twain is a great American classic to some, and to others, seen as a disgrace to literature all because of the disagreements over the ending. Some see the ending as a perfect way to end such a great book, but others see it as a total waste and it doesn't satisfy them at all. The ending to Huckleberry Finn has caused much argument to whether it's appropriate to the rest of the book or not, but actually it could go either way, being very much appropriate or also being completely different to the rest of the book.

Some people might say that the ending doesn't go with the rest of the book because the change in plot and the characters. The whole plot changes when Huck reaches the Phelps's house. They stop going on adventures through the river and briefly stopping in towns. The whole setting evolves around the Phelps's household and not the river. Also, although Huck is still narrating the story, it seems as though Tom Sawyer is the new main character. He is always leading the way and telling people what to do.

This seems a bit wishy-washy—by the time you get to the end of the paper, you will probably have a clearer point to make, and you can rewrite this. For example, you could explain the reasons the ending seems inappropriate but then argue that it really does work.

It would be useful to recap the situation—King and Duke gone, Jim sold into slavery again, etc. Then you'll need to illustrate what you say above and contrast it to what came before. You'll also need to outline some main reasons why the ending doesn't or does fit—there should probably be some preview of these in your intro.

Figure 5.4. Jeremy's partial draft.

people even thought it was offensive and completely inappropriate to the rest of the book. As a reader myself, I thought the ending to such a well written and entertaining book was boring, unsatisfying, and most of all, inappropriate to the rest of the book.

Despite being a bit redundant, this opening paragraph establishes a direction for the essay, and the lead sentence of each body paragraph moves it another step forward:

First off, why did some readers see the ending so great and perfect? Some might have thought that it satisfied the rest of the story when …

To contradict these reasons, there are some reasons why the ending was boring and not exciting. Right before the final stretch of the book …

Along with the fake dullness of the ending, it was also extremely unsatisfying for a reader. Throughout the whole entire book …

Not only was the ending to *Huckleberry Finn* boring and unsatisfying, but also it didn't fit with the rest of the book because the characters had different traits.… (emphasis added)

The strong transitions in this final version of the paper reflect the logical pattern of reasoning that Jeremy developed as he revised from his partial draft. His essay turned out as well as it did not because of the brilliance of my intervention but because of its *timing*. Submitting a partial draft allowed him to pause and take a step back from the writing and allowed me to offer some feedback and suggestions when they could still do some good.

Another benefit to reviewing partial drafts is that I can see the full range of problems that students are facing early on and prepare a mini-lesson focusing on the most common ones. After reading a set of drafts, I prepare a list of revising and editing tips like the one in Figure 5.5 and use it for a workshop session, focusing primarily on the first five items. Later, when students have completed their papers, I ask them to take out the list again and use the last five items to check mechanics and formatting. I prefer giving out customized suggestions to distributing a generic checklist because they come directly from the students' writing. Some items show up every term, but others vary according to the experience of the students and the nature of the task.

Tips for revising and editing your *Huckleberry Finn* paper:

1. Don't be wedded to your partial first draft. The easiest and most effective approach to revising may be to start again, using pieces of what you have already written.

2. Make sure that your topic and your overall direction are clear at the beginning. Don't make your purpose a mystery.

3. Don't assume that your reader recalls all of the details of Twain's novel exactly as you do. Include a synopsis of the facts that are relevant to your topic.

4. Develop a plan before completing your draft. Think about all of the parts that need to be included and allot a certain amount of space to each one (such as a page or a paragraph).

5. Ground your analysis in the texts. Include quotations from *Huckleberry Finn* to support your assertions. Don't leave quotations hanging, assuming that their significance is obvious. Lead into each quotation with a point you want to make and follow up with an explanation.

6. Cite quotations properly, using author-page: (Twain 37). Note that you close the quotes before the parentheses but put the period after them: "Blah blah blah" (Twain 22).

7. Don't change tenses: when analyzing literature, it's usually best to use the "historical present" (recount events in present tense).

8. Handle titles correctly: novel titles are placed in italics or underlining (which are the same thing). Titles of articles and other short pieces are placed in quotation marks.

9. Give your paper a meaningful title, not a generic one. Do not underline it. Be sure to include a heading (name, date, course).

10. Proofread carefully to eliminate stylistic and mechanical errors!

Figure 5.5. Revising and editing suggestions.

There are many techniques that can result in meaningful revision, but they all depend on motivation. Students who are engaged and feel that they have some choice and control are more likely to embrace revision as a meaning-making strategy than those who see it as another weary step on a forced march through "the" writing process. We can encourage students to take the more positive view by acknowledging that *re-vision* of a topic can occur at any point and that different writers have different needs on different occasions. This means keeping our classroom procedures flexible and timing them to provide support when it is needed the most.

> **Your turn.** Try "sitting on your own shoulder" as you work on a demanding writing task to "observe" your strategies for revising (the Track Changes feature in Microsoft Word might help). Think about how your personal approach compares to what you teach your classes about revising. Also ask your students to talk about their approaches to and feelings about revision. Do they engage in *re-vision* or merely correct errors? When are they most willing to revise? When do they find revision a chore? Reflect on how you could modify your methods to make revision a more natural and helpful part of the writing process in your classroom.

Incorporating Publication as a Writing Strategy

There is probably no better way to motivate students to improve their writing than to make it public in some way. The benefits of "writing for real" are well known, but for too many student writers, the teacher is still the only audience. Publication projects can be labor intensive, so it's not surprising that they don't happen more often in English classrooms. But students need regular opportunities to write for authentic purposes and natural reasons to revise their work. Publishing provides both, and it doesn't have to be an onerous job. In Chapter 2, I gave several examples of "high-stakes" writing assignments that give students a public voice, including classroom anthologies, school newspaper articles, and letters to public officials. In Chapters 7 and 8, I give some examples of digital media production and public speaking, respectively. Here I would like offer a few observations about publishing as a strategy for teaching writing.

My definition of *publication* is pretty expansive. When students share drafts in response groups, they're "publishing" their work in a small, secure way. When I invite students to get up and read finished pieces to the entire class, I'm giving them a higher-stakes opportunity to "publish." The same is true when I ask a student if I can use his or her paper as an exemplar for another class. These informal occasions for sharing writing with a wider audience all "count." But something special happens when publication is the purpose from the beginning of a project. Students approach the work with an urgency not usually exhibited for "academic" assignments. Some even go above and beyond the requirements because the writing really matters to them. I've witnessed this phenomenon many times as advisor to the school newspaper as students discover the power and responsibility of the press, and I've also seen it when students create individual publications based on personal or family experiences. Primary school children are excited when they have the chance to make "published books" out of their stories, and high school students are no less enthused by the opportunity to exercise their artistic flair.

Students have come up with all kinds of ideas for their own publications. One created a booklet on the American West as depicted in *My Ántonia* and *The Donner Party* that included a series of original illustrations and a comparative essay. Another assembled a history of Utica, New York, her family's hometown, using photos, artifacts, interviews, and secondary sources. I think that my favorite self-publishing projects are my ninth graders' multigenre autobiographies, which I described in Chapter 2. Each time I look through a stack of these booklets, which are shared with peers and parents and, I hope, kept forever as mementos, I am reminded again how powerful is the human urge to tell one's story and establish one's identity. Every project has a colorful, artistic cover that shouts "Here I am!" and a range of unusual genres: in one, a concert poster showcasing the student's talents; in another, a "field guide" describing the writer's habitat and behaviors. Many of the projects are quite moving, revealing the hardships and complexities of students' lives, and most demonstrate that the writers have stretched themselves.

Jalisa, a special education student who often struggled with writing, put together a collection that showed both the revealing and the stretching characteristics of multigenre projects. She included a haibun (a combination of descriptive prose and haiku) on the disappointing coldness of an early spring day, a diary entry on an exhausting afternoon at the Laundromat, a letter to her apartment manager complaining about the "loud, mean, and obnoxious" kids living on her hallway, and this fretful vignette entitled "The Car!":

Out of everything in my mom's car all I notice is the speedometer gage. I'm always looking at it wile my mom is driving. The speedometer has a long orange needle with a black background, tells me the miles per hour. As my mom drives the needle moves to the right then decreases rapidly as she comes to a red light. If my mom seems anxious the orange needle flutters back and forth. Sometimes my mom is mad when she is driving so I look at the speedometer and the needle is increasing more and more to the right. I find myself looking out the window to see what the speed limit is. I notice that my mom is way past the speed limit. The orange needle moves to the left as she is slowing down. Then I see the needle at zero when she's at a complete stop. I get out of the car and wonder how fast or how much to the right that orange needle gets to when I'm not beside her.

Significantly, Jalisa illustrated this piece with a stop sign and a diagram of the speedometer emphasizing the orange needle. Her frequent repetition of "orange" made me think of the Homeland Security advisory system used after the September 11 attacks: orange means that the threat level is high, and that's what the speaker seems to feel about her own "homeland security" as she assesses her mother's stress. In assembling her project, Jalisa poignantly (though perhaps unintentionally) represented all the tensions in her day-to-day world. I think it was the act of publishing that drove her to dig deep.

> **Your turn.** How do your students respond to opportunities for publishing? What effects do you see in their writing? Pull out the writing program grid you completed in Chapter 2 and look again at your high-stakes writing assignments. How many involve publishing (in any form) for audiences other than the teacher? What other kinds—print, oral, visual, or digital—might you include as group or individual projects? How could you develop a "culture of publication"?

Recursive Teaching

The more we learn about writing through personal reflection and scholarly research, the harder it is to reconcile our understanding of this complex, recursive process with the linear model of writing usually taught in schools. The gap between theory and common practice poses a real dilemma for English teachers. We need to acknowledge how messy writing can be and how different the process looks for different writers, but we also need to teach essential skills explicitly. For me, the best way to do both is to focus on *strategies*. Instead of presenting writing as a sequence of *steps* to be checked off—each one resulting in a product—we would do better to help students develop a repertoire of techniques addressing all *aspects* of writing process, to be called on whenever they are needed. Invention, response, revision, and publication should be embedded in writing instruction, but not necessarily in the same order or in the same way for every assignment. Our teaching of writing strategies should be as recursive and personal as writing itself. Returning repeatedly to reusable heuristics, adding often to their toolkits of techniques, and reflecting regularly on their own composing practices will help students to become strategic writers, to develop flexibility and control.

Recommended Reading

Collins, James L. *Strategies for Struggling Writers*. New York: Guilford, 1998. Print.

> Drawing on extensive research, this helpful book demonstrates methods of teaching writing strategies that draw on the cognitive and cultural strengths of resistant writers.

Dean, Deborah. *Strategic Writing: The Writing Process and Beyond in the Secondary English Classroom*. Urbana, IL: NCTE, 2006. Print.

> Like Collins, Dean holds that writing instruction should focus on teaching strategies that give students control. She critiques the rigid, step-by-step "process" method and presents strategies for inquiry, drafting, and product.

Johnson, T. R., ed. *Teaching Composition: Background Readings*. 3rd ed. Boston: Bedford, 2008. Print.

> Though intended for college composition teachers, this collection includes many articles useful to the secondary teacher, especially in Section 2, "Thinking about the Writing Process." Among the thirty selections are foundational pieces on composition theory as well as perspectives on issues such as grading, grammar, technology, and diversity.

Newkirk, Thomas, and Richard Kent, eds. *Teaching the Neglected "R": Rethinking Writing Instruction in Secondary Classrooms*. Portsmouth, NH: Heinemann, 2007. Print.

> This lively collection includes practical essays on a wide range of topics: teaching the composing process, exploring genre, digital writing, writing outside the classroom, and teaching difference.

6

Encouraging Response to Literature

The *what* and the *why* of teaching literature were the subject of Chapter 3; now I address the *how* and the *who*. In the earlier chapter I focused on program design, and here I turn to the daily challenge of encouraging students to respond to literature in thoughtful, positive ways. The *how* aspect of this chapter is its attention to strategies for fostering engagement. The *who* aspect is its insistence that students play the central roles in literature activities.

In my early years of teaching, my evening preparation for literature lessons nearly always followed the same pattern. I would make detailed marginal notes on the assigned reading and reflect on larger thematic questions, just as I had learned to do in college. Then I would prepare an agenda: the points I wanted to cover, the passages I wanted to review, the questions I wanted to ask. I loved doing this work because I learned so much from it; I really *knew* the piece I was teaching by the time I was done. But I was often flustered by the way the lesson went the next day. Sometimes I would pose what I thought was an interesting question, but no one would volunteer. Sometimes a student would raise a key point early in the period that I had planned to introduce at the end, spoiling my "big finish." Often the "discussion" was a ping-pong match between me and a few class members, who responded to my prompts but rarely to each other.

The problem was that my lessons weren't discussions at all—more like interactive lectures. I wrote the program, and I ran the show, which was always focused on explication of the text. On the rare occasions that students worked with each other, it was to answer study questions that I'd prepared. Eventually I realized that "less is more" and loosened up a bit, leaving some space for real student input. I also heard this from a wise, veteran teacher: never ask a question in class if you already know the answer. That got me thinking about the purposes of class discussions: were they for students to explore ideas, or more to demonstrate to me that they had done their homework? Finally I learned how to design productive group work and made the tough decision to move off center stage as frequently as possible.

It's easy to fall into the rut of traditional, teacher-led textual analysis. We enjoy using New Critical practices because we're good at interpreting books this way. But a steady diet of close reading can kill the enjoyment of literature for some students. This chapter explores the possibilities of using other critical lenses (feminist, Marxist, etc.) and suggests incorporating small-group work through literature circles, jigsaws, and art activities. It also offers strategies for designing effective literature-based writing assignments and for teaching literary concepts.

Critical Theory and Group Interaction

In Chapter 3, I mentioned the growing interest in teaching critical theory at the high school level. When I first heard of this idea, I was skeptical. What I had seen of contemporary theory at the college level seemed too esoteric—more concerned with philosophy and ideology than literature. But through the example of two of my Amherst Regional High colleagues, Danae Marr and Kristen Iverson, I became aware of some accessible and practical treatments of critical theory, including some designed specifically for high school students. I have already cited Lois Tyson's *Critical Theory Today*, a relatively new and readable college textbook, and Deborah Appleman's *Critical Encounters in High School English*, a creative adaptation of critical theory for the secondary classroom; both provide clear explanations and specific applications of a range of critical approaches. Another valuable resource is Lisa Schade Eckert's *How Does It Mean? Engaging Reluctant Readers through Literary Theory*, which explains how the author built a "general" (i.e., not college-prep) world literature course with units focused on five critical approaches. Eckert sees literary theory as a fundamental tool for skills development:

> Learning theory gives [students] a purpose in approaching a reading task, helps them make and test predictions as they read, and provides a framework for student response and awareness of their stance in approaching a text. . . . They discover how they are constantly interpreting signals whenever they read, even though they may not be aware of doing so. They can develop an awareness of the meaning-making strategies they already employ or can learn to employ for improved comprehension and appreciation of text. (8)

Just as practicing a range of invention strategies helps students become more conscious, flexible writers, using a variety of critical lenses helps them become more deliberate, insightful readers.

One of the invention strategies I recommended in Chapter 5 was based on Kenneth Burke's "dramatistic method." Robert McMahon's *Thinking about Litera-*

ture: New Ideas for High School Teachers develops a provocative approach from the essential questions in Burke's theory. "The power of these questions," McMahon writes, "lies in their making explicit what skillful readers already do" (xiii). Among the prompts included in his "Summary of Basic Questions" are four deceptively simple ways to inquire into structure (What goes with what? What versus what? What follows what? What becomes what?) and these evaluative probes:

> TRUTH. *Examples*: Is this character's understanding of her situation true or false, and why? In what ways is it true (accurate, adequate, valid), and why?

> GOODNESS. (a) MORAL CHARACTER. . . . Is this character a good person, or a bad one, and why? In what ways is this character a good person, and why? In what ways is he a bad one, and why? (b) ACT. Is this act good or bad, and why? In what ways is this act good, and why? In what ways is it bad, and why? (xx)

Subsequent questions invite the student to consider both the character's purposes and the act's consequences. McMahon demonstrates his technique in interpretations of texts as diverse as the biblical parable of the prodigal son and Alice Walker's short story "Everyday Use."

Another approach based on contemporary critical theory is presented in Barbara King-Shaver's *When Text Meets Text: Helping High School Readers Make Connections in Literature*, which focuses on the concept of *intertextuality*, the notion that "[when] we read a book, a short story, a play, a poem, or an essay, we are reading every other text we have ever read. Likewise, when an author writes a text, he or she is writing every other text he or she has ever read or written" (4). The idea of intertextuality is as old as reading, but its modern theoretical roots are in the transactional model of reading, semiotics, and poststructuralist criticism (2–6). All three suggest that the meaning of a text depends on context, and particularly the reader's experiences. "In the English classroom, teachers help build content knowledge by introducing information, both written and visual, that addresses the subject being studied. In addition, they can orchestrate intertextual studies to help students make connections by introducing paired texts for study in a supportive environment" (7). King-Shaver shows how intertextual units can be developed for the study of genres, themes, authors, and archetypes. I gave some examples of these kinds of connections in Chapter 3, and I offer some ideas for creating multicultural literary "conversations" in Chapter 9. Any time we create a syllabus, we're laying a foundation for intertextuality, so it makes sense to arrange texts to facilitate conceptual connections. It's important, though, that we teach students how to do the connecting rather than do it all for them.

King-Shaver links intertextuality to the schema theory of learning, which is also the basis of an influential book on reading: *Mosaic of Thought: Teaching Comprehension in a Reader's Workshop*. Its authors, Ellin Oliver Keene and Susan Zimmermann, outline a powerful approach for improving children's comprehension that includes teaching them to make three types of connections: "text to self," "text to text," and "text to world" (55). All three could be called intertextual in the sense that students' experiences and the world are, like books, "texts" to be interpreted. I have found this method extremely helpful in teaching high school students how to respond to literature, and I encourage them to use any of the three types of connections as jumping-off points for their literary response papers.

The *Mosaic of Thought* connection strategy is one of many helpful teaching techniques I have learned from elementary and middle school colleagues. Others include several forms of group work designed originally with younger students in mind. The educational advantages of having students work on problems together are well established, as Elizabeth G. Cohen explains:

> When the groupwork assignment demands thinking and discussion and when there is no clear, right answer, everyone in the group benefits from that interaction. People of any age deal with the uncertainty of a challenging task better if they consult fellow workers or students than if they try to work by themselves. This is why the frequency of interaction in the task consistently predicts individual and group learning when groups are working on discovery problems. (11)

The intellectual benefits can occur even when—or especially when—there is disagreement in work groups, which also have obvious potential for improving oral language proficiency and social interaction. The principal reason that I decided to adopt group-work strategies is that they multiply the learning opportunities in the classroom. If we learn by verbalizing our ideas, then everyone needs to have lots of chances to talk. Even the most equitable whole-class discussion can't provide them—just do the math. But well-managed group work can.

"Well managed" is the key. Teachers get frustrated with groups because some students don't stay on task, do their share of the work, or cooperate with their peers. Many students also get frustrated for the same reasons, especially when they receive group grades. I've seen all of these problems in my classroom and come close to giving up on group work at times. But on reflection I've realized that when things go badly it's because I haven't prepared students well enough or provided the right kind of structure. Fortunately there are many researchers and practitioners, such as Cohen, in the field with helpful strategies for fostering cooperation, assigning leadership roles, staging tasks, and other key steps in creating successful group interactions.

One model for group work that I've found particularly effective is the "jigsaw" (see Aronson). This strategy requires a bit of engineering, but it gives students the opportunity to work in different groups, as learners and as teachers, and makes them accountable to their peers. If a class has thirty students, the teacher might create six heterogeneous "home" groups of five students each (let's call them A, B, C, D, E, F) and five distinct learning tasks. Each member of a home group joins an "expert" group (1, 2, 3, 4, or 5) to accomplish the task with peers from the other home groups. Then the home groups reconvene with each member now an expert on one aspect of the lesson (for example, A1, A2, A3, A4, A5), and the students teach each other what they have learned. The teacher can conclude the lesson with a large-group discussion or a more formal assessment. The beauty of this strategy is that it can be applied to a range of learning tasks, and once a class has learned how it works, it can be organized fairly quickly.

Perhaps the most promising group strategy for the English classroom is literature circles, a technique supported by Lev Vygotsky's sociocultural learning theory and Louise Rosenblatt's transactional reading theory (Day and Ainley 158–159). Popularized by Harvey Daniels and practiced by thousands of teachers, literature circles work like adult book clubs (except that students actually read the books). Literature circles take many forms, but Daniels lists several "official" criteria:

1. Students choose their own reading materials.

2. Small temporary groups are formed, based on book choice.

3. Different groups read different books.

4. Groups meet on a regular, predictable schedule to discuss their reading.

5. Kids use written or drawn notes to guide both their reading and discussion.

6. Discussion topics come from the students.

7. Group meetings aim to be open, natural conversations about books, so personal connections, digressions, and open-ended questions are welcome.

8. The teacher serves as a facilitator, not a group member or instructor.

9. Evaluation is by teacher observation and student self-evaluation.

10. A spirit of playfulness and fun pervades the room.

11. When books are finished, readers share with their classmates, and then new groups form around new reading choices. (*Literature* 18; emphasis original)

At the secondary level, the literature circles strategy has to be adapted to accommodate required books (159), but I've found that I can make it work by offering two to four similar titles (slave narratives, Victorian novels, etc.), then following up with the jigsaw technique for sharing.

One controversial aspect of literature circles has been whether to use "role sheets" specifying the tasks to be performed by each member of the group. Daniels recommended these tools "as a way of showing kids how smart readers think" and as a means of capturing their responses in writing, ensuring that the groups would have plenty to discuss ("What's the Next" 11), but many teachers have rejected them as too mechanical, favoring reading journals, sticky notes, and other kinds of preparation (12). I'll offer my take on this question later.

Literature circles and jigsaws provide useful structures for teaching critical theory. The goals of introducing multiple critical lenses and organizing group work are really the same: to open up the possibilities for response and to be inclusive. This isn't to say that a teacher-led close reading of the text is never appropriate, but it certainly shouldn't be the default lesson plan.

Looking at Literature through Critical Lenses

The idea of applying a variety of critical theories to works of literature isn't entirely new. I had been doing it unconsciously for years—when I introduced my ninth graders to the heroic journey archetype or asked them to reflect on the portrayal of female characters in *The Odyssey*, for example—before deciding to name the practice and make it a regular feature of my literature instruction. Students don't need to master the complex apparatus of archetypal criticism or understand all of the ideology underlying feminist criticism to appreciate the insights that come from looking for recurring plot structures and character types or examining gender roles in literary works, but it is helpful for them to know that a wide variety of critical lenses is available to them, and that each one will bring out different aspects of a piece.

For instance, when students read Rebecca Harding Davis's nineteenth-century novella *Life in the Iron Mills*, which tells the tragic story of Hugh, a poor immigrant mill worker with no opportunity to develop his considerable talent as a sculptor, they have no trouble applying the Marxist lens—without even knowing what it is. Some of the story's dialogue focuses explicitly on the power of capital, the oppression of workers, and the possibility of revolution, so the text invites a class-based analysis. But another story emerges when I direct students' attention to the female narrator and the circumstances of the author, whose career as a writer was impeded by her gender. This is one of several suggested topics I give them for an informal response paper:

> Though this novella focuses primarily on the lives of mill workers, the story can be
> seen as a metaphor for the wrongs suffered by women. Try interpreting the no-
> vella as a feminist tract, with particular focus not only on the women characters
> but also on the message of Hugh's statue, "the korl woman."

Created from mill waste (korl), the statue seems to ask questions about suffer-
ing—the artist's, and the author's, too. The story becomes much richer when viewed
through more than one lens.

Unlike Eckert, who introduces critical theories one at a time over the course
of the year, most English teachers at Amherst Regional High have adopted the
practice of presenting several at once, at least in junior/senior courses. In doing so
we probably sacrifice some of the depth that Eckert achieves in favor of exposing
students to the breadth of contemporary interpretive strategies and offering them
choices for their own experiments with literary criticism. Coming up with clear, suc-
cinct summaries of the various theories is a challenge. Tyson's book offers a helpful
overview of the questions that the various schools of criticism ask (423–425), while
Appleman's includes a handout with more detailed explanations of nine theories
(155–158).

The best way I've found to teach the concept of critical lenses and the various
critical approaches is to have students apply them to a short, accessible text. A familiar fairy tale is always a good starting point; stories such as "Cinderella" and "Little
Red Riding Hood" have no shortage of suggestive material for reader-response,
psychoanalytic, archetypal, feminist, and Marxist interpretations. Another work I've
found useful for this purpose is Anton Chekhov's short story "A Nincompoop." In
this 1883 piece the narrator, a member of the gentry, summons his children's governess, ostensibly to pay her, but then proceeds to make a series of spurious deductions
from her salary until there is almost nothing left. When she thanks him nonetheless,
he flies into a rage, chiding her for being "spineless" and "silent." In point of fact, she
has spoken up several times, but he hasn't heeded her protests. In the end, he says
that he was only trying to teach her a "cruel lesson" about standing up for herself
and gives her all she is owed. As she goes out at the end of the story, he muses (in
sadness for downtrodden humanity? or twisting his moustache?): "How easy it is
to crush the weak in this world!" (22). Despite or perhaps because of its brevity, this
is a rich, ironic, enigmatic story, open to many readings.

A jigsaw activity serves well as an introduction to the critical lenses. When using
the Chekhov story, for example, I start by doing a dramatic oral reading, sometimes
asking a student to read the governess's lines (since the narrator sees himself as a
teacher, the role-playing adds an interesting dynamic). Then the students discuss
the story in their home groups, sharing their opinions and questions. When they
move to their expert groups, I do a mini-lesson for the whole class on the four or

five critical lenses they will be using and assign one lens to each table. The students read and discuss the story again, focusing their attention on the kinds of issues such critics would raise. If a group is doing historical or biographical criticism, one or two members may go to the computer or a reference book to do some quick research on nineteenth-century Russia and/or Chekhov. Each student is responsible for taking detailed notes so he or she can share the expert group's insights after returning to the home group for a third discussion of the story. Ultimately, I bring the whole class back together for a debriefing on the process. Two points I always reiterate at this point are that (1) critical theories are ways to view a work, not part of the work itself (in other words, a story need not have a feminist agenda to yield to a feminist reading) and (2) different critics using the same lens may come up with different readings (whether "A Nincompoop" challenges or reinforces patriarchal norms is open to debate).

At least once each term, after students have developed some familiarity with critical theory, I ask them to write an analytical essay using a particular lens (see Figure 6.1). For these assignments, students who choose the same critical perspective become a "literature circle" (or perhaps a "criticism circle") devoted to examining the assigned reading through that lens. They help each other work through the nuances of the theory and its applications to the work, and I meet with each of the groups to monitor the students' progress and address their questions.

Eventually each member of the group develops a tentative thesis and writes a partial draft, as described in Chapter 5. When I respond to these drafts, I try to help them focus their lenses and, if necessary, narrow their views to something manageable. The final products vary in depth and sophistication, but they almost always offer interesting interpretations, as in this opening paragraph from Aviva's feminist analysis of "Rappaccini's Daughter":

> In his short story "Rappaccini's Daughter," author Nathaniel Hawthorne took a strange twist on the biblical Garden of Eden. The only prominent female in the story is the titular character, Beatrice. She is an interesting take on the popular concept of a femme fatale, an alluring seductive woman who leads men into dangerous situations. Unlike the femme fatale's, Beatrice's "temptation" is inadvertent. She does not know of her father's plan to make Giovanni similar to her; she only wishes for his company. Although Beatrice is a femme fatale in the literal sense of the term, she is actually controlled and manipulated by the different men in the story, and each is involved in some type of power struggle with her. Her role as a victim becomes apparent when seen through the lens of the original biblical Fall.

Although Aviva was one of several students in her class using the feminist lens for this essay, no one else in her group approached the story in quite the same way.

Today we'll be reviewing some of the lenses critics use to study literature and applying them to "Rappaccini's Daughter." Working in a self-selected group, you'll examine the story from one of these perspectives to see what it reveals. Eventually you will derive a thesis from your chosen perspective and develop an analytical essay on Hawthorne's tale and its biblical source.

1. **Historical Criticism:** Historical critics are interested in what was happening at the time the tale was *written*. They might ask: How do the historical facts of nineteenth-century America affect our understanding of the story? A historical critic might see in Rappaccini's garden, for example, a symbol of the scientific revolution going on in Hawthorne's time, when all things seemed possible. What does the story seem to "say" about tampering with nature? Are there places human beings shouldn't go? Is Hawthorne's meaning consistent with that of Genesis?

2. **Marxist Criticism:** Marxist critics are interested in power relationships between classes and in the uses and abuses of capital. They might ask: How is power distributed and exercised within the story? Who has power in Padua, and what counts as "capital" in this university town? How do the powerful use their power? Who doesn't have power and why? Are there any parallels to the Genesis story?

3. **Psychological Criticism:** Psychological critics apply the insights of psychology to literary characters. They might ask: What traditional aspects of human personality (heart, mind, and soul) are most prominent in each of the characters? What modern psychological concepts, such as the unconscious (hidden desires and meanings), defense mechanisms (displacement, denial, projection, etc.), *eros* and *thanatos* (love and death), and aspects of the mind (id, ego, and superego) can help us understand what goes on in the story? How do you account for Giovanni's varying responses to Beatrice? What motives drive her responses to him? What other relationships are important? How can they be explained? How does Hawthorne's presentation of characters compare to the Genesis story's depiction of human nature?

4. **Feminist Criticism:** Feminist critics are interested in gender issues, including power relationships between men and women, sexual stereotyping, etc. They might ask: How are the events of the story related to gender? To what extent is Beatrice in control of her life, and to what extent is she controlled by others? How does Hawthorne present her in contrast to the other characters? Does she have any strengths that they don't have? Does Hawthorne raise the same or different gender issues from the Genesis story? Does "Rappaccini's Daughter" ultimately challenge or reinforce gender stereotypes and patriarchal norms?

5. **Structuralist Criticism:** Structuralist critics focus on the underlying patterns that help us understand a text. These include the basic elements of story "grammar" applicable to any narrative. They might ask questions like those in the "Summary of Basic Questions" on the back (which are derived from the work of Kenneth Burke). How do these questions apply to "Rappaccini's Daughter"? What do they reveal about the story's structure, conflicts, and character development? Structuralist critics are also interested in archetypes, or original patterns (such as myths). They might ask: How does Hawthorne's story fulfill or deny the reader's expectations arising from knowledge of the Genesis story?

Figure 6.1. Critical approaches to "Rappaccini's Daughter."

Members of each criticism circle seem to encourage each other to develop original applications of the critical theory.

While all students at Amherst Regional High get regular practice using critical lenses, those who choose to participate in our Honors/AP program work with them in depth. All of the classes in my department are untracked, but we do offer enrichment options within each course. Students who fulfill the enrichment requirements successfully receive Honors designation, and those who complete Honors projects in two junior/senior literature courses receive AP credit. These Honors/AP assignments stress critical theory. Each student reads a book independently (sometimes choosing from several options), then engages in a multistep process leading to a substantial analytical paper using a critical lens. The first time a student goes through this process, one of the early steps, after reading and discussing summaries of several critical theories, is to write three one-page responses to the work, each from a different perspective.

For example, as part of his project on *The Grapes of Wrath*, William wrote feminist, Marxist, and reader-response commentaries. In the first, he focused on the role of Ma Joad, "the woman who took charge and showed how women can be leaders and just as good as men." In the second, he turned his attention to Tom, "the poster boy for Marxism in this text," who tried to "unite all the workers into one spirit that will fight for their rights." The reader-response lens gave him the most trouble; his only specific observation (arising from his experience as a person of color, perhaps) was that "the book doesn't include African-Americans as main characters."

After completing the three-perspectives assignment, the student (with the teacher's feedback and guidance) chooses one critical theory to study in more depth and to use as the lens for the final paper. William chose Marxist analysis and focused on Steinbeck's critique of capitalism. The second time a student does an Honors/AP project, the process is similar, but he or she is required to read published criticism of the work and integrate it into his or her paper.

> **Your turn.** Using one of the titles cited in this chapter or an online source, review the essential elements of the main contemporary critical theories, then try applying several of them to a work that you teach regularly. Which of these lenses are you currently using (perhaps unconsciously) in your lessons on literature? Which others do you think your students could benefit from trying? How do (or might) you introduce the concept of using multiple lenses to your classes? Draw up a lesson plan and try it out, then revise as needed.

Energizing Literature Discussions with Group Activities

In the last section I suggested using the jigsaw technique to introduce critical lenses. There are many other ways this versatile strategy can be incorporated into literature instruction. I've organized poetry discussions this way—by assigning each expert group a different poem by Emily Dickinson in a one-day lesson, or a different Romantic poet in a one-week mini-unit—as well as end-of-course reviews of major themes. And the jigsaw is only one group-work strategy. Another simple but powerful activity is the carousel brainstorm, in which students move around the room in groups responding to prompts posted on chart paper. This technique has the twin advantages of getting students out of their seats and creating a visible public record of their thinking. No-name strategies can be valuable, too, like putting students into work groups to review and discuss a particular chapter or excerpt of a text. As I noted earlier, what's different about this approach from whole-class discussions is that everybody has a chance to participate actively since the available "air time" is divided among a much smaller number of people, not including the teacher, who tends to monopolize it. Or, put another way, there's no place to hide.

My students' favorite group activities are probably the ones that involve art—studying it or creating it. Studying visual art—and music, too—helps students grasp literary and philosophical concepts that can be elusive in print. For instance, the central ideas of transcendentalism become much clearer to my American literature classes when they study my collection of Hudson River School prints (most of them saved from a calendar and laminated) in small groups. They can *see* Emerson's ideas about nature as beauty and language and spirit and his concept of the Oversoul in these paintings. The images also provide another way to understand terms such as *symbol* and *mood*. In Renaissance and Modern Literature, I use images from art books to help students make the transition from one era to the next. For instance, comparing Michelangelo's *David* with Bernini's illustrates clearly the differences between Renaissance and Baroque sensibilities. I ask students to find parallel differences in the literature we are studying, and they always come up with valuable insights. Music also works well as a nonverbal exhibit of changing styles, and students enjoy picking out and discussing distinctions they hear among representative selections.

Creating art—well, drawing pictures—is an equally valuable group activity. By "group activity" I don't mean having a group of students create a single work, though that's valuable, too, but rather having them work on their own pieces as they sit in a group. It's the cross-talk that happens as they work with markers and colored pencils that matters. For example, let's go back to the transcendentalists. One strategy I use frequently to help students make sense of Thoreau's ideas is to ask them to pull out quotations from *Walden* that they find provocative or intriguing and write about them. A variation of this activity is to ask students to illustrate their quotations instead, and they often do so in suggestive ways. One student chose the passage in which Thoreau discusses the laying of "sleepers," or ties, for the railroad and comments that the workers, now dead, are the sleepers: "The rails are laid on them, and they are covered with sand" (67). The student captured Thoreau's point effectively by drawing a set of tracks in which the ties are, in fact, people, with a train running over them. Meanwhile, she was sharing her ideas about the quotation with her peers, as they shared their ideas about their quotations with her.

Another helpful application for drawing is having students use it to visualize and capture the meanings of key scenes in a novel or images in a poem. When a group works on illustrating the three scaffold scenes in *The Scarlet Letter*, for example, the participants gain a much deeper understanding of the characters, the symbolism of the letter *A*, and the structure of the novel. Hester, Dimmesdale, Chillingworth, and Pearl are present each time, but their positions and relationships change. To create accurate images of these scenes, students have to study the text. To present their drawings to the class afterwards, they have to develop a coherent explanation of their interpretations. This work is excellent preparation for discussion and analytical writing. A fascinating alternative to illustrating scenes on paper is re-creating them in living tableaux. In this activity, each group has to come up with a way to represent the meaning of its assigned passage using only stage position, body language, and facial expressions—no words or actions. It's interesting to watch students prepare these performances and to listen as the class dissects them.

As I noted earlier, one of the most authentic ways to incorporate group work into the English classroom is to organize literature circles. This strategy has several advantages, in my view. It allows me to expand the syllabus by including four novels, say, when there is only time for one. None of the students will read all four, but they will hear about them and become aware of their contents. Also, scheduling litera-ture circle units once or twice a term gives students some choice in their readings, something they crave. Even more important, since it's neither possible nor desirable for me to lead all of the group discussions, students get to take more responsibility for their learning and apply the skills they have developed in other units.

There are some logistical challenges in setting up literature circles. One is estab-lishing the groups. It's important that they not be too small or too large—I think six is about right. Since it's unlikely that equal numbers of students will choose each book, when I give my book talks, I give each student a note card on which to write his or her first and second choices—or to write "no strong preference." The note cards work better than passing a sheet around, which sometimes creates a bandwagon effect. This procedure gives me some flexibility as I sort out who goes where, and everyone usually seems pretty happy. A bigger challenge is preparing the students to work effectively in their groups. Daniels notes that many teachers have given up role sheets to assign responsibilities. I still use them, at least for the first few meetings of each group, to ensure that certain activities happen at each meeting. I've adapted some roles from Daniels's work and made up some of my own (see Figure 6.2). Each student is expected to take on a different role each time, prepare accordingly, and pass in his or her notes (as in Figure 6.3).

Having designated roles is helpful at the beginning because, even though the students all know each other, they haven't necessarily worked together before. They usually find that the work they have prepared for discussion overlaps; the open-

	Sept. 29	Oct. 2	Oct. 4
1. **Discussion Leader:** Responsible for keeping conversation focused, making sure that everyone participates. He or she needs to plan an agenda and submit a report at the end of class.	1. _____	_____	_____
2. **Open-Response Question Writer:** Responsible for preparing and explaining a thought-provoking question for open-response writing during the discussion period and leading a follow-up discussion.	2. _____	_____	_____
3. **Background Researcher:** Responsible for finding and reporting background information (topics: slave rebellions, Fugitive Slave Law, abolitionists).	3. _____	_____	_____
4. **Character Tracker:** Responsible for making a list of important characters and their roles and sharing it with the group for discussion and clarification.	4. _____	_____	_____
5. **Quotation Finder:** Responsible for preparing and introducing a list of important quotations from the reading for discussion by the group.	5. _____	_____	_____
6. **Recording Secretary:** Responsible for keeping and typing up minutes of the discussion, including major points and questions raised and views exchanged.	6. _____	_____	_____

Figure 6.2. Literature circle roles for *Incidents in the Life of a Slave Girl*.

Life of a Slave Girl Quotations

p. 109 "It is always better to trust than to doubt."

I found this quote surprising to come from someone who was trapped in slavery and no white person could seem to keep their word on anything. Still, it is an important quote that more people should try to live by.

p. 168 "The heavenly father has been most merciful to me in leading me to this place."

After everything that happened with Christianity in the South that to her there was still a God.

p. 174 "Hot weather brings out snakes and slaveholders and I like one class of the venomous creatures as little as I do the other. What a comfort is, to be free to say so!"

This seemed like an appropriate quote because she was finally free in the South and that included freedom of speech, which offered her endless possibilities to what she was used to.

Figure 6.3. Quotation finder preparation for literature circle.

response question writer's prompt may connect to one of the quotation finder's passages, which may relate to an observation made by the character tracker, and so on. Sometimes the discussion leader nervously checks the agenda and the clock after one of these lively exchanges only to find that most of the points have been covered. My hardest job during these sessions is to stay out. Naturally I want to listen in and ask a probing question or two, but if I pull up a chair, it almost always kills the student interaction. So I do my best to avoid hovering, trusting the groups to make their way forward.

There's a difference "between hovering and wisely intervening" in group work, as Cohen points out. There is "nothing . . . to be gained from letting a group struggle onward":

- When the group is hopelessly off-task
- When the group does not seem to understand enough to get started or to carry out the task
- When the group is experiencing sharp interpersonal conflict
- When the group is falling apart because they cannot organize themselves to get the task done. (108)

Or when some group members have come unprepared. Even in such problematic circumstances, I try hard not to take over, striving instead to facilitate students' efforts to find solutions.

One more thought about setting up group work. For informal day-to-day activities, I let students form their own groups or have them count off if I want to mix things up. But when planning sustained group work (for long-term projects, perhaps), I like to be more deliberate in choosing who works with whom. When there isn't an obvious reason for putting students in certain groups (as in literature circles), there can be suspicion or discontent about the teacher's grouping decisions. I learned a great strategy for avoiding this situation years ago—I don't remember where—and I've used it ever since. I ask for a number of volunteers from the class equal to the required number of groups to serve as the selection committee. I give them a class roster and send them out into the hall to decide what the groups will be. Here's the catch: I tell them that *I* will choose what group each of them will join, so they have a strong incentive to create congenial groups with good potential for success. I'm always impressed with how seriously they take this task and how imaginative they are in pursuing fairness and balance.

A final observation about assessment: most students hate group-work grades, and I don't blame them. A common grade for all participants often leaves the hardest workers feeling resentful, and separate grades are always invidious. Better not to grade group work at all, I say, except as part of an overall class participation evalua-tion, in which consideration of individual efforts is natural and appropriate. Groups should assess themselves, however, preferably through writing and sharing at the end of each meeting, not to find fault but to figure out how to improve.

> **Your turn.** What role does group work play in your classes? How often do stu-dents work in groups? For what purposes? With what results? What do you think would improve the quality of the students' interaction? What other kinds of group strategies would you like to try? Starting with one unit in one class, develop a plan to convert some whole-class activities into group activities. Keep in mind that doing so may mean modifying the goals of the lessons.

Encouraging Voice and Specificity in Students' Writing about Literature

Literature study always goes hand in hand with writing, usually of analytical essays. Students generally don't enjoy writing these papers because they don't feel con-nected to the topics, and teachers don't enjoy reading them because the papers tend to be lacking in voice and specificity. I suggested one possible solution earlier in this chapter: basing analytical essays on "critical lens" interpretations of assigned read-ings. In Chapter 2, I argued that creative writing based on literary works (narratives written in minor characters' voices, "missing" or additional chapters, original pieces using similar styles, etc.) is also a legitimate product of critical analysis. I would like now to offer a few more suggestions for making writing about literature more appealing and useful for students and thus more gratifying for the teacher.

One idea takes its cue from Keene and Zimmermann's *Mosaic of Thought*. If skillful reading involves making connections between the text and the self, other texts, and the world, why not make such associations the explicit goal of some writ-ing assignments? For several years now I have been including in the mix of writing tasks in my literature courses informal papers that ask students to respond to the assigned readings by relating them to personal experiences, other works of litera-ture (in the broadest sense of the term), and world affairs. Sometimes they do a little of each, as in Caitlin's initial response to *Moby-Dick* (see Figure 6.4).

Students make all kinds of connections in these papers. The assignment seems especially helpful when students are reading ancient literature (read: more than thirty years old). Otherwise remote texts such as the Bible are brought closer to home: the Cain and Abel story sheds light on a soured sibling relationship; the endless warfare in the book of Joshua over rival claims to the same land illuminate

A Change in Opinion

"We're reading what?" I exclaimed as my eyes lost their E-period glaze. Mr. Penniman glared at me from across the room. I mentally chastise myself for not paying more attention . . . again. He repeats the statement.

"We'll be reading Moby-Dick at the end of the term, if the class is up for it." Oh I was. I was totally and utterly up to reading Moby-Dick. It was the greatest American novel ever written, and it was one that I would never read without such encouragement as deadlines and grades. A copy of Moby-Dick had sat in my house for as long as I could remember. Its prodigious presence loomed over the rest of the measly paperbacks on my father's antique bookshelves. I took it down from time to time and admired the contrast of the gold leathering with the red leather cover. It simply screamed 'intellectual feat.'

I wanted to read it, but I was afraid to even start. My father warned me of its inaccessibility, its depth, and its utter overabundance of whale terminology. I needed to prepare to read such a book or, as my father suggested, be bored out of my mind.

Yet, despite all of this I was excited when I found out it was part of my English syllabus. Here was a chance to conquer a childhood fear, and ~~a chance~~ to dive into potential symbolism and twisted allegory. It might be boring, but at least I would have read it.

Surprisingly, Moby-Dick possessed a humorous and adventurous plot. The opening sentence of "Call me Ishmael," drew me in immediately. I appreciated the biblical reference and wondered if Ishmael had the character of his namesake. (He did.) As Ishmael described his inn in New Bedford I started laughing. I loved that he preferred to sleep on a short plank than with a questionable bed fellow. I never expected to laugh at a novel written in the 1800s. (One time I smiled while reading *Pride and Prejudice*, but in general the Victorian era is not amusing.) The story, with omens, death, Indians, and mysterious captains, is a swashbuckling adventure. The book that I feared to start is a veritable page-turner.

Moby-Dick may be humorous and exciting, but these are not main reasons for my appreciation of it. In light of conventional opinions of the Victorian era, Herman Melville's novel is scandalous. Just reading it in context of the time it was written makes me feel wicked! Ishmael befriends a cannibalistic savage, Queequeg, and they practice both of their religions together. During this period of Western imperialism, Christian missionaries embarked to all parts of the globe to spread their message. The message essentially stated pagans will not be saved, convert immediately. For Melville to imply that not only were all religions similar but to worship along with non-Christians displayed respect to one's fellow man went against Western culture's core beliefs. Melville's beliefs were unpopular as well as unique.

Moby-Dick is a revolutionary ~~novel~~ story for the Victorian ~~novel~~ era. A book which I feared would bore me to tears has become the most exciting part of my homework load. Melville's ~~novel~~ work really is America's greatest novel, and I enjoy reading it.

Figure 6.4. Caitlin's response paper on *Moby-Dick*.

the current Mideast conflict. The students' experiences and worldview inform their understanding of the literature and vice versa. When selecting items for their course portfolios, students often choose these pieces, and because their understandings have changed since writing the initial drafts, they usually revise them substantially.

Another kind of writing about literature I've come to value is analyzing a short passage. This assignment addresses two of our most frequent complaints as English teachers: that students don't read closely enough to grasp the meaning of challenging works, and that they don't cite specific evidence from the text in their analytical writing (or the evidence isn't relevant). One of the reasons, I think, is that though we often *tell* them to do close reading and to integrate textual evidence, we don't *teach* them how. My colleague Chris Herland and I tried to tackle this problem when we co-taught Renaissance and Modern Literature. We put together a multistep project for the first reading of the term, *King Lear* (see Figure 6.5). The reasoning behind this assignment was (1) if students are to get better at close reading and citing evidence, they need lots of teacher- and peer-mediated practice and support, (2) if they focus on relatively short passages, they won't be overwhelmed by the task and thus will be able to analyze the excerpts thoroughly, and (3) if they are successful in their close readings, they will gain insights that will help them comprehend the work as a whole. This approach proved successful. Even Shakespeare-phobic students systematically decoded and drew inferences from their passages, while stronger readers wrote penetrating essays with ample textual support.

I have adapted this method for several other uses, including both low-stakes analytical exercises for ninth graders and in-class writing assignments for older students. In each case I turn the four-part analytical process in the *King Lear* handout (or a slight modification) into a worksheet that students use first in groups and then individually to examine short poems or excerpts from plays or novels. Sometimes I ask the ninth graders to write up their notes in paragraph form, thus producing a "no big deal" analytical mini-essay, a real confidence booster for some students. For similar reasons, I occasionally have older students write brief analytical essays during class, especially if they have struggled with this form of writing. After some group practice analyzing passages, I ask each of them to choose a piece to examine individually using the worksheet. Then I schedule the computer lab for one or two days. Working from their prepared notes, the students write their essays in class, where they can get support from each other and from me. These conditions—plus the knowledge that the assignment will be drafted by the end of class—seem to help some students overcome their fear of analytical writing.

> **Your turn.** Are you satisfied with your students' writing about literature? Do you hear their voices in this writing? Does it demonstrate close reading? Original interpretation? If you would like to see improvements on these or other points, what changes might you make to your assignments? Can you see applications in your courses for informal response papers on text-to-self, text-to-text, and text-to-world connections? What about close-reading essays? Critical lens analytical papers? What modifications would you need to make to implement such assignments?

Teaching Literary Concepts and Terms

I'm of two minds about teaching terminology. It's useful to be able to call things by their proper names, but part of me says it's our emphasis on literary argot that

The goal of this assignment is for you to learn the process of close reading. To fully understand a text, you must be able not only to comprehend the literal meaning but also to infer what is implied while analyzing the nuances of the language. In this assignment we will focus on passages from the first act of *King Lear* to develop a deeper understanding of the characters and to practice the close-reading process. Then you will write independently a two- or three-page essay analyzing a short passage from acts 2–5.

STEP ONE: *Annotate act 1, scene 1.*
As a class we will examine lines 38–141 in which Lear asks each of his daughters to declare her love for him and be rewarded with a portion of his kingdom. I will model the reading of Lear's first speech, and then, in small groups, you will annotate later speeches by Goneril, Regan, Cordelia, and Lear using the following guidelines and report your findings to the class for further discussion:

1. Paraphrase the content of the passage (literal meaning).
2. Determine what is suggested or implied by the speaker's tone, the connotation of the language, figurative language, etc.
3. Offer an analysis of the character and his or her relationship with other characters.
4. Anticipate future events based on your analysis of the passage.

STEP TWO: *Annotate other passages from act 1 and jigsaw.*
In a small group, you will annotate and discuss one of the following passages using the process listed in STEP ONE. Then, using the jigsaw method, you will present your analysis to students from other groups.

1. 1, 2, 1–22—Edmund
2. 1, 2, 128–148—Edmund
3. 1, 3, all—Goneril
4. 1, 4, 120–204—The Fool
5. 1, 4, 282–296—Lear
6. 1, 4, 303–317—Lear
7. 1, 5, all—Lear and Fool

STEP THREE: *Select and analyze a passage individually from act 2–act 5.*
As you continue reading the play, you will be responsible for identifying other important speeches and exchanges. You will select one passage as the subject for an analytical essay. Using the analytical method outlined in STEP ONE (except that #4 will be changed to "Connect the selected passage to the development of the character throughout the play"), you will write a rough draft of the essay's contents.

STEP FOUR: *Solicit peer feedback and suggestions.*
Working with your response group, you will share your analysis, give and receive suggestions for improvement, and discuss plans for organizing your essay.

STEP FIVE: *Prepare a working draft of the essay for teacher feedback.*
Using the results of your response session, you will write a working draft of your paper. In addition to the four-part analysis, the paper should include an opening paragraph identifying the character(s) and the purpose of the essay as well as a concluding paragraph. You will submit the draft for my comments.

STEP SIX: *Write the "final" draft of the essay.*
After reviewing my comments, you will revise your draft to improve the clarity, depth, and style of your analysis in accordance with the assignment criteria and submit the paper for final review. You will have a chance to revise it further if necessary, and/or you may decide later to revise it for your course portfolio.

Figure 6.5. *King Lear* passage analysis.

makes literature feel so inaccessible to some students. The danger is especially great with poetry, to which so many kinds of specialized language are applied, and from which students feel especially alienated.

Take your average Shakespearean sonnet. You know that it's a *sonnet* because it has fourteen lines, including an *octave* that sets up a problem and a *sestet* that resolves it, linked by a *volta* or turn. Since it's a *Shakespearean sonnet* (as opposed to *Petrarchan*), it is composed of four *quatrains* and a *couplet*, with the *rhyme scheme* ABABCDCDEFEFGG. The poem has a regular *meter*, which is called *iambic pentameter* because each line consists of five two-syllable *feet* with the *accent* on the second syllable. To keep the poem from sounding like a nursery rhyme, this pattern may be varied occasionally with the substitution of a *trochaic, dactylic, anapestic,* or *spondaic* foot. Also noteworthy is that some of the lines are not *end-stopped;* Shakespeare uses *elision* to achieve a more natural sound. Besides *rhyme* and *rhythm,* the poem includes other aural effects such as *alliteration, assonance,* and *consonance,* which are created by repetition of sounds; or *onomatopoeia,* which relies on imitation of the sound of the subject being described. Then, too, Shakespeare is known for his beautiful *imagery* and his use of *figurative language,* so *similes* and *metaphors* abound, and there are undoubtedly examples of many other *poetic devices,* such as *personification, hyperbole, understatement,* and *oxymoron,* and perhaps even *metonymy* and *synecdoche.* Ever the wit, the poet may have thrown in a *pun* or two, set up a *paradox,* or used other forms of *verbal irony.* This rich array of language helps establish the *mood* of the poem and offers clues about its *tone.* Other hints about its meaning come from the *connotations* of the words he chose, the *allusions* to history and mythology he inserted, and of course the *symbols* he created. Discerning all of this, you surely have a clear understanding of the sonnet's *theme.* Phew! That's forty-five literary terms for fourteen lines of poetry. I know that no one teaches all of these New Critical terms at once, but none of them is beyond the pale of high school literature study. And these don't include analytical tools for other forms of verse, much less the ones that apply exclusively to fiction, drama, epic, and so on. Is all of this apparatus necessary? Shouldn't we dump it and concentrate on fostering appreciation?

That's one side of the issue. There's another part of me that says it *is* important to teach literary concepts, and not just because they appear on high-stakes tests. Appreciation of anything is enhanced by knowing how it works. It's true for art and music—and biology and physics—and it's true for writing. In some ways I don't think we challenge students enough to learn about the artistry of literature. The only terms that many students use with any confidence are *simile, metaphor,* and *personification,* which we seem to teach year after year, like the parts of speech. Can we move on to other concepts without killing students' interest and confidence?

It's hard to strike the right balance, and I still have a tendency to overdo it sometimes. Whenever possible I introduce terms and concepts at natural points in the discussion, particularly when a student has noticed something interesting and doesn't have a name for it. That's a great opportunity for a mini-lesson. Otherwise, I ask myself what kinds of literary vocabulary will be most helpful and appropriate for comprehending the works being studied and reaching the goals of the unit. When teaching *Romeo and Juliet*, for example, I teach terms such as *prologue* and *chorus*, since they appear on the first page of the play, and introduce the concept of *comic relief*. I also explain the structure of a five-act tragedy. Does knowing this structure help ninth graders "get" Shakespeare? I think so. In Oral Communication, the poetry unit focuses on performance, so I stress terms and concepts related to sound and form: *alliteration, meter, internal rhyme, blank verse, stanza, dramatic monologue*. Another criterion for selecting terminology is what will be useful to students in their writing. In ninth grade one of the major assessments is an original short story. To help students become more conscious of the elements of good story, I ask them to analyze other writers' works with those elements in mind (see Figure 6.6). Finally, I look for figurative language and literary forms in everyday speech and popular culture—and encourage students to do the same. "Give me a hand" is a *synecdoche*; television dramas, like epics, often begin *in medias res*. It's not important that students remember all of the terms, but it is valuable for them to see how versatile and creative human beings can be with language.

Studying literary vocabulary is a scaffolded group activity in my classroom. Whether the purpose is identifying examples of short story elements in Alice Walker and Amy Tan stories, as in Figure 6.6, creating a plot diagram of *Romeo and Juliet*, or tapping out the rhythm in a Robert Frost poem, students learn better and get less frustrated when they work together. I try to keep this work playful by making it relatively low stakes. When I do give a quiz on terms, it doesn't count much, and it's structured to capitalize on what students know (see example in Chapter 4).

> **Your turn.** How do you select the literary concepts and terms that you teach? Do they come from textbooks, or do you choose them on your own? Since there are far too many to "cover" in any course, what criteria do you use to prioritize them? What activities have you found most useful for building students' understanding of literary language? What changes would you like to make in the ways that you manage this aspect of literature instruction?

Participatory Learning

When I reflect on the changes I've made since my early days as a literature teacher, I realize that more than my method has evolved. I see the purpose of literature instruction differently now. Wanting to pass on my own appreciation of the works I

Group work: Fill in the following table using examples from "Everyday Use" and "Rules of the Game."

Topic	"Everyday Use"	"Rules of the Game"
What **point of view** is used in the story? How does the point of view affect the story?	First person narration—Mama tells the story. She knows her daughter Maggie well, but she doesn't completely understand her daughter Dee.	
Explain the **plot structure** of the story by identifying the exposition, rising action, climax, and falling action.	Exposition:	Exposition: Waverly describes her childhood in Chinatown and relationship with her mother.
	Rising action:	Rising action: Waverly learns to play chess and becomes a national champion featured in *Life* magazine.
	Climax:	Climax: Waverly tells her mother not to show her off because it's embarrassing and obvious.
	Falling action:	Falling action: Waverly's mother won't acknowledge her when she comes home after running away.
What methods of **characterization** does the author use (description, speech, actions, comments by the narrator)? Give several examples for the character listed.	Dee:	Mother:
How does the object listed serve as a **symbol** in the story?	Quilts:	Chess set:
What is the **setting** (time and place) of the story?		
What is the **mood** of the story, and what factors help to create it?		
What examples of **irony** can be found in the story? What kind are they?	Situational: Dee says at the end that Mama doesn't understand her heritage, but Mama is the one who has *lived* it!	
What do you think is the main **theme** of the story? (Several possible answers)		
In a passage of **dialogue**, how does the author indicate a new speaker?		

Figure 6.6. Short story worksheet and literary terms review.

was teaching, I used to be concerned that I "cover all of the key points" about them in my lessons. My initial doubts about using multiple critical lenses and relying on group work may have been in part a worry that students would "lose something" if I gave up control of the discussions. And they do, in a way. When students meet in groups and connect literary works to their experiences and view them from a variety of perspectives, they *don't* necessarily "cover" everything that I think is important or interesting—not that they would remember my brilliant interpretations very long, anyway. What they gain is much more enduring: the confidence and capacity to make books their own, to be full participants in the transaction of reading. I still have plenty of opportunities to guide their literary journeys, but the point is that they are doing the traveling, and not just listening to my travelogue. And I hope this leads to a wanderlust that will last a lifetime.

Recommended Reading

Cohen, Elizabeth G. *Designing Groupwork: Strategies for the Heterogeneous Classroom*. 2nd ed. New York: Teachers College Press, 1994. Print.

> Cohen develops a rationale for group work, explains its key principles, and provides in-depth advice for implementing the practice successfully. It is written for the teacher who wants not only to design interesting ways for students to interact but also to understand the theory behind peer-mediated learning.

Eckert, Lisa Schade. *How Does It Mean? Engaging Reluctant Readers through Literary Theory*. Portsmouth, NH: Heinemann, 2006. Print.

> This book describes a full-year course focused on literary theory. It includes handouts on critical lenses and examples of student responses.

McMahon, Robert. *Thinking about Literature: New Ideas for High School Teachers*. Portsmouth, NH: Heinemann, 2002. Print.

> Applying Kenneth Burke's literary theory, this book includes a universally applicable "Summary of Basic Questions" about literature and detailed analyses of five works demonstrating their use, as well as recommended teaching strategies.

Moon, Brian. *Literary Terms: A Practical Glossary*. Urbana, IL: NCTE, 1999. Print.

> Moon's glossary, the first book in NCTE's Chalkface Series, is not your typical handbook of literary terms. It includes entries on conventional topics such as *imagery*, but it also features items derived from contemporary critical theories: *binary opposition, patriarchy, hegemony*. Each entry includes an opening exercise, a theoretical explanation, a practice activity, and a summary.

7

Making the Most of Media and Technology

True confession: I am not a technology pioneer. I held out for years against buying cable television ("It costs *how much*? Broadcast is *free*!"). I was not the first on my block to carry a cell phone (I thought that walking and driving were things you did to *escape* from the telephone). Early in my teaching career, I learned how to show a filmstrip, but I never quite mastered the 16mm film projector. I've come a long way since then, but I'm still a bit baffled when I hear my technophile friends raving about the latest Internet gizmos.

It's not that I'm a Luddite or a technophobe. I often use electronic media and computer software in my classes, competently enough that some of my colleagues call on me for advice and support. However, my usual approach to technological innovation is to watch and wait long enough to make an informed decision about whether and how a particular device or application will help me to do my job more effectively and efficiently—to do a cost/benefit analysis, in other words. I like to incorporate powerful new tools whenever feasible, but only if I believe that the time and effort required on my part and my students' is justified by the likely gain in knowledge, understanding, or skill. So I catch the back of many waves—and miss a few entirely.

In general, English teachers have been eager to embrace electronic media and technology for educational purposes. At Amherst Regional, our department was the first to take classes to the computer lab to learn word processing, and now the demand for lab time is so high that we have to sign up weeks in advance. We never seem to have enough DVD players or camcorders to go around. Students are doing more and more electronic projects and presentations. Most of this activity is wonderful, but are we certain that the advantages of using media and technology are commensurate with the costs in time and resources? Not always. Parents and administrators sometimes complain that English teachers show too many movies, and we probably do. Have you ever popped in a video on a hot Friday afternoon because everyone felt too weary to work? I'm sure most of us have. When you take classes to the computer lab, are your students learning digital collaboration or publishing skills, or just typing? Too often the latter, I expect.

The intent of this chapter is to prompt you to do some strategic thinking about the uses of media and technology—about why these tools should be included in the English curriculum and how they can support its literacy goals. Don't look for instructions on particular types of hardware or software. Instead, you will find illustrations of technology-related activities that provide rich opportunities for skill building and critical thinking—that move beyond the "now that we've read the book, let's watch the movie" syndrome into media analysis and production.

Teaching in Exponential Times

The pace of change is constantly accelerating, especially in information-related fields. Keep in mind that the World Wide Web is less than twenty years old. I can't even imagine the kinds of technological adaptations my grandchildren will have to make. That's the point of the "Did You Know?" videos that have "gone viral" on the Web (see Fisch and McLeod): we're living in "exponential times," educating students to live and work in a world we can barely contemplate.

Chances are that our students are more cognizant of and comfortable with what's happening in the realm of technology than we are. The gap is particularly wide in computer applications. Should we just acknowledge that we can't keep up and relinquish the field to our tech-savvy students, a majority of whom are actively *contributing* media content, not merely *consuming* it? Not according to a recent paper prepared for the MacArthur Foundation:

> There are three core flaws with the laissez faire approach. The first is that it does not address the fundamental inequalities in young people's access to new media technologies and the opportunities for participation they represent (what we call the *participation gap*). The second is that it assumes that children are actively reflecting on their media experiences and can thus articulate what they learn from their participation (what we call the *transparency problem*). The third problem with the laissez faire approach is that it assumes children, on their own, can develop the ethical norms needed to cope with a complex and diverse social environment online (the *ethics challenge*). Any attempt to provide meaningful media education in the age of participatory culture must begin by addressing these three core concerns. (Jenkins et al. 12; emphasis original)

Participation, reflection, and ethics are certainly within the English teacher's baili-wick. We may have to learn from our students how certain technologies function, but we are well positioned to help them develop the communication skills needed to get fully involved in online participatory culture, the analytical habits of mind required to understand how media shape our perceptions, and the ethical standards necessary to become responsible content creators. The MacArthur report argues that the core competencies for the new literacy "should be seen as social skills, as ways of interacting within a larger community, and not simply an individualized skill to be used for personal expression" (20). These skills range from role-playing and multitasking to judging information sources and negotiating differences in perspectives and norms.

Most schools are still a long way from placing media literacy for the twenty-first century at the center of English classroom activity. Even so, many teachers are developing strategies that integrate technology in meaningful ways (as opposed to adding on "media for media's sake" assignments). The September 2007 *English Journal* featured several authentic approaches to incorporating new literacies, including, for example, Karen E. Moynihan's multimodal research project on collectibles and the subcultures they spawn. In this engaging but challenging endeavor, Internet research, digital photography, data management, graphic design, and PowerPoint presentations complement more conventional research and reporting methods, such as interviewing and writing. In the same issue other teachers wrote about successful uses of podcasting, virtual worlds, threaded discussions, online reviews, and more. To these could be added animation, digital storytelling, blogging, and many other possibilities (see, for example, Herrington, Hodgson, and Moran). English class is exploding with technological possibility.

Which prompts me to raise a troubling question: possibility for whom? The MacArthur report cited previously raises concerns about the "participation gap" caused by unequal access to new media. This is a serious issue for English teachers who are trying to foster twenty-first-century skills and habits of mind in their classes. Despite a variety of federal, state, and local efforts to bridge the "digital divide," what Charles Moran and Cynthia L. Selfe wrote a decade ago is still true: "Emerging technologies make visible, and perhaps increase, the gap between rich and poor and the related gap between races in this country" (48). Many of my students lack computers and Internet connections at home. They do have access to technology during the day—each classroom has a work station, and the computer lab and library are available during and after school—but they are still clearly at a disadvantage when compared to classmates who enjoy easy access on evenings and weekends. Exacerbating the technology gap is the fact that the students without computers are more likely to be the ones who have to work or care for younger siblings, limiting the time they can spend after hours at school. So they get less experience using the new media, and the gap widens. I'm acutely aware of this problem whenever I develop an assignment that requires or that would be facilitated by technology, and I try to structure the project to give my digital have-nots a fair chance to succeed. That usually means making time during class for students to use school facilities and offering some viable low-tech alternatives.

My approach to media instruction (and instruction with media) has been to focus on four broad goals. The first is to incorporate nonprint texts into the curriculum to be studied as and in conjunction with works of literature. These can include a range of genres, from audio recordings to graphic novels, but typically they are films, undoubtedly still the most common media used in English other than books. My second purpose is to promote media literacy, to increase students' awareness of the ways that messages are created and the influences that they have on individuals and society. Available subjects include everything from magazine advertising to network news. The third goal is to enhance students' research skills, particularly to encourage effective and responsible use of the Web. For too many young people, Internet research doesn't get beyond Google searches and copy-and-paste; I want them to learn more tools and better options. My final aim is to create authentic opportunities for students to learn techniques of media production. These techniques can be as simple as including tables and images in word-processed documents, or they can involve a complex array of skills, as in desktop publishing, PowerPoint presentations, and website design. The four sections that follow illustrate my approach to these four goals.

Approaching Films as Literary Texts

As I noted in Chapter 6 in regard to teaching art and music in conjunction with literature, studying nonprint forms can provide another path to understanding concepts central to our field: mood, tone, theme, style, and so on. The medium that offers the readiest and perhaps richest connections to the works we teach is film. English teachers have long understood the benefits of linking books with movies, and the wide availability of current and classic films in video formats has made the practice almost universal. Sometimes the reasons are questionable—showing the movie essentially as a reward for reading the book, as I used to do on occasion, is a dubious use of class time—but there are many legitimate ways to incorporate film in the English curriculum, creating stronger students of literature and wiser consumers of mass media.

Probably the most common method of integrating film is comparing the book with the movie—looking at how a director interpreted the text. I'm not as big a fan of this approach as I once was. Students who engage with a book always seem to be disappointed by the changes, and those who don't connect with it (or don't read it) aren't motivated by the screen version, either. There are effective strategies for teaching critical viewing through comparison. For example, John Golden prepares his students by introducing them to the *cinematic* elements (shot type, angle, camera movement), *theatrical* elements (costumes, props, sets, lighting), and *literary* elements (characterization, setting, symbolism) of film (25), and by showing them the difference between *directly filmable* and *indirectly filmable* elements of text (26). He teaches them to focus on the effects of the transformation from text to film, and he even asks them to translate movies into text (29–30).

When I do show video versions of titles that I teach, it tends to be for purposes other than comparing them with the texts. For instance, one of my major objectives in teaching *Romeo and Juliet* to ninth graders is to convince them that, despite their misgivings, they *can* understand and connect with Shakespeare. This play is usually their first encounter with the Bard, and of course they find the reading difficult. By the end of the unit I have them acting out cuttings, but at first they struggle too much with the language to perform the lines fluently. To help them hear the meaning and emotion embedded in the script and visualize how the play can be staged, I show them clips from Franco Zeffirelli's 1968 adaptation and Baz Luhrmann's wacky 1996 version. *Clips* is the operative word here—the idea isn't to present complete interpretations of the text but to illuminate particular scenes. The nurse's long discourse about Juliet's falling on her face as a child (1.3) is a good example. Students often bog down when reading this speech, but seeing it performed reveals its humor—and the nurse's character. Viewing the clips always leads to discussions of the directors' decisions, especially about omitting lines: was it just to save time, or were the lines unnecessary because they served as scenery in Shakespeare's theater?

Comparison *is* among my goals when using my favorite strategy for incorporating films: pairing them with books on related subjects. I use the word *related* somewhat loosely here. The connection may be historical or geographical or cultural, or it may be thematic. In Chapter 3, I mentioned linking Michael Moore's *Roger & Me*, a seriocomic documentary on the effects of the General Motors plant closing in Flint, Michigan, with Ralph Ellison's novel *Invisible Man*. At first students don't know what to make of such a crazy film, but soon they understand that the unemployed auto workers are invisible for the same reason that Ellison's unnamed protagonist is: people refuse to see them. Another literature-film association I make that might seem like a stretch is Voltaire's *Candide* with Roland Joffe's *The Mission*. The surface connection is setting: Candide travels to South America, where he visits the utopian kingdom of El Dorado, which is home to people so content that they need not pray. They resemble the Guarani of *The Mission*, peaceable natives of Argentina who are ultimately annihilated due to a political feud in Europe. The film, like the novel, raises complex moral and philosophical issues and leaves them similarly unresolved. It also serves as a useful transition in the Renaissance and Modern Literature course. It takes place in the eighteenth century, as *Candide* does, but its depictions of unspoiled nature and corrupt civilization anticipate the themes of Romanticism.

In ninth grade I use a literature/film link as the basis for teaching the comparison/contrast essay. One of the core readings in that year is Elie Wiesel's *Night*, a devastating memoir of the Holocaust. Most students have some prior knowledge of the events, but they are overwhelmed by Wiesel's depiction of them. I have tried a variety of movie pairings with this book, but the one I have found the most successful is with Roberto Benigni's *Life Is Beautiful*. This film provides some much-needed comic relief in a gloomy unit, and for many students it offers an introduction to foreign films with subtitles. But its real value (for my purposes) is that it shows, when contrasted with *Night*, that the same materials can be used in pursuit of different artistic visions. Wiesel's story documents his loss of faith in God and humanity, while Benigni's pays tribute to the power of love. To prepare for writing the comparison/contrast essay, students take extensive notes and engage in wide-ranging discussions. They point out a variety of similarities and differences in plotline and setting. They recognize, too, that the movie's depiction of the Holocaust is unrealistic, and some of them wonder whether it's disrespectful to treat such a serious subject with humor. I work on getting them to go deeper than the surface connections into what the works have to say about human relationships, human nature, life itself; into the writer's and director's purposes and the choices they made to fulfill them. Using the multistep process outlined in Figure 7.1, each student selects a basis for comparison and assembles key evidence. In an essay focusing on the depictions of the camps, Carla reached this conclusion:

> It's surprising that two interpretations of the same event could be quite so different. The two stories were meant to affect people in different ways. *Night* depressed me and put me in a state of shock and disbelief—I hadn't been aware of just how dire the situation was. *Life Is Beautiful* was uplifting and heartening, it made me feel like "*La vita e bella*": Life is beautiful. I prefer the latter, and I know that I am not the only one. However, the story must be told.

Carla's response to the unit is fairly typical in that it highlights the idea of interpretation. Some students don't prefer the film to *Night*, but most see that both works represent artistic intentions.

Using films as literary works presents some logistical challenges in the school setting. I try to provide as much of a cinema experience as I can (minus the Coke and candy). If possible, I use one of our weekly long periods to allow for sustained viewing time. I do quite a bit of preteaching and lead many follow-up activities, but I interrupt the films as little as possible and only at logical breaks. Another problem with showing movies is ratings, some of which seem out of whack. If I feel that an

Writing Assignment for *Night* and *Life Is Beautiful*   Name_____*Carla O*_____

The writing assignment for *Night* and *Life Is Beautiful* will be a two- or three-page comparison/contrast essay. You will have the opportunity to choose the focus of your comparison, which will require using specific evidence from the book and the film.

Step 1. From the list of similarities you compiled in your notebook and other ideas you have thought of since then, **write down several ways that *Night* and *Life Is Beautiful* could be compared and contrasted**. Do you want to compare the father and son relationships, for example? Or perhaps the messages that the two works convey about life? Or maybe their relative effectiveness in communicating the meaning of the Holocaust? An example is provided to get you started:

a. *Night* and *Life Is Beautiful* are both about father-son relationships in the concentration camps.

b. *In both stories, the fathers die but their sons live, but the relationships under which the fathers die are very different.*

c. *The camps are very different in Night and L.I.B.*

d. *L.I.B. is very unrealistic and Night is true, but they both follow a similar plotline.*

Step 2. Decide on one focus area for your comparison/contrast essay (put a check next to the topic above). Then, using the chart below, **list several details from the book and the film** that are related to your topic and indicate whether they are similarities or differences (+ or –):

Topic	*Night*	*Life Is Beautiful*	+ or –
Peoples' physical condition	emaciated, weak, gaunt	a little bit skinny and sad	–
Morale	hopeless, faithless, self-centered	always some hope, full of faith in God & human spirit, helping each other	–
Nazi officers	harsh, unsympathetic, apparently emotionless & w/o personality or individuality	"	+
Living conditions	overcrowded, desperately little food & water, unsanitary & unhygienic	"	+
Affect on relationships	disintegrated them all, every-man-for-himself mentality—will to survive overrode loyalty and caring	strengthened them—"hard times bring out the best in men" attitude—people looking out for each other	–
Daily life	predictable & monotonous: got up, "breakfast," work, "dinner," sleep—no free time/ energy	similar but w/ inexplicable free time/energy for "games", sharing food w/ hidden child	–

Step 3. After you have selected several details, you should **write a partial working draft** of your paper (about one page), including at least the opening paragraph and some examples.

Step 4. After getting some feedback on your partial draft in class tomorrow, you should **finish it over the long weekend**. You can organize your paper by discussing one work and then the other in parallel order, or you can compare them point by point. These two methods will be demonstrated in class. You will be expected to use some direct quotations in your paper.

Step 5. The final step (due Jan. 22) will be to **revise the paper and make a final draft**. Make sure that you carefully check the organization and evidence in the paper and edit to eliminate mechanical errors.

Figure 7.1. Literature/film comparison essay worksheet.

R-rated film (such as *Shakespeare in Love*) has value for my students, I write a letter to parents explaining my purposes in showing it and requesting their permission. They almost always approve, but they do appreciate being asked.

Your turn. Using a table like the one below, make an inventory of the movies that you show in your classes and reflect on why and how you incorporate them into the curriculum.

Film	Course/Unit	Purpose(s)	Clips or Whole	Activities

Do you use film adaptations of books that you teach? If so, what are your goals? How do you ensure that discussion of the films goes deeper than how they differ from the written texts? Do you also include films as artistic works in their own right? How do you relate them to the works of literature they accompany? Are there other instructional goals you would like to pursue using films as texts? What films would serve best? Search online and ask colleagues for suggestions.

Cultivating Critical Media Literacy

Young people are voracious consumers of media: movies, television, games, music, Internet. As much as we might like them to spend more of their free time with books, all indicators point to students' lives becoming even more saturated with electronic messages, some of them not very positive. We can't control what they hear and see, but we can teach them how to be critical listeners and viewers, to interpret the explicit and implicit meanings of media productions and identify the techniques used to create them. There are many useful resources for teaching media literacy, such as the documentaries on gender, race, and other issues developed by the Media Education Foundation (http://www.mediaed.org/). But it's also important—and fairly simple—to assemble your own materials and to get students involved in the investigation.

During the nearly twenty years that I served as newspaper advisor, I taught dozens of journalism classes—at Amherst Regional the course is open to everyone, not just the newspaper staff. In addition to teaching the techniques of news reporting and writing, I focused on fostering critical awareness of the ways news is reported. I wanted students to learn to recognize balance and bias in newspapers and other media. They kept current events journals throughout the term in which they analyzed coverage of particular issues. At the end of the course, I asked them to write an analytical essay on television news. To prepare them for this assignment, I recorded two evening news programs from the same day. At least one was a commercial broadcast, such as the *CBS Evening News*; the other was often from public television or a cable network. Before showing the programs in class, I created a two-column chart on the board and asked students to do the same in their notebooks. We used these charts to keep track of the story lineups and take notes on the coverage. At each commercial break we stopped to compare observations and discuss their implications. Students were often surprised by the results of our research: by how much the selection and treatment of stories varied; by how thin the coverage was, especially of international affairs; by the amount of time devoted to puff pieces and teasers. I remember one particularly startling comparison. In 1985 I happened to record two broadcast news programs on the day of the Mexico City earthquake. Each devoted the entire show to the disaster. The basic facts and the pictures were the same, but the narratives were very different. On one network the underlying theme was "Mexican people unite to battle adversity"; on the other it was "shoddy construction practices multiply misery." One of the conclusions that students almost always reached in their analytical essays was that no one should rely on a single source of news.

Advertising is another rich source of material for teaching critical literacy, especially in connection to social justice issues. Gender stereotyping is still rampant in promotions of everything from toys to food to underwear. So is racism. When reading *Invisible Man*, many students are appalled by Ellison's descriptions of a coin bank in the shape of a grinning black man and Sambo dolls being sold on the street. They are even more shocked when they recognize how pervasive ethnic stereotypes still are in commerce. I've collected lots of examples, including ads for collectible dolls from Sunday paper magazine sections: Buckwheat, the wide-eyed "pickaninny" from the *Little Rascals*; an "authentic" Indian princess in buckskin and beads; and Pablo, the "siesta-loving" Mexican boy, complete with sombrero and serape. I tack these and similar items on the bulletin board and invite students to look for more. Newly aware, they find plenty of examples, not only in magazines but also on television and online. My colleagues who teach African American Literature and Women and Literature have entire walls devoted to such images. Sadly, there is no shortage of stereotypes in the popular media.

The key to increasing critical awareness is teaching students to "read between the lines" of nonprint texts, just as we do with printed ones. In network news a message may be imparted as much by a raised eyebrow or a skeptical tone of voice as by the words spoken. In advertising, an appeal may be based on the juxtaposition of image and text or on allusions to cultural icons. Each form has its unique language and conventions, as well as some rhetorical features shared with traditional print genres. The expanding world of electronic media presents many promising opportunities for analysis—video games, "reality" programs, Internet sites, popular songs—any of which can serve as objects of study in the writing and literature classroom.

> **Your turn.** What forms of nonprint media do you use in your professional and personal life? What benefits do you gain from them? How do these texts convey meanings? What strategies do you use to "read" them? Are you aware of any biases or stereotypes that they contain? Try doing a critical analysis of one example—an episode of a television show, a song, a favorite Web page. Then develop a lesson in which you lead students through a similar process with the media that inhabit their lives. What do you and they learn from this analysis? What additional ways do you see of incorporating media literacy into the curriculum?

Encouraging Responsible Internet Research

Sometimes I introduce research projects by telling students that I'm going to acquaint them with a powerful new technology that will enable them to access a wealth of information that they can have at their fingertips wherever they go. After a few more minutes of dramatic buildup, I reach into my bag and pull out . . . a book. I'm only half-kidding. Students rely almost exclusively on the Internet for research. One member of my college class, a junior, recently told me that he had never been to the campus library. But I must admit that I too now turn to the Web initially when I need to look something up. So I don't try to dissuade students from doing research online, but I do try to teach them how to use Internet sources effectively and ethically.

One of the most important lessons for students to learn is that there are different ways to search the Web and more authoritative sites than Wikipedia. Many high school and even college students never get beyond typing their topics into Google or some other search engine. That's fine for a quick reference—if they need to find out, as I did when writing an earlier section of this chapter, who directed a particular film—though they would be wise to check more than one source. A Google search may also serve as a starting point for deeper investigation, as an introduction to the breadth of information available in a field and as a portal to academic and professional websites. It may also turn up thousands of irrelevant and questionable sources, and students need strategies for sorting out what is and isn't valuable.

Part of the sorting process involves narrowing the results using appropriate keywords and applying Boolean logic (truth OR consequences, peaches AND cream, shaken NOT stirred). Sara B. Kajder offers this useful strategy for developing keywords: "divide a sheet of paper into three columns: Must, Might, and Mustn't. Brainstorm within these columns those aspects that *must* be located in your search, those that *might* be helpful, and those that *mustn't* enter into the search" (57; emphasis original). Once students have identified what they're looking for, they can list concepts to be used as search terms. School librarians are usually very good at demonstrating how to select keywords and apply Boolean operators, and I've found it helpful to schedule a lesson in the library when students have focused their topics and are ready to begin their research in earnest (but not before—their eyes glaze over during research "orientations").

Another key step in sorting search results is evaluating websites' credibility. Students don't automatically make a distinction between scholarly sites and fans' or advocacy groups' pages. For example, when my students in Bible and Related Literature do research on biblical texts, many of the websites they find are sponsored by religious organizations. This doesn't mean the sites aren't valuable, but it's important that students understand that the interpretations they're getting are based on particular sets of beliefs. Kajder presents a "scoring rubric" for Web pages that includes items such as determining the author's expertise, learning more about the sponsoring organization, and checking the date of the information (138). If a site doesn't supply this kind of information, it may not be reliable. She also suggests finding out what other pages are linked to the one being evaluated (you can do this by searching on *link:* followed by the site's URL). Amherst Regional High's library website provides a similar guide for judging Internet sources ("How to Evaluate a Web Site"). Students are unlikely to engage in any vetting process, however, unless they get strong teacher guidance. The message I try to convey about the Web is *caveat emptor*—or, as Ronald Reagan often said, "Trust, but verify"—by checking other sources.

Among the other sources I encourage students to use are articles indexed in subscription databases such as Infotrac and Proquest. Libraries pay substantial fees for access to these searchable, full-text materials, but many students don't even know they exist. Demonstrating what these databases have to offer is another good topic for a workshop by the school librarian. And then there is the online catalog, which leads students to that remarkable bit of technology I mentioned at the beginning of this section. I always insist that students include print materials among their sources, and I teach them a tried-and-true search technique: get the call numbers of several books that seem likely to be useful, then cruise the surrounding stacks.

Unfortunately, research projects always raise the specter of plagiarism. Online sources offer especially tempting shortcuts: cutting and pasting someone else's words takes just a few clicks. These transgressions are often painfully obvious: the borrowed material is in a different font, or, in extreme cases, the URL of the source is printed on the bottom of the page. Even when the borrowing is disguised, it's not hard to spot unacknowledged quotations; the syntax and diction just don't sound like the student's language. A Google search of a suspect phrase usually leads directly to the original text. Encountering plagiarism always makes me heartsick, partly because there are serious consequences and a complex administrative process involved, and partly because I know that the student is going to suffer from feeling a loss of trust. But despite the pervasive threat of illicit downloading, I prefer to think of plagiarism as an education problem rather than a law enforcement problem. I would feel uncomfortable asking students to submit their papers to Turnitin (http://www.turnitin.com/), a service used by many schools and colleges to check for originality. Doing so seems tantamount to saying, "I don't trust you."

Though it's obvious that some instances of plagiarism are deliberate and deceitful, most of the cases I've encountered are sins of omission or genuine confusion: failing to keep accurate records of sources, failing to distinguish quotations and reading notes, failing to understand that paraphrased material must be cited, or putting an assignment off until the last minute and leaving too little time to digest the data. These problems are not excuses for plagiarism, but there are steps we can take to help students avoid them. One is to clarify, early and often, the meaning and importance of academic integrity. Easy access to information on the Web has muddied the concept of intellectual property, so students need opportunities to discuss what is and is not ethical research behavior. Another important step is to show students how to *learn* from sources rather than just *copy* from them. Kathleen Guinee and Maya B. Eagleton teach a note-making process that they refer to by the acronym/metaphor "CHoMP"; students learn to

- **C**ross out small words, such as prepositions and conjunctions
- **H**ighlight important information in the remaining text
- **M**ake notes based on the highlighted information by abbreviating, truncating, making lists, using symbols, and drawing instead of writing full sentences
- **P**ut the notes in their own words. (48)

Coupled with accurate documentation, this kind of strategy guards against plagiarism but also promotes synthesis. When students internalize the data they gather, they make connections and gain new insights. They realize that true research involves both pulling in and pushing away: there is a time in each project to compile and catalog what others have said, and a time to clear space to develop an original contribution.

To get better at research, students need more frequent guided practice than they typically get in school. Weeks-long projects culminating in lengthy research papers and/or formal presentations still seem to be the norm. These projects are absolutely necessary and extremely valuable—properly sequenced and supported, they teach a whole range of important skills. But the time and effort they consume guarantee that they will be few. Students can learn many of the same lessons by doing more frequent mini-projects. In American Literature and Nature, I assign a small research project at the beginning of the unit on Melville and Dickinson. Students work individually or in pairs to learn about topics ranging from whaling ships and equipment to life in nineteenth-century Amherst. The requirements are to locate and distill three authoritative sources, to write a one-page report with analysis and proper documentation, and to deliver a five-minute talk. I provide models for all of the steps and coach students as they move through them. The entire process takes about a week. Sometimes I start the ninth-grade Holocaust unit with an even shorter research assignment. Here's the idea: let's see what we can find out online in one class period, reflect on the information tonight, and share our results (both notes and citations) tomorrow. The effect of these mini-projects, I believe, is to make the research process a normal part of learning and to show that using sources effectively and ethically is no big deal.

> **Your turn.** Where does research play a role in your curriculum? If you assign research projects, examine your handouts and reflect on your lessons and procedures. Do they include sufficient instruction on finding and evaluating materials, distilling and synthesizing information, and respecting intellectual property? What aspects of these projects have gone well in the past? What additional resources do you need to make them go better? Do you ever use mini-projects to enhance the curriculum and teach research skills? Could you? Where? Also, look up your school's plagiarism policy to be sure you know all its details. When you encounter academic dishonesty, who has to get involved, and how? Do you have any discretion in handling these matters? What message do you want to convey to students and parents when plagiarism occurs?

Helping Students Become Media Producers

Helping students to become critical, responsible consumers of technology is important, but it's not enough any longer. They also need to become competent *creators* of media content. Teaching the technical aspects of desktop publishing, movie editing, and Web design is beyond the scope of most English classes, but the writing and literature curriculum offers plenty of rich opportunities for student media projects. Sometimes all we need to do is get out of the way.

For example, in American Literature and Society, students work in self-selected groups studying poems by Gwendolyn Brooks. Each group is asked to choose one poem and develop an interpretive presentation in any medium the group chooses—dance, music, slide show, etc. Four boys, all recent immigrants, decided to make a video based on "We Real Cool." They created a script in which several young "punks"(played by themselves) skip study hall and slink uptown to shoot pool. The boys borrowed a camera from the technology department, recruited the detention monitor to be part of the cast, and recorded scenes that showed the main characters ditching class, sneaking around corners, hiding behind cars, strutting into the pool hall, and finally looking empty and sad. Their video was the best-designed project in the class.

Another example: In Bible and Related Literature, every student compiles an annotated collection of biblical allusions found in popular culture. The traditional presentation mode for this collection is a decorated notebook, but I decided to open it to other formats. Hannah, who happened to be taking a Web design course the same term, decided to apply her new digital skills to the Bible project. She created a handsome, image-rich website that enabled the user to scroll through her examples sequentially or navigate to particular sections (see Figure 7.2).

Like the boys who produced the "We Real Cool" video, Hannah was doubly motivated: she was glad to have the chance to do her English assignment in a cre-

Figure 7.2. A page from Hannah's Bible reference website.

ative, high-tech format; she was also grateful for the opportunity to apply her technical know-how to an authentic problem. I'm not particularly skilled at either video production or Web design, so I couldn't offer much advice on nuts-and-bolts questions (though other students could). I could give ongoing feedback on how well these media creations were fulfilling the criteria for the assignments, keeping the students' attention focused on the primary purposes of the work rather than on the technology.

Knowing that students have unequal access to electronic media, and that some have little inclination to work with digital tools, I make the use of technology mandatory in some projects. Since PowerPoint has become a ubiquitous presentation format—and since it is often used so poorly—I try to teach students how to create effective slide shows using this software. My instructional method follows the Show Me/Help Me/Let Me model I referred to in Chapter 3. I show a range of examples from my collection of previous students' work. By studying and critiquing these models, students gain a sense of what is possible and what does and doesn't work. As a class we derive a set of guidelines for PowerPoint compositions: how much and what size text should appear on a page, what kinds of visual elements support the message, whether and when animation should be used in transitions. Then I help students create their own productions by teaching them how to storyboard a presentation, demonstrating the basic design of the program, and coaching them as they proceed. Finally, I let them go: to figure out how to incorporate all elements of the assignment, to develop a visual style, to troubleshoot problems, and above all to learn from each other. They always end up teaching me PowerPoint features I haven't tried. But the process doesn't end with creating the slides; they also have to learn and practice how to make their shows complement (rather than be) their speeches.

I teach PowerPoint in part because I have used it quite a bit myself and feel comfortable explaining it to others. The same goes for desktop publishing software. One day I hope to feel confident enough to demonstrate Web design programs as well. But the type of technology doesn't matter as much as the acknowledgment that digital literacies are indispensable elements of twenty-first-century communication, and they belong in the English classroom alongside reading and writing. That message can be carried by all kinds of media: podcasts, digital photography, blogs, and even the advanced features of word processors.

> **Your turn.** What opportunities for media production do students have in your classes? Are there other assignments that could be opened up to new technologies? Do you include media projects as required elements in any of the courses you teach? If so, how do you approach teaching the technical aspects? How satis-

fied have you been with the results? How do you think they might be improved? If you don't currently assign media projects, think about the forms of technology you yourself use to create digital content. With which of these do you feel most comfortable? Could you design a project involving this medium? What other digital literacies would you like to acquire? Pick a project you would like to try and then find a mentor to help you.

Moving Forward

The world of technology grows larger and moves faster every day, and our students are among its most active citizens. Keeping track of the latest gadgets and lingo is challenging for teachers, and we may feel contrary impulses when considering how to make electronic media part of the English curriculum. The "cool" factor is undeniable—students are clearly motivated by opportunities to work with new digital tools and applications. On the other hand, taking more time for technology means crowding something else—probably traditional literacy activities. The way forward, in my view, is to think of media study not as competition for reading and writing instruction but as exposure to innovative literary genres and practice with contemporary tools for composing. Ideally, technology use will become fully integrated rather than added on. As you consider modifying your practice, it's fine to go slowly: better to incorporate a few media effectively, with clear connections to the curriculum, than to serve up a smorgasbord of incongruent activities. But we do have a responsibility—especially to students on the wrong side of the technology gap—to make media literacy, both receptive and productive, a priority in English. Interpreting and creating high-tech forms are the twenty-first-century's basic skills.

Recommended Reading

Christel, Mary T., and Scott Sullivan, eds. *Lesson Plans for Creating Media-Rich Classrooms*. Urbana, IL: NCTE, 2007. Print.

> This resource includes sections on media and literature, popular culture, and persuasion, with detailed plans for media literacy and production lessons. The accompanying CD contains classroom handouts and teacher and student work samples.

Firek, Hilve. *10 Easy Ways to Use Technology in the English Classroom*. Portsmouth, NH: Heinemann, 2003. Print.

> This book's context-rich chapters present strategies and materials for incorporating a range of technologies, familiar and new, into the English curriculum.

Gerster, Carole, ed., with Laura W. Zlogar. *Teaching Ethnic Diversity with Film: Essays and Resources for Educators in History, Social Studies, Literature, and Film Studies*. Jefferson, NC: McFarland, 2006. Print.

> This collection includes historical chapters on representation of people of color on film and recommendations for teaching ethnic-American literature on film and as film.

Herrington, Anne, Kevin Hodgson, and Charles Moran, eds. *Teaching the New Writing: Technology, Change, and Assessment in the 21st-Century Classroom*. New York and Berkeley, CA: Teachers College Press and National Writing Project, 2009. Print.

> In nine example-rich essays, elementary, secondary, and college teachers describe their strategies for teaching writing through technology (blogs, multimedia projects, etc.), and the editors provide context and conclusions.

Kajder, Sara B. *The Tech-Savvy English Classroom*. Portland: Stenhouse, 2003. Print.

> A good place to start in this clear and helpful volume is the appendix, which includes tools for evaluating your classroom tech-savvy. The chapters present rationales and classroom strategies for including technology in logical steps and nonthreatening language.

Profiles in Practice: Digital Storytelling with Teacher Consultants from the National Writing Project. 2008. Web. Pearson Foundation and National Writing Project. 28 June 2009.

> This website explains digital storytelling and highlights several projects created to improve student writing. The site includes a variety of student work samples, links, and attachments.

Supporting Development of "Basic Skills"

8

I put "basic skills" in quotation marks here because I don't like the way the term is used in some public discussions of the English curriculum. I think that writing for authentic purposes is pretty basic; so are connecting personal experience with literature and using digital technology to communicate effectively. But when people bring up "basic skills," they're usually referring to discrete aspects of language and literacy, such as punctuation and vocabulary—particularly the aspects that get tested on high-stakes assessments—and what often follows is a real concern that schools don't do an adequate job of teaching these skills. I rarely get through a back-to-school night, for example, without addressing a parent's anxiety about grammar.

I'm not suggesting that the "basics" aren't important. All of the above-mentioned skills, plus comprehension, spelling, and more, are essential elements of writing and reading that *should* be addressed in the English classroom. The real question is how. The traditional paradigm of instruction isolated these facets of language arts: grammar lessons focused on naming of parts, unconnected to ongoing writing assignments; weekly vocabulary lists and tests, unrelated to current readings. The clear trend in the field over the last several decades has been to integrate the teaching of "basic skills" into a unified composition and literature curriculum. However, the question is far from settled. Although the holistic approach has gained wide acceptance among English teachers, there are still compelling calls for direct instruction targeting particular skills. The content and format of state assessments have given this matter special urgency, and many schools have reverted to traditional teaching methods to boost scores. I don't see the business of skills instruction as an either/or proposition, however. I'm a strong advocate for an integrated curriculum, but I believe there is adequate space within it for authentic activities that focus on improving key language arts abilities. The trick is to make this work connected, not canned.

In this chapter I offer some recommendations for providing the skills instruction students need without fragmenting the program of study—on the contrary, by incorporating activities that reinforce it. Some of my suggestions come in the form of connected lessons or major projects, but most take advantage of "teachable moments" in formats such as mini-lessons and group work. Two sections of the chapter focus on perennial concerns of the English teacher: grammar (including linguistic analysis and editing skills) and reading (including vocabulary and comprehension). Another section addresses a new set of "basic skills" in the English program: test-taking strategies. Finally, I propose renewed attention to an untested (and thus largely neglected) skills domain: oral communication. But first, some viewpoints from the field.

Getting a Handle on the "Basics"

Before we can decide how to teach "basic skills," we have to be sure we understand what they are. That's no easy task, considering the amount of controversy that some skills questions have generated. The Great Grammar Debate is the prime example: English teachers have been fighting for more than a century over whether formal grammar instruction is beneficial. Decades of experimental research seem to show that it has no positive effect on student writing. Yet, says Patrick Hartwell in a much-quoted *College English* article, we never resolve the issue because the opposing sides, working from different assumptions, disagree on how to interpret the results (106). Even if this question were settled, the debate would undoubtedly continue; many teachers would argue that language study has intrinsic value, apart from any influence on writing ability.

Clouding the controversy is the fact that *grammar* has multiple meanings, as Hartwell explains (109–110). *Grammar 1* is the set of language patterns that all native speakers of a language have in their heads by the age of five or six—*the* grammar, in other words. This is the grammar that tells us to say "big red barn" instead of "red big barn" without knowing why. *Grammar 2* refers to theories developed by linguists to describe Grammar 1. There are many such theories, each of which could be referred to as *a* grammar, and their descriptions vary. For example, when I first started teaching, I was surprised to find out that in modern transformational grammar, words that I had learned as articles and possessive pronouns are labeled "determiners," words that signal a noun is coming. *Grammar 3* is not really grammar at all, but linguistic etiquette. When we point out or try to correct errors in "bad grammar," we are referring to usage. *Grammar 4* is Hartwell's term for school grammars—the versions of Grammar 2 taught in textbooks—which may be derived from but do not always accurately reflect scientific analysis of Grammar 1. For instance, there seems to be a rule in English that calls for the object case when a pronoun appears at the end of a sentence, even after a linking verb: when someone asks, "Who's there?" most people instinctively reply, "It's *me*." But traditional school grammars (which were derived from Latin) prescribe the unnatural-sounding "It is *I*." *Grammar 5* refers to the use of grammatical terms to teach prose style, as in Strunk and White's popular handbook, *The Elements of Style*. A lesson based on this definition might show students how to combine short sentences by embedding descriptive material in appositive phrases or relative clauses.

Does that clear things up? I doubt it, but this much is certain: we need to think carefully about our purposes and students' needs when considering approaches to grammar. The deep and surface structures of language and the ways linguists have described them (Grammars 1 and 2) are legitimate subjects for study, but textbooks (Grammar 4) may not be that helpful in teaching about them. Nor is linguistic analysis likely to improve students' writing. If that is our primary goal, we should concentrate on usage and style (Grammars 3 and 5). What is the best approach to teaching these aspects of writing, and how much grammatical knowledge is necessary?

In reality, a good deal of "grammar" instruction focuses on teaching students to avoid error. But such efforts may be misplaced. A simple but powerful insight I gained years ago from Mina Shaughnessy's *Errors and Expectations: A Guide for the Teacher of Basic Writing* has stayed with me: students write the way they do "because they are beginners and must, like all beginners, learn by making mistakes" (5). Errors are rarely random or illogical; they often reveal that students know more than they are able to represent in the surface features of their writing. Sentence fragments and comma splices, for instance, do not result from lack of understanding of the sentence but rather from lack of awareness of how to punctuate its complex and compound forms, which students acquire intuitively without learning their names. Thus errors in punctuation may be indicators of progress toward a more mature style. Worksheets on subjects and predicates will not help students move forward. Nor will marginal corrections or commands such as "Proofread your work!" "Such strategies ram at the doors of their incompetence while the keys that would open them lie in view" (Shaughnessy 5). Those keys are the students' implicit knowledge and the teacher's ability to bring it into the open, where the appropriate fixes can be applied.

Constance Weaver, a leading authority on grammar, advocates a "less is more" approach: teaching "a minimum of grammar for maximum benefits." Her "scope-not-sequence" chart enumerates five broad goals to be pursued "between kindergarten and graduate school":

- Teaching concepts of subject, verb, sentence, clause, phrase, and related concepts for editing;

- Teaching style through sentence combining and sentence generating;

- Teaching sentence sense and style through the manipulation of syntactic elements;

- Teaching the power of dialects and the dialects of power;

- Teaching punctuation and mechanics for convention, clarity, and style.
  (21–23)

Weaver argues for teaching linguistic concepts in the context of writing, when there is the best chance of transfer to students' work. She recommends "incidental lessons," in which grammatical terms are introduced casually while the class discusses literature or student writing; "inductive lessons," in which students are guided to notice patterns and make generalizations; and "mini-lessons," in which the teacher presents new information and students try it out in collaborative activities; as well as teaching grammatical points in writing conferences (26). These indirect, minimally invasive measures can be easily integrated into the curriculum.

Not as loud but just as vigorous as the grammar debate has been the discussion of reading instruction in the secondary classroom. Some ask: Should reading skills even be taught at the high school level outside of remedial classes? Aren't students supposed to learn them in the elementary grades? But the common view of reading—that it is "a set of basic skills, widely adaptable and applicable to all kinds of texts and reading situations"—is changing, according to literacy researchers Timothy Shanahan and Cynthia Shanahan (40). Recent national efforts to boost early reading have improved younger students' performance, but these gains do not seem to last beyond middle school. Giving students a literacy "vaccination" in the early grades doesn't make them immune to failure in high school when the reading demands become more complex. The conclusion: "Most students need explicit teaching of sophisticated genres, specialized language conventions, disciplinary norms of precision and accuracy, and higher-level interpretive processes" (43). Shanahan and Shanahan's model of literacy development is a pyramid with three levels. At the lowest level are the most basic and most generalized skills: decoding, knowledge of high-frequency words. At the middle level are intermediate skills such as generic comprehension strategies and basic fluency. Most students have attained this level by the time they enter high school, though many have not. At the top level are the most specific, discipline-based skills, signified by the narrowing of the pyramid (44–45). The processes required for comprehending a short story are not the same as those needed to understand a biology textbook. But high schools generally do not have systems in place to teach these high-level skills. "By the time adolescent students are being challenged by disciplinary texts, literacy instruction often has evaporated altogether or has degenerated into a reiteration of general reading strategies . . . most likely to benefit only the lowest-functioning students" (45). The implications are clear: English teachers *must* be reading teachers, not just to improve the "basic skills" of students below grade level, but to facilitate all students' acquisition of the higher-level skills that are basic to our field. When students complain that English teachers "read too much into" a work of literature, they may really be saying that they need advanced reading instruction.

One point of difference among English teachers is over the kinds of books to use in class, especially in an era when more and more students seem to have reading problems—weak skills or just a lack of interest. One school of thought is that texts should be highly engaging and immediately accessible to adolescents—"easy reading," if you will. Based on her experience with reluctant readers, Kylene Beers recommends these features in fictional texts: thin books and short chapters, white space, illustrations, well-defined characters, plots with a lot of action that begins right away, mysteries, funny books, characters that are the students' age or slightly older, characters who face tough choices, realistic language, easily defined conflicts (285–288). Young adult novels often (but not always) fit these criteria, and Beers offers hundreds of examples in an appendix. A contrary view is offered by Carol Jago, who suggests teachers choose more demanding fare:

> Students need to be working in Vygotsky's Zone of Proximal Development. Ideally, instruction should be aimed at the level where students learn with the aid of a teacher or more knowledgeable peers. The texts chosen for classroom study should be ones that students are unable to read without you. In too many cases middle and high school instruction is aimed at what I call the ZME, or the Zone of Minimal Effort. In this instructional zone, the texts are as short as possible, and if possible, humorous; every day's lesson stands alone to eliminate reliance on homework reading; and basic skills are retaught ad nauseam. . . . While seemingly responsive to student needs, this kind of instruction in fact leaves students who are working below grade level farther and farther behind. ("Understanding" 307)

There is something to be said for each of these points of view. I certainly agree with the idea of stretching students beyond what they find familiar or comfortable—the challenge itself can be a source of motivation—but I don't think that short or humorous texts necessarily signal minimal effort or hinder growth. As noted in Chapter 3, I think it's essential to vary the lengths and difficulty level of readings, as well as to give students some choices.

Beers and Jago would agree that reading needs to be taught rather than merely assigned. Both recommend a variety of activities, such as activating prior knowledge and acting out passages with difficult syntax, to help students connect with texts. Both also recommend steps for teaching vocabulary, the strategy English teachers turn to most frequently to improve reading comprehension. William Nagy, a leading researcher in the field, argues that vocabulary and comprehension have a complex, reciprocal relationship. "Having a big vocabulary does contribute to being a better reader. But being a good reader also contributes to having a big vocabulary"—because good readers read more (34). The implication of this hypothesis is that vocabulary instruction, including "building word consciousness, helping students to identify morphological and semantic relationships among words, increasing their sensitivity to words with multiple meanings and to contextual variations in meanings" (42), should be integrated with comprehension strategies and activities promoting fluency and motivation. Thomas B. Smith outlines a comprehensive approach to vocabulary building that includes creating "word-rich environments" in the classroom, choosing words that are helpful for talking about assigned readings, and spending "less time, more often" on word-study activities (21–25). Smith's article appears in the March 2008 issue of *English Journal*, which is devoted to vocabulary instruction. Other pieces advocate approaches ranging from synonym mapping to an "old school" emphasis on Greek and Latin roots. One feature these perspectives have in common is *intensity*—rich and repeated exposure to words. Research supports this approach: according to Nagy, a student needs as many as twelve instructional encounters with a word to take real ownership of it (28).

In contrast to the rich and robust discussions of grammar and reading in professional publications, little attention has been paid to oral communication in recent years. It should have been otherwise: writing in 1998, Nancy Rost Goulden worried that teachers might be overwhelmed by "an expanded English curriculum that includes not only the traditional language arts of writing and reading but also the 'new' language arts of speaking, listening, and media literacy" (90). The anticipated expansion was the product of new state and national standards that elevated the oral arts into a prominent place in the English curriculum. But then along came testing. Since speaking and listening can't be assessed on paper exams, the urgency to improve instruction in these essential skills rapidly diminished. That's a shame. With the advent of new communication technologies, having the confidence and competence to speak effectively in the public arena may be needed more than ever. It's not that students don't give oral performances in English class, but they usually do so in service of literature or composition: reporting on research, reading parts in a play, sharing a piece of writing. These activities certainly provide valuable experience, but they don't necessarily foreground public speaking skills.

Goulden offers some helpful ideas for teaching the formal speech, including repeated "oral drafting" of the text and presenting in the extemporaneous mode, i.e., without a script (93). She emphasizes the importance of the relationship between the speaker and the audience: "The real secret to effective delivery is attitudinal rather than behavioral. Successful speakers who appear natural and comfortable focus on the message and getting that message to the audience, not on how they look and feel" (94). These insights are mostly intuitive, but creating conditions in which students can gain them (planning, rehearsal, and feedback) amid many other demands on class time is a daunting challenge for the teacher. Gregory Shafer uses a creative approach to developing oral literacy in his weekly "Tell Me a Story" project. Dissatisfied with conventional speeches and debates, he sought a more democratic, constructivist alternative. "Speaking had to excite and empower—to touch the lives and excite the imaginations of my classes. Instead of emanating from my desk, the activities should be more congruent with the naturally playful lives of my students" (102). After building a class consensus on what constitutes a successful story, he assigned five students per week the task of telling one in the form of an original narrative, dramatic reading, or literary interpretation. Shafer reports that minority students especially felt liberated by the project: "The arbitrary and oppressive policies that have traditionally required minority students to try to emulate the majority culture did not exist for Tell Me a Story" (105). Like Goulden, Shafer emphasizes the connection between speaker and audience, which is key to making a public speaking assignment a lesson in *oral communication* (rather than a composition presented orally), whether the task is performing a piece of literature or presenting a slide show.

My journey in teaching "basic skills" reflects many of the debates and trends in the field. I'll give some examples of how I approach grammar, vocabulary and comprehension, and public speaking in the following sections. Since some of these "basics" figure prominently in state assessments, I'll also include some suggestions for preparing students to take standardized tests.

Grappling with Grammar

In my recollection, seventh-grade English was all about grammar: five days a week of learning linguistic terms and diagramming sentences. The experience wasn't unpleasant, just unrelenting. Subsequent courses were less intense, but lessons on the parts of speech and many types of phrases and clauses, usually from the venerable *Warriner's* handbook, always played a prominent role. I started out teaching the way I was taught: in ninth-grade classes especially, I emphasized the importance of learning the structures of the English language and the rules of usage, punctuation, and spelling. I used a variety of textbooks, including some based on modern linguistic theory. But the outcome was always about the same: half the students, the ones who came into the course with solid background knowledge, made progress; the other half made little or none. I began to wonder if there was a grammar gene that some people had and some didn't.

These results, plus graduate work in composition theory, language acquisition, and sociolinguistics, led me to question my practice. I learned that teaching the names of linguistic features would not improve my students' writing, that they already had implicit knowledge of the structures I was trying to elucidate, and that some of the "rules" I was promulgating were just aspects of the dominant dialect. Over time, I changed the focus of language study in my classes and clarified my goals. I cut back significantly the amount of terminology I expected students to learn, concentrating instead on building awareness of linguistic patterns so they could manipulate them more deliberately. I stopped teaching isolated lessons on mechanics, switching to seizing errors as openings to conduct mini-lessons for the class, small groups, or individuals. I also became a language diversity crusader, pouncing on any opportunity to give an impromptu lecture or demonstration on dialects and power, features of African American English, and so on.

For example, when reviewing parts of speech (which always seems necessary, though students learn them in grade school), I now concentrate on function rather than classification. A noun is not a "person, place, thing, or idea"; it's a *name*, but it's also a *role* in the sentence: subject, object, etc. A word that serves as a noun in one context may serve as an adjective in another. To reinforce this point, I assign exercises like the one in Figure 8.1. If I give a quiz on parts of speech, I'm apt to use Lewis Carroll's "Jabberwocky" or something similar as the text; since most of the words are made up, students have to pay attention to their forms and functions.

Whenever I read student work, I keep on the lookout for potential mini-lesson ideas. If a student makes a particular kind of error repeatedly, I make a comment about it on the paper and try to sit down with him or her for a quick conference the next day, perhaps with another student having the same difficulty. But if I notice the same pattern of error in several students' writing, I plan a ten-minute mini-lesson to open up the problem and explore alternative solutions. I mentioned earlier the sentence fragment and the comma splice. Sharing examples of these from students' work allows me to show them that their mistakes may be signs of sophistication; changing a period to a comma here or a comma to a semicolon there transforms an error into an artful construction. As Weaver suggests, I mention only incidentally

Identify each underlined word's part of speech		(answers)
1. The football team made another first <u>down</u>.	_____	(noun)
2. You have to <u>down</u> the medicine, even though it tastes terrible.	_____	(verb)
3. Don't look <u>down</u> when you're standing on the edge of a cliff.	_____	(adverb)
4. Go <u>down</u> the hill, turn left, and you'll be there.	_____	(preposition)
5. Never go up the <u>down</u> staircase.	_____	(adjective)

Figure 8.1. Exercise on identifying parts of speech.

what the structure is called: a participial phrase, an adverb clause, a compound sentence. I tell students they can use the term to impress their friends. These discussions often bring up questions of technical correctness versus style. When is a fragment *better* than a complete sentence? (See Schuster for some examples.) Or consider this instance of lack of agreement between pronoun and antecedent: "Fear has been around since the creation of man. They were not able to explain this feeling. . . ." The student who wrote this passage probably chose *they* because he sensed the plural nature of *man* and intended it to be gender-inclusive. In the previous paragraph he had written, "An athlete might fear that his/her opponent has a higher success rate than him/her." Neither of this writer's answers to the indeterminate-gender pronoun problem is terribly elegant, but they present an excellent opportunity for exploring the linguistic (and political) issues and seeking solutions.

To introduce the element of play into language study—and to create more occasions for mini-lessons—I sometimes start class by putting a problem on the chalkboard for students to work on in their notebooks: a sentence-combining exercise or a short passage to be edited. Ninth graders especially seem to enjoy working out these puzzles. I often make up examples, but the Daily Language Workouts books published by Great Source (Sebranek and Kemper) are also, well, a great source of material. These books include dozens of "MUG shot" (mechanics, usage, grammar) sentences and paragraphs that provide useful practice in spotting and fixing common mistakes. When students share their solutions, I probe their reasoning a little: "Yes, there should be commas around that phrase. Why do you think they are needed? What would happen to the sentence if we removed the phrase? What if the sentence were written this way instead? Would it need commas then?" Besides providing answers to the problems, these discussions help to make language patterns more visible. Sometimes I supply a grammatical term ("By the way, that's called an appositive"), but I rarely require students to learn it. Once in a while I give them a real poser, like this gem a colleague passed on to me years ago:

> The following is a single complete sentence. Add the necessary punctuation:
> "Mary where John had had had had had had had had had had a better effect upon the teacher." (Hint: Mary and John just got back a test on verb usage.)

Give up? Here's the answer: "Mary, where John had had 'had,' had had 'had had'; 'had had' had had a better effect upon the teacher." Occasionally I even throw them a curve on a quiz:

> Choose the correct word from the pair in parentheses:
> "Amy, you don't _____ (seem, seam) well," said the sewing teacher.
> George appeared to be dead, but he had only _____ (fainted, feinted).

Having some fun with grammar takes away much of the fear and loathing that most students associate with the subject, relaxing their resistance enough to internalize a few key concepts.

One aspect of language that I'm very serious about is dialect. I teach a number of texts that include nonstandard dialects, such as George Bernard Shaw's *Pygmalion* and Zora Neale Hurston's *Their Eyes Were Watching God*, in part because they provide opportunities to discuss language differences from both scientific and social perspectives: though all dialects are equally capable of expressing ideas, power dynamics elevate some and disparage others. I always have my antennae up for comments about "bad English" or "ghetto language" so I can point out the baggage such terms carry and show students how to unpack them. I give mini-lessons on features of African American English to demonstrate that it is governed by rules, some more refined than those of Standard English. For example, while the Standard English sentence "She's working at McDonald's" is ambiguous, meaning either "She's working right now" or "She has a job," African American English distinguishes the present action from the habitual action: "She workin' at McDonald's" versus "She *be* workin' at McDonald's" (for more on habitual *be* and other aspects of African American English, see Redd and Webb). Equipping students with this kind of information helps them develop a greater appreciation for dialect-rich literature and prepares them to challenge the stereotypes they encounter in the media and society.

None of the types of language instruction I've discussed requires teaching from textbooks, though it's good to have a few on the teacher's desk. The explanations and examples they provide are valuable for *us*, especially when questions about unfamiliar aspects of grammar come up and when we need to check on rules that still feel a little fuzzy. Most students are overwhelmed by the amount of information in grammar books, and they don't really need it. What they need is a spirit of inquiry, a curiosity about language, a willingness to experiment. That kind of openness comes from engagement, not drill.

> **Your turn.** Reflect on your "grammar story." What were you taught? How did you learn? How comfortable do you feel with the way you teach grammar now (or don't)? What skills do you think students need most? Create a (brief) list of priorities for your classes.

Boosting Vocabulary and Comprehension

The best overall approach to building students' reading skills is to get them *involved* in reading: in reflecting on the literature assigned in class and connecting it to their own lives, in viewing texts through multiple lenses and discussing their interpretations with peers, in writing creative and analytical responses to deepen their understanding, and in pursuing personal literary interests independently. In Chapter 6, I suggested some strategies for facilitating this kind of involvement. That said, I believe that it's also important to enhance students' reading experience with skills activities that focus their engagement with challenging literary texts. Nagy's description of the reciprocal relationship between vocabulary and reading comprehension suggests that intensive work with words is one productive method (33–41).

Word study was not my favorite part of high school English. Vocabulary "instruction" consisted of assigning twenty words from a random-words-every-student-should-know booklet every Wednesday and giving a quiz on memorized definitions the following Wednesday. Sometimes I did the work, sometimes not, but in either case most of the words I had "learned" were forgotten by Friday. In my teaching, I have moved further and further away from this shotgun approach. My current thinking can be summed up in three basic principles:

- *Vocabulary awareness should be embedded in all classroom activities.* During class discussions, group work, and writing workshops, I constantly call attention to interesting and unusual words, comparing them to more familiar ones and explaining their nuances. I frequently send students to the dictionary to research and report on unfamiliar words that come up during a lesson. I do my best to notice and applaud when students take risks in oral or written word choice.

- *Vocabulary chosen for class work should be relevant and useful.* Most of the words I assign come from readings, from lists I compile as I prepare to teach the texts. Sometimes I substitute words that I want to introduce—societal concepts such as *miscegenation* or cultural terms such as *Baroque*. In either case, I try to select "Tier Two" words, "high-frequency words for mature language users" (Beck, McKeown, and Kucan 210), interesting words that are at the edges of students' awareness or that surely will be in the future (see Figure 8.2). Occasionally I ask students to create their own individual lists, but generally I prefer group learning.

- *Vocabulary assignments should adhere to the doctrine "less is more."* I have cut back the number of lists I assign (no more than three per trimester) and the number of words per list (usually about fifteen). My reasoning: if students do more work with fewer words, they may actually learn them.

Vocabulary assignments typically span two to three weeks. At the beginning of the process, students spend substantial parts of two or three class periods looking up the words in the text and in the dictionary. I used to make this stage a home-

1. betrothed 44	6. brigands 78	11. indignity 142
2. pretense 49	7. serenely 82	12. apathetic 192
3. acrid 65	8. malodorous 100	13. puritanical 193
4. admonished 71	9. successive 103	14. vulnerable 193
5. presumptuous 72	10. jauntily 115	15. scrutinized 195

Figure 8.2. Vocabulary assignment for *The Joy Luck Club.*

work assignment, but I've changed for several reasons: some students don't have dictionaries at home, others are apt to download definitions from the Web, and nearly all have trouble making sense of the words independently. Now I encourage them to work in groups and to take their time as I circulate among them and answer questions. I want them to study the contexts in which the words are used, and I want them to digest the definitions, finding the relevant ones and rendering them in language that they understand. I ask them to record (or figure out) the parts of speech to reinforce grammar skills and to aid in determining usage. The next stage is crucial: composing original sentences (or sometimes a connected narrative) using the vocabulary words. This work starts in class and continues as homework. The results are generally mixed; getting the sense of a new word is a process of trial and error. My policy is that students can and should revise their sentences until they have them all correct—and this work "counts" in the quiz grade. Meanwhile I spend a few minutes in class each day pointing out spelling traps, breaking words into parts, explaining origins and analogues, inviting questions, and giving illustrations. Students continue to confer with each other as they move toward proficiency. By the time the quiz day arrives, they have spent a lot of time with the words. I don't test their knowledge of definitions, because I know that "owning" a word doesn't require memorizing the meaning but rather developing a feel for the way it is used. I usually dictate the list, which serves as a word bank. Students then fit the words into sentences (or analogies or a story) with blanks by using contextual clues (for instance: "AIDS attacks the immune system, leaving its victims _____ to a variety of infections."). The scores are almost always high. When they're not, I meet with the students to figure out what went wrong and how to fix it (including new study skills and possibly individual accommodations). I also offer a do-over. During and after this process, I make a point of using the words in conversation, and I always notice when students use them in speaking or writing.

While vocabulary work can play a key role in boosting reading comprehension, it's not the only kind of help students need to negotiate challenging texts or to develop the advanced, discipline-specific skills at the top of the literacy pyramid. Many students' eyes glaze over when they encounter dense passages of narrative or description, especially in texts that are written in unfamiliar styles and forms (think of *Jane Eyre* or *The Odyssey*, for example). Admonishing them to "Concentrate!" or "Read it again!" isn't likely to improve the situation unless we also offer some strategies to increase motivation, problem solving, and stamina. Reading specialists have taught us what these should be: setting a purpose for reading, previewing, activating prior knowledge, visualizing, monitoring meaning, annotating text, rereading, retelling, reflecting, and many more (see, for example, Beers or Tovani). Add to this list the specialized skills required for "literary" reading of texts: awareness of genre conventions, interpretation of figurative language, recognition of allusions, attention to ironic and symbolic meanings, and so forth. Even enumerating these features of effective reading is overwhelming, and it speaks a danger—of treating reading skills as a checklist of steps to be mastered rather than an organic process. The apparatus that accompanies the selections in some anthologies verges on this approach, and I can't think of a surer way to kill students' interest in literature. In my view, the best method of promoting comprehension strategies is to model what *we* do as readers, to make visible the kinds of thinking we engage in when we delve into a text. Many students have the mistaken idea that teachers have magical powers, that we never get bogged down or confused. If only that were true! It took me three tries to get past the opening chapters of Toni Morrison's *Beloved*. It's important to share our struggles with students, but also to show them how we work around them. Doing so encourages them to share their struggles and strategies as fellow readers.

Short texts such as the prologue to *Romeo and Juliet* work especially well for "visible readings" because they allow me to take students through the entire process. Ninth graders are usually excited by the prospect of reading the play but tend to be deflated by their first encounter with Shakespeare's language. I remember one boy who, after I read the prologue aloud on the first day of the unit, asked, "Is the whole play going to be like this?" It was a perfect opening to my lesson, which focused on how to read challenging texts. I took the class through the prologue a little at a time, explaining the observations I had made and the questions I had raised as I read. For instance: "I noticed that this whole passage is only three sentences, but it's hard to figure out what each one is about. The subject of the first sentence is 'two households,' but what about them? Where's the verb? Here it is: 'From ancient grudge *break* to new mutiny.' What does that mean? Oh, wait: there's a footnote note here saying that 'mutiny' means 'violence.' That's an odd definition. Now I get it, though: two old families in Verona are feuding again" (Shakespeare 41). As I moved on to the second and third sentences of the prologue, which focus on the "star-crossed lovers" and the content of the play, I invited students to contribute their observations, questions, and strategies, and together we constructed an interpretation, noting features that make reading Shakespeare difficult: inverted syntax, obsolete word meanings, and so forth. This lesson didn't solve their problems, but I think it boosted their confidence.

Often I use this approach with texts that are new or still puzzling to me, such as certain Emily Dickinson poems. Students respond positively when I admit that I'm not sure what to make of a particular passage. "Okay, I get the part about life being a 'loaded gun'—that could be unfulfilled potential—but who is the Owner? And what are they hunting?" (Dickinson 341). Seeing that it's normal to be perplexed at times, students feel freer to acknowledge their own bewilderment—and to posit potential interpretations. This technique also works with sections of longer texts, particularly the opening pages of modern novels, which tend to conceal as much as they reveal. *The Great Gatsby* is a good example; the beginning is tough going, and without some guidance many students would give up on the book, never getting to the compelling story.

"Visible reading" sessions work best as group activities, relying on student interaction and collective meaning-making. Some students face challenges that are beyond the scope of these methods. I'll offer some ideas about individual interventions in Chapter 10.

> **Your turn.** Review the vocabulary assignments and tests that you use in your classes. What are the explicit or implicit goals of this work? How well do you think it supports your students' growth in reading comprehension? Do you see other possibilities for vocabulary study? Also reflect on the challenges your students face in reading literature. What aspects of the reading process do they seem to struggle with most? How might you use "visible reading" sessions to demonstrate your own reading strategies, especially for overcoming confusion?

Demystifying Standardized Tests

English teachers have always been responsible for two of the three Rs, but now it seems we have another to contend with: readiness for high-stakes assessments. It's hard for me to think of practicing for standardized tests as a legitimate aspect of the language arts curriculum, but the reality is that state exams will be with us for the foreseeable future and students' prospects will hinge in large part on their test performance. We have an obligation to help them do their best. That doesn't mean that we have to turn our classes into test-prep academies, however. I know that many districts now require teachers to spend inordinate amounts of time on practice tests. This strikes me as a panicky and wrong-headed response; it may boost the number of passing scores, but it seems to set mediocrity as the measure of success. I believe that a rich and diverse writing and reading program is the best preparation for standardized tests, and I'm fortunate enough to work in a school that allows teachers to pursue that approach.

This is not to say that I never have students rehearse for the state assessment. I want them to be familiar with the format and to have some experience navigating it. In Massachusetts the tests are released every year, so it's easy to show classes the kinds of questions they will be facing. Even this step is reassuring because most of the items are quite accessible. For example, the tenth-grade long composition always takes the form of an open-ended prompt about literature:

> In many works of literature, a character must adjust to life in a new environment. From a work of literature you have read in or out of school, select a character who must adjust to life in a new environment. In a well-developed composition, identify the character, describe how the character adjusts to life in a new environment, and explain how the character's adjustment relates to the work as a whole. ("English" 201)

Students are quick to see how such a question can be applied to works they have read in class, and I usually ask them to try one or more of these prompts. More important, I'm *always* asking them to respond to open-ended questions about literature, so they already know what to do. The real task is to determine what a "well-developed composition" looks like. The state provides a rubric and work samples, but students can also figure it out for themselves in group discussions.

A little harder to prepare for are the passage-analysis portions of the test. I almost never use multiple-choice items, so students don't get much equivalent practice as part of the regular curriculum. There are plenty of examples online from previous state assessments, and we do look at those, but I also develop some for texts we are reading in class. For instance, I created the quiz in Figure 8.3 and gave it to my tenth graders a couple of weeks before they sat for the big exams. The contents reflect the mix of questions found on the Massachusetts tests: some on "language" (vocabulary or grammar), some on comprehension and inference, and some on literary devices. I also included open-response items, which accompany most passages on the state tests. Students are plenty familiar with these from class work, but they tend to get tripped up by them in high-pressure situations, especially the requirement to use "relevant and specific evidence." Because custom-designed quizzes like this one serve an authentic purpose in the course, students take them more

Quiz on *Chronicle of a Death Foretold* (MCAS style)   Name_____

Multiple Choice (10). Circle the letter of the correct answer:

1. The <u>best</u> definition of the word *chronicle* as it is used in the title of the novel is

    a. A chronological history of events
    b. A watch or clock
    c. A detailed narrative record or report
    d. A prophecy of things to come

2. The sentence, "I returned to this forgotten village, trying to put the broken mirror of memory back together from so many scattered shards," is an example of what literary device?

    a. Iambic pentameter
    b. Metaphor
    c. Onomatopoeia
    d. Consonance

3. What does "scattered shards" refer to in the sentence quoted above?

    a. Pieces of Santiago Nasar's body after he was murdered
    b. Members of the Vicario family who left town after the murder
    c. Eyewitness accounts from townspeople who were there that day
    d. Hundreds of letters from Angela Vicario to Bayardo San Roman

4. Why did Angela Vicario return home on her wedding night?

    a. She realized that she was in love with another man
    b. The sheets of her marriage bed were stained with blood
    c. She was upset because her brothers had committed a murder
    c. Her new husband rejected her because she was not a virgin

5. When Placida Linero saw the Vicario twins coming toward her house with knives, "she ran to the door and slammed it shut." What is *ironic* about this act?

    a. She prevented her son from reaching safety
    b. They were actually trying to kill Santiago Nasar
    c. They were probably after the wrong person
    d. She had just been to the dock to see the bishop

Open Response (40). Answer each question thoroughly on the back of this sheet.

6. The "death" referred to in the title of the novel is "foretold" on the first page. After "giving away" the ending, how does the author manage to create suspense in the book? Use relevant and specific evidence to support your answer.

7. What consequences did the Vicario twins face for the murder of Santiago Nasar? Why? What cultural values are evident in their act and in the law's reaction to it? Use relevant and specific information to support your answer.

Figure 8.3. Reading quiz in state assessment format.

seriously than practice tests. Reviewing the results provides an opportunity not only to wrap up discussion of the reading assignment but also to examine the structure of the questions and consider strategies for selecting or constructing the best answers.

> **Your turn.** Search online for recent releases of (or practice tests for) your state's high school English language arts assessment (or, if you prefer, sample items from the English SAT or ACT). Do an informal analysis of the questions. What kinds of skills do they test? What kinds of items predominate? Which ones would likely give your students the most trouble? How might you create some authentic opportunities to practice such items in class? List several possibilities for linking test preparation with your curriculum. If you are required to teach from commercial test-prep materials, think about how you might foster connections between them and the content of your courses—by asking students to create their own test items, for example.

Paying Attention to Public Speaking

I mentioned earlier that I think it's unfortunate that oral communication skills get so little attention in English class. I'm sure that standardized testing is partly to blame for this neglect—skills that are assessed are naturally the top priorities—but another reason may be that public speaking is a little outside our comfort zone. Communication theory isn't typically part of the English major, and until recently most high school speech courses were conducted by specialists. That was true in my school for many years, but now our tenth-grade Oral Communication requirement is taught by everyone. I'm glad that I've had the chance to work with students in this context. They are usually scared to death at first, but the shared experience unites them. I've never seen stronger peer support than in that class. It's possible to capture some of that spirit in a regular English course, too, if students have regular opportunities to present *and* if there is a public speaking curriculum—that is, if there is explicit instruction and practice in how to prepare a speech and connect with an audience.

As a guide for planning lessons in Oral Communication, I still find it useful to remember the five canons of classical rhetoric: invention, arrangement, style, memory, and delivery. The first three have become elements of the writing curriculum—discovering ideas, illustrations, and arguments; organizing them into a logical sequence; and choosing effective language. These tasks are somewhat different when the medium is speech and the audience is looking at you. Today we don't place as much value on memory as the ancient Greeks did, but I still make it a goal to move students in stages toward extemporaneous speaking. Delivery— intonation, pacing, posture, gestures, facial expressions—is the crux of it all and the hardest set of skills for students (or teachers!) to master. A key challenge in teaching public speaking is convincing students that rehearsal is real work, deserving the same kind of time and attention as writing and reading assignments. To make sure that focused practice happens and that it results in meaningful revision in arrangement, style, and delivery, I schedule paired rehearsal/critique time in class when students are preparing speeches. This activity looks and sounds a bit chaotic—with partners occupying all parts of the classroom, and some tucked into nooks and crannies of the hallway—but it's the best way I've found to encourage students to make multiple "drafts" of their speeches. The repetition also helps them to feel comfortable speaking aloud, on their feet. Another element I include in all speaking assignments is video recording—for the student's eyes only. Watching and listening to themselves and then reflecting is the best form of feedback.

The first formal talk that I assign in Oral Communication is a perennial favorite in my department and could be used in any class. The "object of value" speech, originally introduced to the course by my colleague Jane Baer-Leighton, is part personal experience narrative, part icebreaker. Students generally have a lot of fun with it, both as listeners and as speakers. The objects they select range from stuffed animals to sports equipment to family photos. The assignment sheet (see Figure 8.4) explicitly outlines the steps in preparing and practicing the speech to ensure that everyone takes the work seriously and has a successful outing. Since it's the first speech of the term, I allow students to use a full text. That means devoting instruction and rehearsal time to techniques of working with a script (highlighting, inserting reminder notes, sliding rather than flipping pages) and maintaining eye contact (looking at all parts of the room, memorizing some parts of the speech, sliding a finger down the margin to keep track of one's place). Even so, most students list "looking up more" as a goal when they review the video recordings of their speeches, and they soon get a chance to improve. The next assignment, with somewhat higher stakes, is to deliver a tribute or eulogy. Many of these talks are about parents, and most amazingly poignant.

In addition to public speaking, the Oral Communication course includes assignments in oral interpretation of literature. These include an extensive poetry unit, in which each student develops a presentation with several poems by a particular author or on a common theme, and a drama unit, in which small ensembles rehearse and rehearse and eventually perform cuttings from a play (I generally use Arthur Miller's *All My Sons*). One of my favorite projects, though, is the readers theater project I have developed for Gabriel García Márquez's short novel *Chronicle of a Death Foretold* (see Figure 8.5), which involves adapting prose fiction for the stage (or the screen). I divide the class into five groups and give each one the task of presenting one of the book's five chapters. It's a complicated job: students have to deal with multiple perspectives, uncertain events, and frequent flashbacks. The

1. Select an object that has a significant meaning in your life. Use common sense in selecting an item, since you will be showing it in class. Large or bulky items, weapons, animals, or any other objects that would be inappropriate for the classroom are not allowed. Choose something that can be easily displayed and with which you associate important memories or that figures prominently in an important regular activity.

2. Begin by taking notes on your object (in your spiral notebook) in five categories:

   a. Physical description of the object
   b. The way the object derived its meaning
   c. The feelings the object produces
   d. The object's significance in your everyday life
   e. How the object represents you or certain qualities you have

3. Write a clear, well-organized speech from these notes. Be sure to include the five categories (not necessarily in order), and feel free to add creativity and humor as well. Have some fun! The finished speech should be two to three minutes long, which is about 1½ pages double-spaced.

4. After you have rehearsed the speech with a partner and received feedback, revise the text to improve its content, clarity, and flow. Practice it aloud again and again, in front of a mirror, to a pet, to your family. Be sure that you are looking up, making regular, prolonged eye contact with your audience, speaking slowly and clearly, and using emotion and enthusiasm to convey your message.

5. Prepare a speaking script of your object-of-value speech (double-spaced, 14-point type, not stapled) with appropriate highlighting and speaking notes—and keep practicing!

6. This (and future) speeches will be recorded so you can review your performance. After your speech, view the video and write a detailed commentary using the feedback form provided.

7. Evaluation will be based on successful completion of **all** of these steps. At this stage especially, the preparation process is just as important as the final product.

Figure 8.4. Object-of-value speech assignment.

process they go through to decide what to include and what not to include, what to narrate and what to dramatize, and how to capture the spirit of the chapter involves them in deep textual analysis and intense negotiations. Since the writer/adapters are also the performers, they can tailor the parts to their strengths. I remember one group that included an English language learner who was still having trouble with

Your group has been assigned one chapter from Gabriel García Márquez's novel *Chronicle of a Death Foretold*. Your task is to select portions of that chapter to present to the class as readers theater, which is a combination of oral reading and acting based on a prose text. You will need to modify the text to do this effectively. Some parts can be read by a narrator, but others should be acted out, with the characters saying lines taken from the text or invented but based on the text. The presentation should have an appropriate introduction that sets the stage and identifies the characters. The performance should run approximately ten minutes, with everyone in the group having a significant role. To make this project a success, everyone must do his or her part! NOTE: The group must submit one clean copy of the script with all parts clearly marked.

Figure 8.5. Readers theater assignment for *Chronicle of a Death Foretold*.

oral English. He got the dramatic final scene, in which the main character says little but dies dramatically and slowly. The student's over-the-top performance stole the show.

It's nice to have the luxury of a whole term to teach oral communication skills. Making time for this kind of work in a regular English course is challenging. But assignments like the object-of-value speech and the readers theater performance relate to and reinforce composition and literature standards, as the PowerPoint presentation I mentioned in Chapter 7 connects to media goals. The secret to restoring (or establishing) public speaking as an integral part of the English curriculum is not adding more projects to an already too-crowded syllabus but using oral communication skills as a lens to examine—and possibly reorient—units we're already teaching.

Your turn. Do an inventory of the speaking assignments that are currently part of your courses. What are the main goals of these projects? Do they include explicit instruction in oral communication skills? If so, which skills? If not, how could the assignments and related lessons be modified to include public speaking goals? Start by focusing on one project per course.

The Integration Challenge

If you've been completing the Your Turn prompts in the boxed sections of this chapter, chances are you have quite a to-do list. Any one of the topics covered in this chapter could be the focus of an entire course, and you may be wondering, "How can I set aside enough time for instruction in grammar, vocabulary, reading comprehension, test-taking strategies, public speaking, and who knows what else when I'm already scrambling to give adequate attention to the core subjects of writing and literature?" It's a fair question with no easy answer. One solution, as I've tried to suggest, is to stop thinking "set aside" and start thinking "integrate." Even the best "basic skills" lessons will be ineffective if they are not connected to the larger curriculum. It's also important to establish priorities. It's not possible to do everything in every course, so you have to decide what will benefit your students the most. What-skills-to-address-when is a great conversation to have with your department. You can't do it all in your classes, but you and your colleagues can collectively introduce and reinforce a great many important skills over time.

Recommended Reading

Beers, Kylene. *When Kids Can't Read, What Teachers Can Do: A Guide for Teachers 6–12.* Portsmouth, NH: Heinemann, 2003. Print.

> This volume covers all aspects of reading instruction with classroom illustrations, strategy suggestions, and thorough discussion. The book's "if . . . then . . ." index helpfully directs the reader to the most relevant chapters for specific problems.

Tovani, Cris. *I Read It, but I Don't Get It: Comprehension Strategies for Adolescent Readers.* Portland, ME: Stenhouse, 2000. Print.

> Designed to help teachers move reluctant students from "fake reading" to proficiency, each chapter illustrates a common problem and recommends strategies for addressing it. The appendixes include a variety of classroom forms and handouts.

Weaver, Constance. *Grammar for Teachers: Perspectives and Definitions.* Urbana, IL: NCTE, 1979. Print.

> Anyone who missed the Great Grammar Debate, never studied linguistics, or just feels shaky about grammatical concepts and terms will benefit from this book, which includes chapters on grammar's relationships to reading and writing and on comparing grammars.

Wheeler, Rebecca S., and Rachel Swords. *Code-Switching: Teaching Standard English in Urban Classrooms.* Urbana, IL: NCTE, 2006. Print.

> This book includes an extensive discussion of the linguistic perspective on dialects, attitudes toward the use of nonstandard English in school, and the features of African American English, as well as specific strategies for teaching students to code-switch. The resources included are valuable for English teachers in all classrooms.

Opening the Door

9

Taking a Multicultural Stance

In Chapter 3, I began a discussion of the possibilities and challenges presented by the ever-expanding and increasingly diverse body of literature available for study. In contrast to the courses I took in high school and college, today's American literature classes are likely to include works by writers representing the rich mixture of cultures in American society, and world literature now comprises more than the classics of Europe and the ancient Mideast. In this chapter I would like to extend the discussion of diversity by looking at the high school English classroom as a site for in-depth multicultural education, as a place where difference is respected and embraced. I will use the broadest possible definition of *multiculturalism* here, to refer to principles for designing content and pedagogy valuing all kinds of human diversity.

I feel fortunate to have spent my entire career in a department and school district with a strong commitment to multiculturalism and diversity. My first department chair, Marilyn Lewis, initiated an African American literature course forty years ago, and it is still a popular choice for our juniors and seniors. More recently, my colleague Sara Barber-Just developed a course in gay and lesbian literature, possibly the first in the country at the high school level. It, too, has been heavily subscribed. These courses, along with a well-established Women in Literature class, were designed explicitly to focus on social justice concerns, but the processes of creating and approving them, along with ongoing districtwide initiatives on multicultural education, have spurred reflection on the content of more traditional offerings, such as American and British literature and the required courses in ninth and tenth grade. We have had many, many spirited philosophical debates about literature: what may have started as a question of whether to replace a canonical work with a contemporary one has sometimes led to rethinking the core themes of a course or even the purposes of the entire program. In many ways our discussions have mirrored the intense national discourse on the literature curriculum. This kind of probing conversation has value in every English program, no matter how many courses it has or how they are organized.

As individuals and as a department, we have learned that committing to multiculturalism entails more than changing the reading list. We have had to change ourselves, too, to recognize the effects of white/male/heterosexual privilege and institutional racism/sexism/homophobia and to develop inclusive and transformative teaching practices and policies. For me, as for most people, this process has been long and difficult. I have experienced triumphant moments, such as the end of tracking in English department courses (discussed in detail later in this chapter), and troubling ones, such as class discussions of sensitive subjects gone wrong. I understand now that implementing multicultural education is a complex business, but the potential for democratizing education and involving students in life-changing inquiry far outweighs the risks.

My purpose in this chapter is to explore the principles and practices of multiculturalism as they apply to English class. Included are strategies for expanding the curriculum by creating "conversations" between canonical and noncanonical texts and for building units in diverse literary "contact zones." I also offer suggestions for managing discussions of difficult topics and for avoiding some of the pitfalls teachers often encounter when taking a multicultural stance.

Canon to Right of Them, Canon to Left of Them

Had Tennyson written his famous war poem in the late twentieth century, he might have called it "The Charge of the *Lit* Brigade" and taken as his subject the protracted battle within our discipline over what books to teach and how to teach them. The imagery would still fit: more than a few high school English teachers have felt "Storm'd at with shot and shell" (235), while professors, parents, and politicians "Volley'd and thunder'd" about the literature curriculum. The central question on this front of the so-called culture wars has been whether to teach the "canon"—the received list of "masterpieces" of Western civilization that "have stood the test of time"—or to create a multicultural curriculum composed of classic and contemporary works by people of all colors and backgrounds and by women as well as men. Like most either/or propositions in education, this one has proved to be a false dichotomy. The canon is alive and well in our schools, though many new voices are being heard in the classroom. But the issue is hardly settled; a range of theoretical and pedagogical problems still need to be addressed. This section highlights several of them as well as some of the larger implications of multiculturalism.

A basic problem in sorting out the literature debate is defining the terms. What, exactly, is *the* canon? Is there such a thing? While certain titles and authors—*The Odyssey* and Shakespeare, for example—appear on most lists, scholars and teachers are far from unanimous on which ones are indispensable. Nor are the lists immutable. "Great" American poets whose works my grandmother memorized in school, such as Henry Wadsworth Longfellow, barely rate a mention in today's anthologies. The Massachusetts English Language Arts Curriculum Framework avoids the word *canon* but defines it implicitly, in Appendix A, as "works reflecting our common literary and cultural heritage." "Our" here is understood to mean "American," and "common" clearly means "Western." Knowledge of these works, which are "the literary and intellectual capital drawn on by those who write in English," according to the framework, ". . . will contribute significantly to a student's ability to understand literary allusions and participate effectively in our common civic culture" (*Massachusetts* 99). Canonical works are valued, then, not just for their literary riches but also for the cultural capital they confer on readers.

The multicultural education movement has forcefully challenged the notion that a mostly white, male, Western canon should form the basis of the curriculum. Significantly, even in the Massachusetts framework "our common literary heritage" now encompasses such writers as Zora Neale Hurston and August Wilson, and the document includes suggested contemporary American and world authors (in Appendix B). But is expanding the reading list the essence of multiculturalism? This term, too, has proved hard to define. A multicultural society, write Suzanne M. Miller and Barbara McCaskill in their introduction to *Multicultural Literature and Literacies: Making Space for Difference*, "means a society committed to resurrect—rather than merely accommodate, or to absorb only then to silence—the neglected literary contributions of America's peoples of color" (10). The "salad bowl" has replaced the "melting pot" as the operative metaphor for America, implying that people of different backgrounds retain their cultural distinctiveness while participating in the larger dominant culture. However, multiculturalism is enacted in classrooms according to a wide range of philosophies. All too common, notes James A. Banks (qtd. in Harris 191–192), are the "contributions" approach (focusing on heroes and holidays) and the "additive" approach (adding works by "ethnic" writers to the existing curriculum). Both of these methods essentially preserve the status quo and reinforce mainstream perspectives. More radical—and thus much more difficult to implement—are the "transformation" approach (restructuring the curriculum to focus on social justice concerns) and the "social action" approach (including community service or political action projects). These last methods clearly take multiculturalism beyond reforming the reading list and into rethinking pedagogy.

It took me a long time to make that transition. For several years I collected new titles to add to my courses without deeply reflecting on why I was including them or on whether the courses themselves needed reorientation. I gradually learned—through reading, antiracist teaching workshops, and especially conversations with colleagues—that authentic multicultural education is complicated and personally challenging. Arlette Ingram Willis says it well:

> Teaching multicultural literature requires (a) a greater understanding of self, history, and the interwoven nature of culture, language, and literature than is found in either a syllabus or a list of readings; (b) an understanding of the sociohistorical and sociocultural events that have given rise to multicultural literature; (c) a willingness to unlearn biases, prejudices, and stereotypes; (d) developing a cultural consciousness that [responds] to difference in a sensitive and thoughtful manner; (e) addressing a history of dominant ideologies and White privilege in education circles; and (f) a commitment to teaching and using multicultural literature for improved educational equity. (Willis and Palmer 216)

Not to mention having the confidence and skills to raise complex, controversial issues in the classroom and manage the consequences. It's a tough journey, and I'm not sure I'm all the way there yet. But I do feel certain that my teaching of literature is now much more relevant to the increasingly diverse world that my students inhabit than it was before I took the first steps.

I have also witnessed firsthand how adopting the principles of multicultural education can lead to "improved educational equity." I have mentioned several times in this book that the courses in my department are untracked. It wasn't always so. Until the early 1990s our students were sorted into basic, standard, and advanced groups. The system was based on parent choice, but it produced the same result as nearly all other tracking systems: dividing students by race and class. As our school became more diverse, the divisions became more troubling. I remember observing two sections of African American Literature that met next door to each other. The standard-level section was about half students of color and half white. The advanced section was all white. Everyone was losing out: students in the lower levels were denied access to our most challenging curriculum, and students in the upper level were deprived of diverse viewpoints.

To make our program socially just and truly multicultural, we realized, we had to bring all students together in heterogeneous classes. After some successful departmental experiments with mixed writing and oral communication classes, Tiina Booth and I decided to team-teach a multicultural, multilevel American literature course. We had more than fifty students from a range of backgrounds, two adjacent classrooms, and a lot of questions about how to teach literature to readers of vastly different abilities. We learned a great deal that semester, and we came away from the experience committed to ending tracking. "We feel that this change is an essential element in multicultural education," we later wrote. "Reading the literature of diversity is good, but learning in the midst of diversity is so much better" (Booth and Penniman 107).

Buoyed by our success, the department decided to make all of our classes heterogeneous, and they remain that way today, despite periodic backlash from some parents and school board members. Like Linda Christensen, who has written movingly of her experiences with untracked classes, we learned that "the notion of great differences in student capacity is false. One of the first obligations of a teacher in an untracked class is to look at student ability in a new light. Teachers must see the gifts that each student brings to the class, not the deficits" (171). We also agree with another of her conclusions: "One of the biggest lies about ending ability grouping is that 'low' students benefit while 'advanced' students languish" (173). We have certainly modified the literature curriculum for our untracked classes, but it most resembles what we used to teach only to the "top" levels, and class discussions are much richer now than when we had separate groups. The basic, standard, and advanced labels no longer exist (they were abolished in the wake of an NAACP lawsuit alleging the grouping system amounted to de facto segregation), but they were replaced with a new set of categories. We are required by school policy to offer Honors and AP options, but we do this through enrichment projects (open to everyone) within our heterogeneous classes (see Chapter 6). The real point of this story is that our departmental effort to create untracked classes was largely a consequence of our commitment to include multicultural literature. Teaching about social justice issues spurred us into action.

For me, making the transition to multicultural content and methods and untracked classes was facilitated by my growth as a teacher of writing. Having in place a classroom infrastructure that encouraged writers to express their ideas freely in a variety of modes, to give and receive response, and to reflect on their progress made it easier to develop a safe and comfortable atmosphere in which diverse students could engage with a variety of challenging issues. Easier, but not easy. Next I share the lessons I have learned in becoming a multicultural teacher.

Avoiding Multicultural Mistakes

When I first decided to undertake the project of diversifying the curriculum, I was long on enthusiasm but short on savvy. I was excited in part because multicultural literature and works by women were mostly new to me—as noted earlier, they hadn't been a significant part of my high school or college education. I signed up for every workshop and attended every conference session I could find that would broaden my knowledge base. I learned about leading African writers and even had the chance to meet Ngũgĩ wa Thiong'o, author of *Weep Not, Child*. I "discovered" neglected women authors, such as Rebecca Harding Davis, who wrote the remarkable *Life in the Iron Mills* in 1861. I encountered the works of Native American writers, such as Leslie Marmon Silko and Louise Erdrich. I couldn't wait to share these finds with my students, and in general I was pleased by their responses. But things didn't always go as planned.

I gradually learned that there are many pitfalls to avoid when introducing multicultural literature, mistakes that can end up reinforcing stereotypes rather than combating them. One of the most common problems is *tokenism*. A well-intentioned effort to be inclusive can turn into a smorgasbord approach to cultural studies: "Okay, class: in the last story, we read about the African experience; now we'll get the Asian perspective." I hate to admit it now, but I've made statements like that in class. Obviously, no single work can represent a whole people or nation, much less a whole continent, so we need to be careful not to present literature that way, explicitly or implicitly. We need to help students see that authors speak only for themselves.

Another potential problem is *exoticism*. Unless the teacher sufficiently frontloads key contextual information, students unaccustomed to learning about other cultures may perceive differences from mainstream American customs as "weird" or "strange." I had this happen in a ninth-grade class when teaching Chinua Achebe's *Things Fall Apart*, which depicts precolonial Igbo society. Since I failed to provide adequate historical background or contrasting images of modern African life, some students took the novel as confirmation of their media-driven notions of Africa as a "primitive" or "backward" place that had little in common with their own world.

The opposite but equally dangerous trap is *universalism*. It's natural to look for what people in diverse circumstances have in common, but it's also important to acknowledge fundamental differences in outlook and belief. There may be eternal human *questions*, but humans' *answers* aren't always the same. We Americans are especially prone to projecting our values onto other peoples; it's partly cultural narcissism, partly a naive desire to connect. Patricia Bizzell warns also that the "universal themes" approach

> has a tendency to produce collections of readings that focus on painful experiences, that often depict people of color as victims, and that can make a reader feel as if an emotional response is being extorted. Students who are members of the cultural group depicted in such a story can be acutely embarrassed by classroom discussion of these episodes; and students who are not group members can be severely alienated, depressed, and "turned off" to the point of rejecting, rather than embracing, any message of tolerance. (165)

To Bizzell's first point, I remember a painful meeting I was part of many years ago in my role as department chair with an African American couple who objected to the black literature we were teaching in our program: works by Richard Wright, Anne Moody, Malcolm X, and others. Hard-working small business owners and active community members, they wanted their children to read more "uplifting" books. I didn't get their point at the time, but I do now. A relentless diet of oppression and humiliation narratives isn't very inspiring. As Bizzell points out, such selections sometimes backfire with white students, too. I've heard this protest more than once: "All we ever read in this school is black literature." The assertion is absurd, but the fact that students occasionally utter it speaks to a kind of empathy fatigue.

What is the best way to introduce diversity into the curriculum, then? Given constraints of time and resources, as well as the caveats discussed earlier, it's clearly impossible to construct a truly *representative* reading list, one that reflects the whole country or world. But it is possible to ensure that a variety of cultural backgrounds and both genders are *present*. It's especially important, I believe, to ensure that the literature curriculum reflects to some degree the diversity of the student body. This point was driven home to me during a lesson in Bible and Related Literature. We were looking at the passage in Genesis 10 that explains which peoples were descended from which sons of Noah. One of the several Korean students in the class looked up and said, "Where were we?" The question spurred an interesting discussion, but I wished I had had the foresight to bring in some East Asian origin stories for comparison that day.

Diversifying the curriculum makes an excellent collaborative project. Working together, members of a department can share expertise and resources and plan for a four-year program that reinforces multicultural concepts and exposes students to an expanding body of authors, works, and societal contexts. In addition to gaining specific knowledge, it's important that students also develop habits of inquiry, questioning conventional thinking and seeking alternative viewpoints.

Your turn. A good way to get started on expanding the literature curriculum in your classes is to broaden your knowledge base, looking for multicultural works that might be linked with titles already in your curriculum. The field of literature is dauntingly broad today, so you have to plunge in somewhere. Ask your colleagues and your school librarian for recommendations. Also look through the anthologies available in your department, and request some sample copies of new ones. Textbooks typically stick to "safe" selections, but they will introduce you to authors whose other works you can explore on your own. If you have a college or university nearby, visit the bookstore and see what literature professors are assigning in their courses. Or look up several course syllabi online and poke around for ideas (for example, Google "African American literature syllabus"). And don't discount serendipity. Once you have your antennae up, interesting works will find you. As you read each piece, make a few notes in a computer file or on an index card. You may not see immediate applications for all the titles you encounter, but you will probably find reasons to come back to them later on.

Enlarging the Literary Conversation

Like many other teachers of multicultural literature, I've found that creating literary "conversations" by grouping works that offer different perspectives on key ideas can be an effective method of stimulating classroom conversations and raising essential questions about diversity. This strategy isn't about creating "debates" or asking works to stand for particular "points"—that approach would be reductive and manipulative—but simply to juxtapose two or more complementary texts and hear what they have to say to each other. To illustrate, let's look at how a unit on the traditional epic can be enhanced to highlight gender issues.

As any teacher of *The Odyssey* or *Beowulf* knows, the worldview of most epic literature is unrelentingly male. Female characters, when they play any role at all, are typically antagonists or distractions. Even the clever and faithful Penelope is confined to a career of "heroic" waiting. Encouraging students to engage in feminist readings of the texts helps to combat stereotypes, but this hardly seems like enough. Pairing an epic with a contemporary work by a female author, such as *The House on Mango Street*, is useful, but the basis for comparison is weak. Instead, I like to present students with something equivalent. For example, the biblical book Judith—the story of a courageous Jewish widow who, with cunning and faith, defeats an invading army and thereby saves her country—is an accessible and effective complement to the traditional epic.

Judith was quite a popular subject among medieval and Renaissance poets and artists—Artemisia Gentileschi's grisly paintings of the story are particularly memorable (see Vreeland)—but the book has received little critical attention in English. This neglect may be attributed to the fact that it is included in the Apocrypha in Protestant Bibles (see Coogan, for example) because it was not part of the Jewish canon. The lack of critical interest cannot be blamed on any lack of suggestive material. Though relatively brief (twenty pages), Judith is a tale of epic proportion, depicting the struggle between good and evil as graphically as *The Odyssey* or *Beowulf*. But it is also a character study, a biblical short story not unlike the more familiar Ruth, Esther, and Jonah.

Teaching Judith in conjunction with or even as an introduction to a unit on epic literature, as I do in my ninth-grade classes, opens up a number of possibilities for comparative discussion. The nature of the hero and his or her role in society; the separation-initiation-return archetype of heroic stories; and stylistic elements such as speech making, hyperbole, and vivid imagery are as central to Judith as to *The Odyssey*. The bonus is that the title character is a thoroughly heroic woman. Unlike most of the female characters in classic epics—think of Kirke (Circe), Skylla (Scylla), and Penelope in *The Odyssey*—she is neither witch nor monster nor damsel in distress.

Judith is a more fully realized character than many of her male counterparts. The unknown author uses dialogue, description, and action to portray her values and personality. Besides characterization, the book of Judith offers other fiction writing techniques to explore. One is that the story gradually zooms in from a wide-angle view of an entire region in turmoil to a close-up of one woman's struggle. Another is the build-up of suspense through a strategy of foreshadowing but concealing key developments, such as how Judith plans to escape after killing the enemy commander Holofernes. Judith has all the narrative complexity of *The Odyssey*, and like that epic, it provides a distant mirror for contemporary issues. The story's principal concerns—evil empires, religious conflict, patriotism, and the power of faith—are today's headlines. Students can deepen their understanding of their world and the problems it faces—including gender stereotyping—by comparing it to the worlds of *The Odyssey* and Judith.

Enlarging the literary conversation involves more than pairing complementary texts. To make space for student reflection and exploration of alternative viewpoints, teachers need to practice what Suzanne M. Miller calls a "dialogic pedagogy," or practices that create real open-forum discussions (as opposed to the typical serial dialogues between teacher and student). In a series of case studies, Miller found that teachers who achieved this kind of transformation "(1) initiated ways of talking which induced a new stance toward texts; (2) provoked collaborative reflection about alternative responses and interpretations; (3) when necessary, scaffolded learning of heuristic strategies for making and examining meanings; and (4) encouraged student-initiated and sustained inquiry" (251). It's hard to sustain this kind of discourse in the classroom, and I can't claim to do so consistently. But giving up authority over the "correct" interpretation, and even encouraging cross-readings, is a start. In the case of Judith, I've had ninth graders argue that her exploitation of Holofernes's lust to get him drunk and kill him (a) demonstrates that she is a master strategist like Odysseus, (b) disqualifies her from hero status on moral grounds, (c) shows that women must empower themselves using any means necessary, and (d) highlights the sexual double standard that exists between men and women. Which reading was intended by the author? Probably none of the above. The story hints that its implicit theme is piety. But students make their own meanings, relevant to their own lives and values, and learn from each other in the process. I'm delighted.

There are numerous possibilities for literary "conversations." The problematic portrayal of Jim in *Huckleberry Finn* can be balanced with escaped slaves' stories: *Narrative of the Life of Frederick Douglass* and/or Harriet Jacobs's *Incidents in the Life of a Slave Girl*. Maxine Hong Kingston's *China Men* can "speak" with Rebecca Harding Davis's *Life in the Iron Mills* about the experiences of immigrant workers. And those are just examples of dialogues about nineteenth-century America. Texts can talk to each other across eras, borders, and genres as well.

> **Your turn.** You probably already have some literary conversations going on in your classes, explicitly or implicitly. Listen to what the works have to say to each other. What could you do in discussions to help students hear their contrasting stories more clearly? What other voices could be added? Are there white male authors for whom you would like to find minority or female interlocutors? Using the strategies suggested at the end of the last section for locating diverse texts, try to make some provocative pairings of canonical and noncanonical works.

Teaching in the Contact Zone

The strategy of creating conversations between multicultural texts on issues connected to social justice can be used to revamp entire courses as well as to enrich particular units. In this section I tell the story of how students and I (with help from my colleague Gene Koehler) engaged the most formidable bastion of dead white males in our curriculum: Masterpieces of Western Civilization. When I was first assigned to teach this course back in the early 1990s, I frankly wondered whether it should still be part of the English offerings. More immediately, I wondered how it could be restructured to be more representative of the world.

The reading list for Masterpieces II, which I focus on here, was exclusively white, European, and male: Shakespeare, Milton, Molière, Voltaire, Rousseau, Dostoevsky, Conrad, Kafka, Sartre, Camus. I love these authors, and my aim was certainly not to eliminate them (though some did get reduced to brief excerpts or relegated to the outside reading list) but rather to balance their viewpoints with those of people customarily treated as "Other": people of color, non-Europeans, and women. Beyond this, my goal was to help students look at the concepts of "masterpieces" and "Western civilization" as cultural and political *processes,* rather than as a set of received "classics" and a single, immutable tradition. I introduced students to the debate concerning the canon during the first class meeting, in discussion and in the course description (see Figure 9.1). Most students had no idea what the canon was at the start of the course and had never thought about how the books they read in school were chosen. We kept this issue on the table throughout the term. I continually stressed that the controversy over what one should read to become educated was current—the subject of intense political wrangling—and important to students on a personal level, since it affected their understanding of the world around them.

To achieve a more balanced view of the world's peoples than is ordinarily provided by a Western civilization course, I employed four basic strategies. The first was to look for opportunities *within the canon* to raise issues of oppression and cross-cultural misunderstanding. Some classic texts speak to these topics explicitly (*Can-*

In studying the classics of Western civilization, we will be taking part in an intellectual endeavor that is both time-honored and controversial. As many previous generations of students and teachers have done, we will attempt to understand the nature of Western culture, unearth its foundations, and explore alongside the great writers of the past the ultimate questions: the nature of God, the nature of humanity, the problem of human relationships, the meaning and purpose of human existence. We will trace the history of Western thought and examine how the creative imagination has transformed ideas not only into literature but also into architecture, visual art, and music.

The controversy surrounding this kind of activity concerns its relevance to the modern world. Some argue that American education is crumbling because students receive too little instruction in the "classics." Others respond that the Western canon is too exclusive, that we should not consider a body of works that is essentially white, male, and European the cultural foundation of our increasingly pluralistic society.

Our approach in this course will be informed by both of these viewpoints. We will examine many of the great works of literature traditionally included in the Western canon, but we will also continually ask ourselves what they omit. Among these are the viewpoints of women, the poor and oppressed, the peoples of the non-Western world. To achieve a better understanding of these viewpoints, we will study a number of works written by and about women and others that investigate the effects of the interaction between European civilization and other cultures. Through critical reading of the works on the syllabus and some outside research, we will attempt to achieve a more balanced perspective than we would gain from a traditional "great books" curriculum. We will also examine the process of canon formation (and reformation) and discuss what makes a work a "classic."

Figure 9.1. Masterpieces of Western Civilization course description.

dide, *The Stranger*). Others need to be "deconstructed" or read against the grain to expose their cultural subtexts. In *The Tempest*, for example, I gave special attention to the character, conduct, and language of Caliban, who, it could be argued, represents all of the "savages" that Europeans encountered in the so-called Age of Discovery.

A useful method for *adding new material* to the syllabus, my second strategy, was to follow Europeans as they "discovered" (read: subjugated) the rest of the world. One example is *Oroonoko, or the Royal Slave* (1688), a novel by Aphra Behn, a prolific but rarely anthologized Restoration playwright, the first English woman to earn her living by writing. *Oroonoko* is the tragic story of an African prince sold into slavery and transported to Surinam (an English colony until 1667). Besides a heroic (though racist) portrayal of Oroonoko, the novel includes a sympathetic description of the native Indian culture and a withering attack on European cruelty.

Another important strategy for broadening the curriculum was to involve the students as *researchers and teachers*. Each one was responsible for investigating and reporting on a topic that would widen the margins of the syllabus. Most focused on literary works, but some covered music, visual art, religion, and even science. One especially interesting set of projects introduced aspects of Japanese culture: Zen Buddhism, martial arts, poetry, landscape painting, and film. The student presentations provided excellent opportunities for comparing worldviews.

My fourth strategy was a combination of the other three: *building units of study* that integrated canonical titles, non-Western works with similar settings or themes, and a series of related oral reports. The "conversations" created by such juxtapositions stimulated lively class discussions and seemed to prompt careful reflection on the central concerns of the course. I called my first integrated unit Into Africa (a play on the title of the then-popular movie *Out of Africa*). In this unit the class grappled with a variety of problems, ranging from sociohistorical issues such as racism and colonialism to questions of literary value and cultural politics. What qualities must a work have to be considered "great"? Should older works be excluded from the curriculum on the basis of racist or sexist content? What constitutes a "good education" in the humanities in the era of the "global village"? The students confronted the same dilemmas we face as teachers of literature and became full participants in the discourse about curriculum.

The first reading was Conrad's *Heart of Darkness,* a novella that represents, perhaps better than any other work of modern literature, the European male's response to his encounter with the African "Other." We spent a number of days working through Conrad's rich, complex language and his multilayered method of narration. We compared the novella's descriptions of Africa and Europe, evaluated its critique of colonialism, and attempted to understand the meaning of Kurtz's disintegration. In other words, we began the unit by examining *Heart of Darkness* on its own terms. Then I dropped a bomb: a scathing essay on *Heart of Darkness* by Chinua Achebe, who argues that Conrad's portrayal of Africa and Africans is thoroughly racist. Following Achebe's lead, we took a closer look at passages from the novella such as this one:

> But suddenly, as we struggled round a bend, there would be a glimpse of rush walls, of peaked grass-roofs, a burst of yells, a whirl of black limbs, a mass of hands clapping, of feet stamping, of bodies swaying, of eyes rolling, under the droop of heavy and motionless foliage. The steamer toiled along slowly on the edge of a black and incomprehensible frenzy. The prehistoric man was cursing us, praying to us, welcoming us—who could tell? . . . They howled and leaped, and spun, and made horrid faces; but what thrilled you was just the thought of their humanity—like yours—the thought of your remote kinship with this wild and passionate uproar. Ugly. (Conrad 105)

On second reading, Conrad's reduction of Africans to a mass of swirling limbs and a "wild and passionate uproar" was shocking to most students. Soon we extended the discussion to other works, including movies and television programs, with dehumanizing depictions of blacks.

Ultimately, we took up the problem of what to do with "classic" works that seem to be grounded in racist perceptions or ideas. Achebe rejects the argument that *Heart of Darkness* is not such a book, that its descriptions of Africa are merely metaphorical:

> Students of *Heart of Darkness* will often tell you that Conrad is concerned not so much with Africa as with the deterioration of one European mind caused by solitude and sickness. They will point out to you that Conrad is, if anything, less charitable to the Europeans in the story than he is to the natives, that the point of the story is to ridicule Europe's civilizing mission in Africa. A Conrad student informed me in Scotland that Africa is merely a setting for the disintegration of the mind of Mr. Kurtz.
>
> Which is partly the point. Africa as setting and backdrop which eliminates the African as human factor. Africa as a metaphysical battlefield devoid of all recognizable humanity, into which the wandering European enters at his peril. Can nobody see the preposterous and perverse arrogance in thus reducing Africa to the role of props for the break-up of one petty European mind? But that is not even the point. The real question is the dehumanization of Africa and Africans which this age-long attitude has fostered and continues to foster in the world. And the question is whether a novel which celebrates this dehumanization, which depersonalizes a portion of the human race, can be called a great work of art. My answer is: No, it cannot. (11–12)

To Achebe's question, I added another: Should *Heart of Darkness* and other books with similar characteristics (*Huckleberry Finn*, for instance) continue to be part of the high school literature curriculum? Students' opinions on the issues raised by Achebe's reading of *Heart of Darkness* varied widely. Conrad had his defenders, who argued that his attitudes were merely reflections of his era, as well as his detractors, who maintained that a "great" writer should be ahead of his or her time. I made no attempt to move the class toward consensus on the novella's literary value. I did press them, however, on whether they thought it should still be taught, and on this point they generally agreed: controversial content should not keep a book from the reading list, but students should be made aware of the controversy and allowed to hear voices on all sides. That seemed like a reasonable position to me—and a mandate to English teachers everywhere.

Giving voice to the long-neglected experiences and perceptions of their peoples is the central aim of many contemporary writers in Africa and other formerly colonized parts of the world. For centuries European observers have oppressed and dehumanized non-Western peoples not only by ignoring their histories and cultures but even by denying them *language,* the essence of humanity. In *The Tempest,* for instance, we are told that Caliban was unable to speak or even think until Prospero taught him language. The nameless Africans in *Heart of Darkness* fare even worse. As Achebe points out, they speak intelligibly only twice, once to voice their cannibalistic desires and once to announce Kurtz's death. The rest is frenzy (8–9).

To counter the stereotype of Africans as speechless, mindless exotics and to enable my students to hear a contemporary African voice, I assigned as the final reading of the unit *The Money-Order,* a novella by Senegalese writer and filmmaker Sembene Ousmane. Sembene (his surname) speaks for the common people: he worked in the fishing and building trades before he began to write (in French) while employed as a docker in Marseilles. *The Money-Order* serves especially well as an antidote to *Heart of Darkness* because it depicts the ongoing consequences of colonialism and highlights the importance of language in matters of empowerment.

The story focuses on Ibrahima Dieng, a poor but pious older man who lives with his two wives in the "Native Quarter" of postcolonial Dakar. Unemployed for a year, Dieng receives notice that his nephew, who is working in France, has sent him a money order. The letter asks him to cash it, give some money to the boy's mother, keep some for himself, and save the rest. Dieng's troubles begin when he learns that he cannot receive the money without an identity card. To be issued a card he must have a birth certificate and three photos. The registry office cannot find his birth certificate because he does not know his exact date of birth. The photographer cheats him, prompting an uncharacteristic burst of anger. And so on, day after day. Meanwhile, Dieng and his wives are beleaguered by acquaintances who think they have received a windfall. Dieng is torn between the needs of his nine children and those of his poor neighbors, to whom his Islamic values tell him he has a profound obligation. In the end, finding that he has been cheated of most of the money by a relative, he sits in the street giving away rice.

Dieng is lost in the bureaucracy and corruption that are the legacies of colonial rule. He faces a system in which he literally has no identity. Its language is French; his is Wolof. Its instincts are selfish; his are generous. Its centering principle is the making of money; his is the service of God. His view of the consequences of this new "money order" is captured best in his reply to his nephew in France: "I beg you not to regard money as the essence of life. If you do, it will only lead you onto a false path where, sooner or later, you will be alone. Money gives no security. On the contrary, it destroys all that is human in us" (130). Since Dieng cannot write, he dictates these thoughts to a letter writer stationed in the post office. Without such intermediaries, he and others like him could not communicate with the rest of the world. Aptly, Sembene played the part of the letter-writer himself in his film version of the story (*Mandabi*).

Students found much to talk about in *The Money-Order*: the familiar theme of immorality in modern life, but also the beliefs and practices of Islamic peoples, the importance of the praise singer (*griot*) in traditional West African societies, and the cooperative relationship between Dieng's co-wives (*veudieus*) and their leadership in time of trouble. Mostly there was the sharp contrast with *Heart of Darkness*. The tables are turned in Sembene's novella: endowed with language, his African characters tell of their struggle to maintain their sanity and their humanity under the corrupting influence of Europe. If there is, to borrow a Conrad phrase, "an implacable force brooding over an inscrutable intention" in Africa, it is surely the legacy of imperialism.

To follow up on the readings and discussions, I asked the students to write papers in which they discussed the experience of reading Conrad, Achebe, and Sembene in juxtaposition. This assignment produced some of the most thoughtful writing of the entire course. The most recurrent theme in students' essays was that reading Achebe and Sembene profoundly changed perceptions of Africa and that no education was complete without such experiences. Finally, to avoid leaving the impression that Achebe and Sembene represent all of modern Africa, the unit concluded with oral reports on works by other writers—blacks such as Buchi Emecheta, Ngũgĩ wa Thiong'o, and Wole Soyinka, but also whites, such as Isak Dinesen and Alan Paton. Like the rest of the unit, these reports depicted encounters between Western and non-Western peoples.

The Into Africa unit is an example of what Mary Louise Pratt calls "contact zones": "social spaces where cultures meet, clash, and grapple with each other, often in contexts of highly asymmetrical relations of power, such as colonialism, slavery, or their aftermaths as they are lived out in many parts of the world today" (qtd. in Bizzell 165). Patricia Bizzell elaborates: "A contact zone is a historical moment when different groups contend for the power to say what's going on, what it all means, what should happen next; so you look at texts produced by these different groups *for* this contention and implicit (or often explicit) dialogue with each other" (166; emphasis original). I would suggest that besides historical moments, contact zones can include societal concerns, geographical locales, and even philosophical questions. The beauty of literary texts is that they can converse with each other—and often do so deliberately—across time and space.

The success of the Into Africa unit—measured not only by students' performance but also by their enthusiastic response—prompted me to develop similar units in other "contact zones," including one focused on India before and after independence and another that connected European existentialists with Akira Kurosawa's film *Ikiru*. Eventually the Western Civilization courses morphed into two new ones with different names and more global perspectives, but the contact zone approach also produced a new offering, Colonial and Postcolonial Literature.

> **Your turn.** Examine the courses you teach for potential contact zones, where you might bring together contending voices for lively dialogues on important issues. American literature is rife with rich historical moments, but so is a course as ostensibly invariable as British literature. Even the eighteenth century, which students typically find dull, offers exciting possibilities: *The Life of Gustavus Vassa* by Olaudah Equiano, the first slave autobiography; *Maria: or, The Wrongs of Woman* by Mary Wollstonecraft, a posthumous feminist novel; plus poems and essays on social justice issues by white male authors such as Daniel Defoe, Thomas Gray, Oliver Goldsmith, Robert Burns, and William Blake. General literature surveys, too, may have camouflaged contact zones. For example, I discovered in our ninth-grade program an unplanned conversation on relationships in families. As you consider your options, keep in mind that the goal is to invite diverse voices into the room but not to tell them their lines. Let them speak for themselves. What resources do you have to create contact zones? What additional resources will you need?

Managing Difficult Discussions

Let's face it: inviting diversity into the curriculum can yield rich results, but it can also produce some uncomfortable confrontations and awkward silences. If we're serious about taking a multicultural stance in the classroom, we have to anticipate these moments—or, better still, craft them—and have strategies at the ready to help students process their feelings of confusion or hurt and grow more tolerant and empathetic. This is hard and sometimes scary work.

Case in point: I have mentioned that I teach *Huckleberry Finn* as a text about race in America. I welcome the chance to introduce the controversies that surround this novel and to let students come to their own conclusions about Twain's portrayal of Jim and whether the book has a racist or antiracist agenda. But I don't look forward to preparing students to encounter the word *nigger* dozens of times. Explanations about dialects, historical biases, and other reasons Twain might have used it so often don't negate the fact that seeing and hearing this word makes most people, including me, squirm. Ignoring its presence in the novel isn't an option, though I admit I used to try to gloss over it quickly and move on to easier topics. Now I bring it up as a topic for discussion even before I hand out the books. After informing students that this epithet appears frequently in the novel's dialogue and narration, I ask them to freewrite anything they want to say about it—feelings, questions, personal experiences. Then I begin a discussion by sharing some of my writing about the word, including how uncomfortable I felt at large family gatherings when older relatives would use it. I invite students to enter the conversation when they feel ready but make it clear that they don't have to share what they have written. What follows is a fruitful, if discomfiting, discussion. Painful memories sometimes come out. Questions about who can use the *n*-word and under what circumstances often arise. African American students may debate with each other about its appropriateness in popular culture and intra-community conversation, and white students get an education about how oppressed peoples can appropriate the language of the oppressor. Meanwhile, I'm on the lookout for anyone who looks really troubled so I can follow up. I end the session by asking the class to reach an agreement about how we will handle the word when it comes up in our analysis of the novel.

The need for discussions of sensitive topics is not always so predictable. Several years ago a huge controversy erupted in our school and the surrounding area over a planned production of *West Side Story*. Some students of color had been requesting this musical for years as an alternative to the typical white-themed Broadway fare. However, as soon as the choice was announced by the directors (one white and one black), some members of the local Puerto Rican community objected on the grounds that the play depicts Puerto Ricans stereotypically. The controversy led to emotional public meetings and caused deep rifts in the student body and staff. It even made the national news. The production was eventually scrapped. Coincidentally, I had planned to teach *West Side Story* that year along with *Romeo and Juliet*, and my ninth-grade class happened to be at that point in the syllabus when the issue arose. I almost decided to scrap my plans, too, but then, I thought, better that the class (a diverse group including Puerto Ricans) be informed. They read the play and engaged in hard discussions about whether the characters were stereotypes or not. They didn't all agree, but they drew their conclusions from analysis of the text—unlike many people on both sides of the public debate, who relied only on the film version.

Race is not the only issue that leads to difficult discussions, of course. Religion can be just as sensitive a topic, and since it is such a common theme in literature, disputes can come up at any time, frequently over the "truth" or the "lessons" of biblical stories alluded to in course readings. In Amherst, students come from diverse religious and nonreligious backgrounds, and their beliefs run the gamut from atheist to fundamentalist. From teaching the Bible as literature I have learned that it's important to establish some ground rules for discussing religion: first, no one gets to scoff at anyone else's beliefs; second, it's not our job as students of literature to decide whether religious beliefs are right or wrong, but only to examine the role they play in the works we're studying; and third, we need to focus on facts, one of which is that people interpret scriptures in many ways. When a student begins a point with "The Bible says . . . ," I say, "Let's look at the text." Or if a comment starts with "Muslims believe . . . ," I say, "Let's look that up." Though somewhat more risky,

I think this approach is more responsible than blocking any talk of religion under the premise that it can't be discussed in public school. It can be and should be, as long as the teacher ensures balance and isn't promoting a particular creed.

A similar approach works for one of the trickiest topics English teachers are called on to address: sexual orientation. The issue is fraught because homosexuality violates the religious beliefs and moral standards of some people, because certain forms of discrimination against gays and lesbians are still legal in most places, and because homophobia remains a "socially acceptable" bias with many students and adults. Avoiding the subject in class may seem like the safest course, but that would hardly be right, and it's not even possible. Even if the literature curriculum doesn't include modern and contemporary titles that overtly address gay and lesbian themes such as E. M. Forster's *Maurice* or Rita Mae Brown's *Rubyfruit Jungle*, canonical works include plenty of explicit and implicit references to homoerotic relationships: Shakespeare's *The Merchant of Venice*, Whitman's *Leaves of Grass*, Melville's *Moby-Dick*, Virginia Woolf's *Orlando*, Willa Cather's *My Ántonia*, to name a few examples. Students are often surprised by gay and lesbian content in literature from "olden times," assuming that sexual orientation is just a contemporary issue. Everyone can benefit from attention paid to this content in class: gay and lesbian students can find some validation in the readings, and straight students can learn that sexual orientation isn't just about sex.

My approach to managing difficult discussions boils down to a couple of tools and a single rule. One of the tools is writing. There is no better way to help students sort out their feelings on sensitive subjects than to give them the chance to write—privately, with the option to share if and when they are ready. The other tool is information. The more students know about an issue, the more likely they are to empathize with those who have different views. If I can't provide the background myself, I find others who can or make it a class project. The rule is for me: "Raise awareness, but don't preach." Naturally I have strong feelings on controversial issues. In some cases these are long-held beliefs on matters of social justice, and in others they are relatively new understandings resulting from considerable reflection. I strive to be honest about my views, but I also work hard to be balanced, often playing devil's advocate to make sure that unpopular views are represented. I also try to remember that it's not my responsibility to resolve complicated social issues; getting students to think deeply about them is enough.

Your turn. What sensitive subjects have you had to handle in your classroom? What strategies have you used to manage difficult discussions? Which ones have been most and least successful? Are there other issues that you would like to introduce? If so, how could you create contexts and processes that would pro-

---

mote openness, balance, and reflection? What background information would you need to assemble? What activities should you include in your plans?

Ongoing Inquiry

I deliberately chose "stance" (as opposed to "stand") for the title of this chapter because I wanted to convey the idea that multiculturalism isn't about having a set position on what to teach or how to teach it but rather about engaging in ongoing inquiry, looking outside to learn more and more about all of the world's people and inside to reflect on our own conceptions and biases. Among the synonyms for *stance* listed in the Microsoft Word thesaurus are *posture, bearing,* and *attitude."* These words are evocative, I think: A *multicultural stance,* they suggest, is a pedagogical body language that speaks openness in the classroom. A multicultural stance isn't politically neutral—it must be grounded in a commitment to social justice—but it is fair and welcoming to all. In this chapter I have tried to show how such a stance can broaden the curriculum; in the next I will address its implications for working with a diverse student body.

Recommended Reading

Christensen, Linda. *Reading, Writing, and Rising Up: Teaching about Social Justice and the Power of the Written Word.* Milwaukee: Rethinking Schools, 2000. Print.

> Loaded with inspiring vignettes, this book is based on the idea that reading and writing are political acts; so is teaching.

Dong, Yu Ren. "Taking a Cultural-Response Approach to Teaching Multicultural Literature." *English Journal* 94.3 (2005): 55–60. Print.

> Acknowledging the fears of (white) teachers, the author describes cultural-response activities that facilitate understanding. This is one of several useful articles in the "Multicultural Literature of the Americas" issue of *English Journal.*

Ramírez, Lettie, and Olivia M. Gallardo, eds. *Portraits of Teachers in Multicultural Settings: A Critical Literacy Approach.* Boston: Allyn and Bacon, 2001. Print.

> The fourteen contributors to this volume share the critical-theory-driven strategies they use to make their teaching inclusive. Articles on literacy, art, technology, parental involvement, and teacher leadership are included.

Whaley, Liz, and Liz Dodge. *Weaving in the Women: Transforming the High School English Curriculum.* Portsmouth, NH: Boynton/Cook, 1993. Print.

> Two veteran teachers offer rationales and strategies for achieving gender balance and a plethora of recommended readings.

Willis, Arlette Ingram, ed. *Teaching and Using Multicultural Literature in Grades 9–12: Moving beyond the Canon*. Norwood, MA: Christopher-Gordon, 1998. Print.

This helpful collection includes essays on multicultural pedagogy and African American, Puerto Rican, Asian/Pacific American, Native American, Mexican American, and Caribbean American literature.

10

Embracing Diversity in the Classroom

I 've always made it a point to study my class rosters before the start of a new term to make sure I can pronounce each student's name correctly. Years ago that just required a little practice, but now it usually calls for some research. Classrooms at Amherst Regional High have become wonderfully diverse, populated with students whose families come from all parts of the world and who speak a wide variety of languages at home. This kind of change has happened or is happening all over the United States. In 1990, fewer than one in seven children under age eighteen belonged to an immigrant family; now the ratio is almost one in four. As a percentage of the total population, the foreign-born population is greater than at any time since the 1920s, with the largest numbers coming from Latin America and Asia ("U.S. Historical Immigration Trends"). Consequently, many schools are scrambling to support a fast-growing number of English language learners (ELLs). Political backlash against immigration has complicated the challenge: in some states (including Massachusetts) restrictions on bilingual education have increased the number of students in mainstream classes who are not fully proficient in English.

Ethnic and linguistic differences are not the only kinds that have affected American classrooms recently. Along with rosters, I find in my mailbox at the start of each term a stack of Individualized Education Plans (IEPs) and 504 plans for students who face difficulties ranging from learning disabilities to Attention Deficit Disorder to Asperger's syndrome to acute chemical sensitivity. Federal, state, and local policies now mandate, as they should, that these students be included in regular classes whenever possible and provided the support they need to succeed. Genuine "inclusion" of students with such needs requires a broad array of accommodations.

That's not all: "regular education" students have diverse needs, too. Research in multiple intelligences has taught us that learners come into our classrooms with a wide range of cognitive abilities and styles (Gardner 6). Their interests, pursuits, and career goals also vary considerably. Socioeconomic conditions, family circumstances, and/or emotional health may influence their performance in school. Teachers must be able to respond helpfully to all of these differences.

Learning, remembering, and meeting myriad individual needs is a daunting logistical challenge. Differentiating instruction relative to the learning style and situation of every student is a worthwhile goal but seems a practical impossibility. To make the demands of diversity more manageable, this chapter promotes the idea of "universal design"—infusing strategies that are often used to make content comprehensible for ELLs and accommodations that are frequently mandated for special education students—into the *basic structure* of the class, along with culturally responsive teaching practices and multiple intelligences theory, to make course-work accessible and relevant to all. The chapter also encourages a flexible approach to student underachievement, focusing on road maps to recovery rather than on threats of failure, and it explores the educational and professional benefits of co-teaching courses with specialists.

Access, Relevance, and Diversity

Access, relevance, and diversity are the bywords of Project Outreach, a National Writing Project initiative to improve the education of students affected by poverty (see "About Project Outreach"). My local site has participated in this program, and as a result I've done a lot of thinking about the implications of these terms. They capture effectively the central themes in the professional literature on responding to cultural and cognitive differences in the classroom.

Access is a major issue for ELLs, who face the huge challenge of studying con-tent in a not-yet-comfortable linguistic medium. "While the number of students with limited proficiency in English has grown exponentially across the United States, their level of academic achievement has lagged significantly behind that of their language-majority peers" (Echevarria, Vogt, and Short 4). One key reason is that it takes four to ten years to develop proficiency in academic English, while the typical English as a Second Language program lasts only two or three (8). Content-area teachers obviously have an important role to play in helping ELLs close the achievement gap. An approach widely used in ESL and immersion programs but also suitable for content courses is sheltered instruction (SI), the practice of weav-ing language and content objectives together in the curriculum through scaffolded lessons. SI teachers

> modulate the level of English used with and among students and make the con-tent comprehensible through techniques such as the use of visual aids, modeling, demonstrations, graphic organizers, vocabulary previews, predictions, adapted texts, cooperative learning, peer tutoring, multicultural content, and native lan-guage support. They also make specific connections between the content taught

and students' experiences and prior knowledge and focus on expanding the students' vocabulary base.... Students are explicitly taught functional language skills as well, such as how to negotiate meaning, confirm information, argue, persuade, and disagree. (Echevarria, Vogt, and Short 14)

The Sheltered Instruction Observation Protocol (SIOP) provides a comprehensive rubric to check lesson preparation, instruction, and assessment for effective scaffolding practices (199–210).

When I learned about the sheltered instruction model from my Western Massachusetts Writing Project colleagues Karen Sumaryono and Wilma Ortiz, I was struck by how aptly it describes good teaching—for *all* students. Who wouldn't benefit from these techniques and practices? Of special importance to ELLs, though, is that school experiences validate their cultural identities. Sumaryono and Ortiz argue that "understanding and supporting the cultural norms of diverse learners help to create a safe and nurturing environment, which motivates students to take the necessary risks to be successful" (16–17). Teachers must find meaningful ways to incorporate students' backgrounds into the curriculum. They recommend saying key words in the lesson in different languages, allowing students to use home languages to respond to informal writing prompts, and using cooperative activities to foster meaning-making in English.

Students who do not feel validated in school may shut down and become invisible. "These are the students," according to Yvonne Freeman and David Freeman, "who do not cause any problems but do not do very well either. They seem to disappear inside the school system, and if they do make their way through the system, they often emerge without the academic knowledge and skills they really need" (5). To combat this too-familiar phenomenon, Freeman and Freeman endorse Carlos Cortés's concept of *multiculturation* (or "multiple acculturation"), rather than *assimilation*, as the goal for ELLs (9). Multiculturation fosters student empowerment through development of its four essential elements: (a) the ability to function in the mainstream, (b) intercultural knowledge and understanding, (c) the collective resources of students from different backgrounds, and (d) civic engagement (Freeman and Freeman 11). Pursuing these aims, which capitalize on home-culture resources rather than treating them as liabilities, can move students beyond mere survival toward real school success.

Multiculturation exemplifies pedagogical practices often referred to as culturally relevant or culturally responsive teaching. These methods, which stress connecting with students and making school relevant to their lives, are widely seen as the keys to closing racial achievement gaps in American schools. Gloria Ladson-Billings, author of *The Dreamkeepers: Successful Teachers of African-American Children*, describes those who practice these methods as follows:

They believe that all of their students can succeed rather than that failure is inevitable for some. They see themselves as part of the community and they see teaching as giving back to the community. They help students make connections between their local, national, racial, cultural, and global identities. . . . Their relationships with students are fluid and equitable and extend beyond the classroom. They demonstrate a connectedness with all of their students and encourage that same connectedness between the students. They encourage a community of learners; they encourage their students to learn collaboratively. . . . They believe that knowledge is continuously re-created, recycled, and shared by teachers and students alike. They view the content of the curriculum critically and are passionate about it. Rather than expecting students to demonstrate prior knowledge and skills they help students develop that knowledge by building bridges and scaffolding for learning. (25)

The role of the student-teacher relationship in the academic achievement of underserved cultural groups cannot be overstated. Teachers must communicate respect and acceptance of students' backgrounds as well as an unflagging determination that they will learn. Sonia Nieto, who has written extensively on the connections between culture and learning, emphasizes the importance of the teacher's role as a "cultural accommodator and mediator" (70). This role includes but is not limited to encouraging students to identify with and draw strength from their home languages and cultural traditions. "In many cases, teachers [also] need to teach children how to 'do school' in order to be academically successful" (71). Some students need this kind of process instruction again and again, all through high school, until they are able to engage with the curriculum.

The teacher must play an analogous role—"*cognitive* accommodator and mediator," perhaps—for students with learning disabilities and other special needs. This role is becoming more demanding as special education evolves from a substantially separate pull-out program to an integrated classroom-based support. Now that inclusion is the gold standard for service delivery, content teachers work with a wider variety of students with diverse needs and often feel swamped by the added responsibility or unprepared due to inadequate professional development. Complicating the situation is the fact that inclusion practices differ from school to school and even room to room. Some, frankly, are not very inclusive: when a student sits in the corner being tutored by a paraprofessional while the rest of the class engages in other activities, it's hard to see the value added by "inclusion" to his or her education. On the other hand, when a special needs student has the chance to interact meaningfully with more capable peers, he or she is likely to experience the full benefits of the inclusion model, among them, improved self-esteem.

Managing the inclusion process successfully in English class begins with the conviction that *all* students can be successful writers and readers; it requires collaboration with parents and special education staff and calls for creativity in lesson planning. A key strategy for meeting a range of student needs is *differentiated instruction*, the practice of individualizing the curriculum according to learners' readiness, interests, and learning styles (King-Shaver and Hunter 6). Any aspect of instruction can be modified to accommodate students' differences: content, process, products, or assessment (4–5). Overworked teachers understandably blench at the thought of preparing multiple activities and assignments for each class, but differentiation can be achieved more efficiently than that. As Barbara King-Shaver and Alyce Hunter point out,

> English teachers are already using many of the teaching and learning strategies that support differentiated instruction. The inclusion of student choice in assignments, such as outside readings and essay topics, supports student differences in readiness and interests. Having small groups of students discuss different texts in literature circles addresses both student interest and readiness in the English class. In addition, English teachers often employ performance assessments with units of study that include multimodal products. (24)

Strategically applied, these and other approaches discussed in this book—writing workshop, flexible grouping, pairing print and nonprint texts—facilitate inclusion without being a burden.

Cooperative learning is a good example of a classroom practice that supports inclusion. Based on the commonsense idea, "When you teach, you learn twice," and supported by extensive research (Kagan 106), this set of techniques is designed to promote "positive interdependence, individual accountability, face-to-face interaction, processing on the social skill, and processing on the academic skill" (107). The original model was based on hundreds of complex lesson designs, but the "new cooperative learning" uses a handful of basic collaborative structures that can be incorporated into any lesson plan—such as Timed-Pair-Share, in which each partner talks and each listens for a specified period (109). Spencer Kagan argues that this flexible approach can also be applied to Howard Gardner's theory of multiple intelligences, the idea that people possess a range of talents—verbal/linguistic, mathematical/logical, visual/spatial, bodily/kinesthetic, musical/rhythmic, interpersonal/social, intrapersonal/introspective, and naturalist—each of which has its own power and value. Incorporating a range of multiple intelligence structures into the classroom can be a key aspect of differentiating instruction.

> Allowing all students in each classroom access to all curriculum through the full range of intelligences, teachers create inclusive rather than segregated learning environments, an opportunity for every student to develop every intelligence, and access for all students to the academic curriculum through their strengths. In the process, all students better understand their own unique patterns of intelligences. They come to celebrate their own giftedness and that of others. When all students see and honor the unique giftedness of every other student, inclusion becomes a reality in every classroom. (Kagan 135)

This sounds like a lofty vision, but again, English is ideally suited to make the most of multiple intelligences. It's certainly a verbal subject, but logic, images, movement, music, interpersonal communication, introspection, and nature can all be integrated smoothly and appropriately.

The more I read in the various professional literatures on classroom diversity, the more I see how compatible they are. Strategies designed to make content comprehensible for ELLs are similar to typical accommodations for students with special needs. Both draw on cooperative learning structures to enhance learning through peer relationships. Culturally relevant teaching's emphasis on getting to know students and empowering them to draw on their own resources has analogues in differentiated instruction and multiple intelligences theory—and in writing process theory as well. These connections suggest the possibility of a unified approach to inclusion.

In that spirit, the Center for Applied Special Technology (CAST) has developed the concept of the universally designed curriculum. Chuck Hitchcock and colleagues explain:

> The idea of creating a flexible environment that serves diverse users originated with the universal design concept in architecture. Retrofitting buildings with ramps and automatic doors to accommodate people with disabilities is costly, marginally effective, and often aesthetically disastrous. Architects have learned that considering the needs of diverse learners when designing buildings saves money and leads to more streamlined, accessible buildings. And as it turns out, universal design works better for everyone. (54)

The curb cut is a good example: designed for people in wheelchairs, it makes life easier for all. "Retrofitting" education for students with diverse needs is also problematic—diminishing the content or making students dependent on "crutches"—so CAST proposes that curriculum be created from the start according to what it dubs the Universal Design for Learning (UDL) principles, which provide for flexible methods of presentation, expression, and engagement. Central to this idea is the process of clarifying the goals that students are to achieve:

> To develop a UDL goal, teachers must first and foremost thoroughly understand what they want students to learn. This sounds simple and obvious, but it is not a given. The language of the goal frequently incorporates a specific means for achievement when that means is not what the student actually needs to learn. In such cases, goals inadvertently specify one acceptable path and exclude all others. Almost any goal can be made inaccessible by unnecessarily limiting the means for reaching it, and conversely, most goals can be achieved if there is flexibility in the means. (Hitchcock et al. 56)

In English, the UDL lens might be used to examine particular writing and reading assignments. Is the real goal to write a five-paragraph essay or to learn the basics of organizing an argument? To read a particular set of short stories or to understand the short story as a genre? The latter option in each case opens up the possibilities for access and relevance. As Hitchcock et al. state, the purpose of UDL is not to reduce effort, but to reduce *extraneous* effort (64).

Universal design is an ambitious goal but a promising alternative to the bewildering array of demands for individual accommodations that teachers now face. If classroom instruction were flexible enough to embrace a wide range of abilities, interests, learning styles, and cultural backgrounds, the teacher could concentrate on getting to know students and helping them to connect with the curriculum, as well as on addressing truly exceptional needs.

Creating Classroom Curb Cuts

I can't claim that I've achieved universal design in my classroom yet, but I think I have moved in that direction. The process began with studying mandated accommodations on special needs students' IEPs. I noticed that several items came up again and again on these educational plans: extra time as needed on tests and papers, access to peer and teacher notes, preferential seating, breaking major assignments into a sequence of steps, and so on. Student A might be entitled to use two of these strategies, Student B a different two, and Student C still another combination. As the number of students with IEPs and 504 plans increased, I found it harder and harder to keep track of who required what interventions, and I worried that I would inadvertently neglect some students' needs. Eventually I realized that I could do a better job of providing support—and make my own life easier—if I made the most common adaptations available to all. I realized, in fact, that in some respects I was close to that policy already. I had always been open to giving students more time when they needed it, so it was a small step to making that option "official" and the process for exercising it more explicit. As a process-oriented teacher, I had always seen assignments as a sequence of steps, but looking at them through the lens of accessibility, I found new ways to make complex tasks more manageable. Some modifications took a little more thought—how to make my notes available to students who needed them or what constituted "preferential" seating—but overall it wasn't that hard to see how I could open the doors of the curriculum a little wider, not just for special needs students, but for everyone.

This change in viewpoint has been liberating. Instead of looking at accommodations as a checklist of duties, or worse, as one more burden in my too-heavy workload, I have come to think of them as natural parts of my teaching practice, as routine as reading papers and preparing lessons. I now look forward to conversations with students who need extra help or adjustments in assignments to make them more accessible because I know that I am enabling these students to connect with the curriculum. Customizing learning isn't about making school easy—in fact, sometimes what students need most is a little "tough love" on the subjects of work habits and effort—but on building confidence, relating assignments to life experience, and formulating realistic plans for success. I have come to understand that accommodating students' individual needs is an ongoing process requiring many and often complex interventions, not just a single implementation of a simple strategy. I also recognize that "success" may look different for each student and that its meaning will change over time. I'll give some specific examples later.

First I would like to explain my current thinking about what universal design should look like in the English classroom and the practical steps I have attempted so far to try to achieve it. Like the architects who have graduated from working around the obstacles found in conventional plans to building in maximum accessibility from the start, I have moved past making exceptions as my primary approach to accommodating differences to adopting practices that embrace them. These practices can be summed up in two words that I have used again and again in this book: *variety* and *flexibility*. To put it another way: something for everyone, everything somehow.

In earlier chapters I commented on the appeal and power of multigenre writing projects. To maximize access and relevance in my classroom, I now try to think of my lessons and units as multigenre teaching projects. In my school, class periods are just more than an hour most days and ninety minutes once a week. That's enough time to include a range of activities, and I do my best to include several every day. Among them are usually some low-stakes writing or draft work on a paper, a partner or small-group activity, and a mini-lesson or teacher-led discussion. This blend always provides some opportunity for me to work with students individually. Technology may also play important roles in daily activities, for the whole class or just a few students. Mindful of how much sitting students do, I try to build in some physical movement: carousel brainstorming on chart paper posted around the room, rearranging the furniture for group work or discussion, or just retrieving folders from files. When I began teaching in this multimodal fashion, I had to be deliberate in designing diverse activities, but now they are part of my pedagogical vocabulary, and I sometimes insert a new element into a lesson on the spur of the (teachable) moment.

Incorporating a variety of learning modes into lesson and unit plans makes it possible to capitalize on most of the multiple intelligences that students possess. I generally prefer not to design instruction around particular intelligences ("Today we're doing visual/spatial learning") or to separate students according to cognitive style ("This activity is for kinesthetic learners"), but rather to ensure that each learning sequence calls on a range of capacities. For example, when I teach the writings of Emerson and Thoreau, which are challenging for most students, I include not only verbal/linguistic activities, such as oral and silent reading, group discussions, and analytical writing, but also tasks that enable students to engage other intelligences: working in teams to find patterns and relationships in nature during a walk around the school (naturalist, mathematical/logical, interpersonal/social); illustrating, miming, or rapping a passage from the text (visual/spatial, bodily/kinesthetic, musical/rhythmic); and making entries on "the meaning of life" in a reflective journal written in a favorite natural setting (intrapersonal/introspective). My students can't always "get" transcendentalism just from reading and discussing "Nature" and *Walden*, but they can grasp its ideas through these other means.

Variety in instructional design goes hand in hand with flexibility, which begins with choice. Even mandatory assignments can make room for different interests and learning styles. Most teachers allow students to select their own topics for writing and research, but what about presentation modes? If a student wants to create a graphic novel instead of writing a short story, is that okay? Or how about composing and recording a ballad? In most cases, I would say, "Absolutely!" Both forms include the essential elements of story structure as well as key writing skills such as crafting dialogue. I wouldn't allow a student to opt for a visual or vocal medium for *every* assignment, but once in a while, when one seems like a suitable alternative, why not?

Flexibility also means being able and willing to modify assignments when necessary. For instance, sometimes students find particular class readings too much of a stretch; the cause may be weak comprehension skills or unfamiliarity with the genre or a combination of factors. I run into this situation quite often in ninth-grade classes, especially when teaching *The Odyssey*. Many students are bewildered by the epic form at first, but reluctant readers are apt to give up before they become accustomed to it. Rather than let them flounder or fail, I try to find an educationally sound and dignified solution. My department owns copies of an abridged, "easy reading" version of *The Odyssey*. They were purchased originally for "basic" classes and are now used mainly by special education students who struggle with reading. But I would be reluctant to hand out this book to a few students in class, saying, in effect, "Here, you take this baby version because you're not smart enough to read the grown-up one." Instead, I bring in a whole stack of these books right at the beginning of the unit and announce to the whole class that they are available to anyone who needs one. I make a big deal of the fact that most ninth graders have never read an epic before, the language is challenging, there are lots of names, etc., so it's normal to be confused. I suggest that students use the abridged version as a preview or review of the readings in the full-text translation. Ironically, the strong readers are often the first to ask for copies of the easy text. Their admission that *The Odyssey* is hard for them makes it easier for inexperienced readers to ask for assistance or for me to quietly offer it. If students are having serious trouble with the book, I may suggest that they do most of their reading in the abridged version and only selected passages in the complete one. No one else has to know, and they can still participate fully in class discussions and learn all the essentials about the epic.

I've used the same approach with slow readers who can't make it through a long novel, such as Ralph Ellison's *Invisible Man* or Dostoevsky's *Crime and Punishment*, both of which are core readings in courses I teach. Rather than have students miss out on these great books completely, I point out the essential sections and provide summaries of the rest. Modifications can work effectively with other kinds of assignments as well. A severely challenged special needs student may find it impossible to write a research paper based on multiple sources, but he or she can probably, with appropriate assistance, write a research *paragraph* based on a couple of articles and thus have access to the same kind of learning as his or her peers.

Your turn. Compile a list of the accommodations required by the IEPs and 504 plans you have received for your special needs students this year. Which strategies appear most often? Are there "regular" students in your classes who could also benefit from these accommodations? What would you have to do to make them available to everyone? Also reflect on how you vary instruction to address different learning styles. Look up "multiple intelligences" on the Internet (at http://en.wikipedia.org/wiki/Theory_of_multiple_intelligences, for example) and jot down activities you use that draw on the various intelligences. What other possibilities can you imagine? Finally, review your policies and practices on modifying assignments. Can you think of ways to make challenging work more accessible without compromising its main objectives?

Plotting Out Paths to Success

In this section and the next, I would like to explore what I see as the principal benefit of universal design: that it allows me to focus on truly individual circumstances. Knowing that the most typical learning requirements are provided for in the basic design of my classes frees my mind to attend to factors that differentiate students at a deeper level—linguistic and cultural backgrounds, family situations, medical or psychological conditions, or school performance histories—aspects of young people's lives that often interact in complex ways to affect their achievement. For me, the best preparation for understanding the real diversity in my classroom has been teaching untracked classes. My department's decision to combine all academic levels into heterogeneous groups (discussed in Chapter 9) has profoundly altered my perception of my students' abilities and needs. No longer blinded by stereotypical labels such as "basic" and "advanced," I have learned to recognize the diversity that was always there, even in so-called homogeneous classes. Everyone has a unique story, and anyone can require special attention.

To illustrate, I'll describe a section of American Literature and Nature I taught recently, which was made up of fourteen boys and ten girls: eleven students of color (African American, Latino/Latina, Asian, Native American) and thirteen white students. Only one was identified as an ELL, but five spoke languages other than English at home. Six class members registered for the AP option, including two of the brightest scholars I have ever taught and three who had never before done advanced work. Eight students were in special needs programs, and four others probably should have been. One student was in a wheelchair, and one was on homebound instruction, so she never appeared in school. It was fitting that one of the course readings was *Moby-Dick*, because the group was as diverse as the crew of the *Pequod*. Luckily, it didn't meet the same fate.

I got to know the students partly through their writing. I always give an assignment at the beginning of the term that invites students to share some details about their lives and to let me in on their thinking. In this case it was an informal piece on their perceptions of and experiences in nature (see Chapter 1). Another course project was an ongoing nature journal, which included personal reflections and philosophical musings. But I also conducted many individual conferences—quick ones in the classroom or the hallway, longer ones after school. Though the purpose of these meetings was always academic, they often ended up being about students' lives.

I'd love to be able to report that due to my brilliant teaching everyone sailed smoothly through the course, but the truth is that several of the students struggled repeatedly, as students often do despite our best efforts. There were juniors who hadn't quite mastered all the academic routines and seniors who were abandoning them to get an early start on the spring slump. Sadly, several students of color had histories of poor performance notwithstanding Amherst Regional's ongoing efforts to eliminate the achievement gap. Some of the special needs students had to work around serious roadblocks in reading and writing. But all of them got involved in the class in their own ways; they shared their experiences and exchanged ideas respectfully on weighty topics such as race relations and environmental stewardship. They also took care of each other. (I'll never forget our field trip to the Mark Twain house in Hartford. Halfway through the tour, the guide said that because there was no elevator, the student in a wheelchair would have to miss the rest. Seeing her disappointment, three of my "underachieving" boys carried her and her chair upstairs.) At the end of the term, everybody was passing, though several had flirted with failure. Honestly, I'm as proud of some of the C's and even D's earned in that class as I am of the A's, because those grades represent, in part, the power of personal attention.

Each class member had a compelling story, but I'll have to let a few vignettes represent them all. (I won't use real names.) I'll start with Valerie, a lively African American senior who chose the AP option for the first time in her high school career. I was pleased by her decision because students of color are sometimes reluctant to participate in the program. However, I soon learned that she faced several major challenges, the greatest being that she was the single parent of a toddler with little time available after school. She was also an inexperienced writer, and she had trouble keeping up with the reading assignments. In some ways she had no business taking on a big project, but since she was determined to try, I was determined to help her succeed. She decided to focus on W. E. B. DuBois's *The Souls of Black Folk*, a book she found difficult but motivating. As she worked her way through it and then drafted her reader-response critique, we stole a few minutes here and there for conferences. In the end, she mustered only four pages of commentary with little close reading, nothing like her classmate Jared's college-level analysis of the same book, but for her the project was more personally affecting. She wrote this of DuBois:

> During [his] time it wasn't that normal for African Americans to attend colleges. Unlike other Blacks he wanted to get to college, he not only forced himself to do it, but he showed others that they can do it as well. I believe that he made an impact on people's lives, especially black males. Growing up as an African American girl, I noticed how young black men struggle with their academics. Here at Amherst High there are few who follow into that category, but most chose to stay that way but there are some who want to exceed in their academic career.

Despite the confusion at the end of this passage, it's evident that studying DuBois prompted Valerie to reflect on her own world. Overall I thought her project was a triumph.

And then there was Adam, a bright but bitter European American senior who had been in special education throughout his school career. He made this comment about his behavior in the reflection letter of his course portfolio: "I know I was noisy, I know I was rude, and a little bit obnoxious but I would take it all back if I could just try again and succeed. I feel bad for all the times I made a ruckus and distracted the class from their ambition and their wanting to learn." The thing is, he didn't *always* make a ruckus; occasionally he offered amazingly thoughtful comments in class discussions. Despite his apparent devil-may-care attitude about coursework and painfully slow reading process, he gradually digested *Huckleberry Finn* and *Moby-Dick* because he valued their drama and humor. He eventually completed most of his nature journal and learned from the experience: "It was cool to see the world change around me and not just the lives I live in videogames. I see now that life is way more fulfilling than some damn idiot box that flashes colors." But he was a trial in class because he was so unpredictable. He and I had many one-on-one discussions, often in the hallway. The turning point came one day when I had reached my limit and said to him, "I never know which Adam is going to show up in class: the rude, disruptive one or the smart, sensitive one who has such great insights. So from now on, if the rude one shows up, I'm just going to ignore him, but if the other one comes, he'll get my attention and support." The comment seemed to affect him, and he promised to do better. He didn't do better at first, and it took all my patience to stay with my plan, but eventually the strategy seemed to work. He contributed more in class and completed more assignments, well enough to earn a B on his final portfolio. At the end of the term he thanked me for sticking with him, and I showered him with praise for his progress. Now he's planning a career in education.

A key factor in my positive experience with Adam was communication with his special education teacher and his mother, both of whom were pursuing the same kinds of academic and behavioral goals with him as I was. I didn't expect them to *compel* him to change—he was eighteen, after all—but it was helpful for us to share information and reinforce each other's efforts. The same was true for James, another student in the class who suffered periodic lapses in motivation. I had frequent conversations with his father, and he supported my efforts by talking to James about his work and encouraging him to keep up. Involving parents and other stakeholders isn't always productive, but it's always worth a try. I think it's a shame when teachers and parents end up in adversarial relationships, because it's usually a result of insufficient conversation.

I don't want to leave the impression here that struggling students are the only ones who need or deserve personal attention. Alice, a brilliant reader and writer, sought me out regularly after school, especially when she was working on her AP project on *The Scarlet Letter*. She didn't need any help on the basics, but she was pushing herself into new lines of thought and wanted to discuss ideas. With some students, I initiated the contact to make sure they were getting appropriate assistance. Such was the case with Yaejee, a hard-working ELL who had successfully made the transition to mainstream courses but still needed some help with her writing—help that she was loath to ask for. Quiet, unassuming students like Yaejee, who always seem to do solid work, often stay below the radar, but we need to notice them. Sometimes a placid exterior masks inner turmoil—or genius waiting to be born.

> **Your turn.** Choose three or four students from a class you are teaching for quick case studies: one achieving at a high level, one at an average level, and one or two usually struggling. Take a few minutes to jot down what you know of their stories, in and out of school. What details seem most relevant to their school performance? What else would you like to know? Also reflect on their individual needs as learners in your classroom. What kinds of personal attention have you been able to give them? What other interventions would they benefit from?

Paving the Road to Recovery

Not long ago the administration at Amherst Regional High instituted a policy requiring that any student in danger of receiving a D or an F at midterm have a "recovery plan," a clear sequence of steps to address the problem(s) resulting in poor performance—usually absences and/or failure to complete assignments—and their underlying causes. I like this idea because it gives a name and a formal process to a philosophy that I have been moving toward in my teaching for many years: that it's (almost) never too late to make up for mistakes.

I used to be pretty hard-nosed about late work: if it's not in on time, it's a zero, period. Frustrated that some students would conveniently get "sick" on major due dates, I once instituted a policy that required them to send their assignments in even if they couldn't come to school—or to call me, so I could come collect the work (no one ever took me up on that offer). These rules didn't spring from mere crabbiness on my part; they were aimed at adjusting too-casual attitudes toward academic responsibilities and even at counteracting a sense of privilege among students whose parents would cover their homework crimes. But I found that I couldn't live with the unintended consequences. Strict adherence to my system meant that a student who got off to a rough start might have no hope of earning credit as little as a month into the term. So after a meeting with the student and his or her parents, I would suspend the rules and agree to grant enough partial credit for makeup work to provide an escape. Eventually I decided to drop the pretense of being tough on "slackers." What was the point? Wasn't it to encourage them to improve? Then didn't I need to make it clear that recovery was possible—and expected?

As a result of these reflections, I've made two significant changes to my grading policies: no zeroes on assignments and no D's or F's on writing folder evaluations. I discussed the latter in Chapter 4. To recapitulate, if a folder is missing one or more papers (the only way it could merit such a low grade), I mark it incomplete and give the student a new deadline for completing the work. When it's finished, I review the folder again. If it doesn't get finished, then a D or F happens. The related no-zero rule is simply a matter of arithmetic. A grade of zero, especially on a major assignment, has a devastating effect on a student's term average. Now I give everyone one free pass on late work. After that, I do penalize lateness, but only enough to remind students that punctuality is important, usually the equivalent of one grade. I do a lot of jawboning, too. Though most students know the expression "better late than never," they haven't heard its sequel: "but better never late." They can recite the whole expression a few weeks into the term, I promise. I've also gotten over my fixation on students' skirting deadlines by staying at home. I know there are some who still grant themselves extensions that way, but now I approach this practice as an ethics problem and present it to my classes as taking unfair advantage. Making it a matter of conscience has been more effective, I think.

Policies alone, even generous ones, do not guarantee recovery from academic disasters. As noted above, building individual relationships with students and working with them one-on-one is the key. I'm careful not to pry into their private business, and I don't try to counsel them on matters beyond my areas of expertise, but I do listen empathically when they confide in me. Unburdening themselves of personal baggage is for some students a critical first step in working out an improvement plan. The next one is usually sorting out and prioritizing what needs to be done. This is the stage of recovery that they typically need the most help with, and it happens to be one of my strengths. As I work with students on solving current problems, I try to teach them a process that they can use again the next time they get overwhelmed:

- First, write down everything that needs to be accomplished without comment.
- Next, perform triage: sort out what has to be done immediately, what can wait for a little while, and what is already past salvaging.
- Next, break the "must do immediately" items into smaller steps.
- Finally, compile a chronological "to do" list, assign a deadline for each step, and specify dates for checking in with the teacher(s).

Making a plan doesn't eliminate anything from the backlog of work (except for unsalvageable projects), but it does make the work feel more manageable. Students almost always leave these meetings feeling more hopeful about their prospects. Obviously, they still have to take many more steps to catch up, and most will stumble along the way. I try to be there to pick them up and set them back on course or, if necessary, meet with them again to plot a new one.

One of the students I used this process with was Jack, who nearly failed the final term of his senior year. Jack was similar to Adam in some ways; he, too, struggled with reading and writing and often became frustrated with school. But Jack was much more reserved and more likely to suffer in silence than to act out. I had worked with him successfully twice before in his high school career, so I was puzzled when he started to accumulate absences and failed to turn in assignments in Bible and Related Literature. His special education teacher was finding him uncharacteristically difficult, too, so something was clearly wrong. When I finally got Jack to open up, he told me that his father had been laid off; for the time being, his after-school income alone was supporting the family. Jack had a good job: he was learning auto repair and planned to go on for advanced instruction after graduation. So at this point, with his family in dire financial straits, he was taking all the hours he could get, even missing school to work. Under the circumstances, I knew that he could never make everything up that he had missed, so I encouraged him to focus on the necessary and the possible: two long-term projects that he had fallen behind on and the readings and papers that still lay ahead during the final weeks of the course. We worked out a realistic plan, and he stuck to it faithfully. His final grade of D+ felt like a victory, especially when I saw him walk across the stage at graduation.

For some students, recovery from academic failure is more than a matter of making up missed assignments; it's a process of making up years of missed education. Several years ago a junior I'll call Jeannine was placed in my fall term American Literature class after transferring from a tough urban school. Her mother, an immigrant, had sent Jeannine to Amherst to live with her sister because she had been getting into trouble at home. I gave her a book, *Huckleberry Finn*, and briefly caught her up on what we had been doing in class. The next day, and several days thereafter, she came into the room saying, "Mister, I don't like to read. I don't know how to read. Can't you just tell me the story?" I suggested an after-school conference, and when we met I learned that she hadn't been attending school regularly nor doing any work for a long time. She said that in her old English class she had just joked around or slept, rarely doing any reading. She volunteered that the fault was largely her own, but whether hers or the school's, the result was that she had become basically aliterate. Jeannine made tentative but important strides that term: she came to class (often tardily), she tried to read the books (usually), she wrote the papers (briefly), and most important, she stayed after school for extra help (regularly). She completed the course successfully, but she still had a long way to go. The next term Jeannine took a class with one of my colleagues, who worked at improving her writing and boosting her self-esteem. When I taught her again in the spring, I could see significant progress in her ability to express ideas, though her drafts were still rife with mechanical errors. She was still a reluctant reader, but she did relate to some of the books, especially Anzia Yezierska's *Bread Givers*, a novel about Jewish immigrants in New York in which the main character is a younger daughter determined to get an education. Apparently Jeannine was developing a similar determination. The next year she continued to progress, and our department gave her an award at graduation. The last time I saw her, she was enrolled in college, planning to major in English literature.

I tell these stories not because I think they should become the plots of feel-good movies and certainly not because I think I performed any miracles. Jeannine and Jack and Adam and Valerie grew significantly in the time that I worked with them, but they were not transfigured. They still faced a host of personal and academic challenges. The credit for their progress should go to the whole team of teachers who worked with them—and mostly to the students themselves. But I do want to underscore the point that all students, however impaired or lost they might be, hunger to learn, and they deserve as many chances as they need to achieve success.

> **Your turn.** Review your policies regarding missing or late work. Do they offer a student who falls seriously behind a realistic chance of recovering? If not, how could you modify your rules to give these students an incentive to keep trying? What procedures do you have in place to help students develop recovery plans? How well is the system working? Are other stakeholders involved? Are there steps you could add or change to improve the process?

Teaching in Tandem

Several years ago, Alan Kasal, a colleague in the special education department, asked if he could talk with me about the ninth-grade English curriculum. He had been teaching a course called Developmental English for students whose language disabilities were considered severe enough to pull them out of the regular program. Alan was uncomfortable with the class for two reasons: (1) he wasn't sure what he should be teaching in writing and literature, and (2) he felt that the students lacked appropriate role models, so they didn't progress as well as they should. Out of that conversation emerged a plan to schedule his course simultaneously with one of my ninth-grade sections in hopes that we could bring all of the students together for joint activities two or three days a week. So began one of the most transformative

experiences of my career. Since then I have co-taught six classes with special education teachers, first Alan and then his colleague Colin Harrington. I am convinced
that this model is among the most promising strategies for meeting the needs of
diverse learners—including those in regular education.

Soon after Alan and I began our experiment, we realized that our goals were
too modest. His students were a little anxious but very happy to be in a mainstream
class, and they quickly rose to the occasion. My students, if they were aware that
Alan's students were "different," soon forgot. Partway through the year, we decided
to make working together the default, with provisions for pull-out instruction when
it was necessary. As the model evolved over the next several years, flexible grouping
became the norm. Sometimes we worked together as a whole class; sometimes in
small groups with each teacher responsible for half of the students; and sometimes
in separate rooms with each teacher leading half of the class, almost always with a
mix of regular and special education students. The presence of two teachers multiplied the curricular possibilities. While I as the English teacher took primary responsibility for laying out the general direction of the course, Alan and Colin each took
the lead in designing units related to their own interests and areas of expertise—the
Holocaust and Japanese poetry, for example. Having the luxury of dividing the class
in two meant that we could not only work with smaller groups on challenging texts,
such as *Romeo and Juliet*, but also offer more choices of readings: two autobiographies, two novels, and so on. We sometimes counseled a special education student
to choose a particular book that we thought was a better fit with his or her interests
or skills, but we never had "high" or "low" groupings. We still had plenty of opportunities to pull students out for special tutoring, but these small groups included
students working on honors projects as well as those with weak writing and reading
skills. More often than not, the pull-out groups were temporary and mixed.

Another aspect of the original plan that was too modest was its objective for the
special education students. We had hoped that they would be motivated by working with more capable peers, but it soon became evident that most of them *were*
just as capable as their peers, or at least not so different as to justify a label such as
"developmental"; they just had some catching up to do. In the middle of the first
year, Alan and I recommended that one of his students be switched to my roster;
her parents were nervous about the change, but she made it successfully and never
looked back. After several more successful transitions, we redesigned the program
with the expectation that all of the special education students would eventually—in
as little as one term or as long as two years—make the shift within the class to "regular" English, which meant that they could complete a majority of the assignments
without wholesale modifications. They still received special education support and
were entitled to all of the accommodations specified in their IEPs, but otherwise
they were doing the same work as mainstream ninth graders. In a few cases, we dis-

covered that students had more severe needs than had been previously diagnosed, and they were reassigned to more intensive literacy development programs.

I know that co-teaching models like ours have been tried in many schools, not always with positive results. Teaching is traditionally an isolated activity, and the cultures of regular and special education are quite different, so working in tandem can be a challenging process. For me, it has been very fulfilling, but I agree with Anne Mungai, who says that the following questions must be asked before teachers are paired up:

1. *Are both teachers flexible?*

2. *What are their personal beliefs about team work?*

3. *Do they value sharing ideas with others?*

4. *Do both teachers view open and frequent communication as a way to strengthen the collaborative process?*

5. *Are both teachers strong advocates of inclusion?*

6. *Do their teaching styles complement each other?*

7. *Do both teachers have confidence in themselves as teachers?* (43; italics original)

The first question is probably the most important. Despite both teachers' best intentions, a lot of planning gets done on the fly in a co-taught class. Daily, dedicated joint-planning periods would be ideal, but they are not realistic in most schools, so the teachers have to want to make collaboration happen. The fifth question above is also critical. Teachers must be committed to inclusion as a matter of social justice. Colin puts it well: "It always feels right to dismantle the segregation of elitist educational policy that values education as a kind of earned privilege that protects success-bound students from their less privileged/gifted peers of differing abilities in public school" (Harrington). He also points out that schedulers can spoil the inclusion model by "warehousing" too many troubled students in a single co-taught section. In my view, two-thirds or more of the students should be regular education, even if that means increasing the class size.

Another indispensable condition for success is that both teachers see co-teaching as an equal partnership. I've known of situations in which the special education teacher was treated as an aide to the "real" teacher. That approach can never work. Both teachers must be open to the possibilities for professional growth. Special education teachers may develop more in-depth knowledge of the discipline, but content teachers stand to gain new insights about teaching and learning. As Colin explains, special educators can stimulate reforms in classroom practice:

Professionally I always see special ed. as cutting edge perspective and practice on the nature of learning as it adds opportunities to the classroom for approaches and surprising responses in diverse learners. This even changes the practice and direction of teaching. It can open methods and create fresh approaches that frees up the learning process for all. It makes teaching more exciting when challenged and challenging students have breakthroughs and raise their personal expectations and expand horizons. (Harrington)

Exciting is the right word. Watching students with poor self-concepts and limited hopes for the future come alive through contact and collaboration with their mainstream peers, and seeing those students open themselves to classmates they may have always treated as "other," is about as good as it gets. But again, co-teaching only works if both teachers believe in it. I suspect that the most successful programs are those created from the bottom up.

> **Your turn.** If your school has a co-teaching program, talk to teachers involved to learn about its benefits and challenges. If you think you are a good candidate for co-teaching, talk to a special education colleague, ELL teacher, or reading specialist about a possible collaboration. Ask yourselves the seven questions listed on page 217, and discuss the needs that a co-taught class might address. If you come up with a promising idea, propose it to your administration.

Grand Designs

I began this book with "backwards design," the practice of starting instructional planning by identifying desired results, and I've finished it with "universal design," the process of creating learning environments in which all students gain access to the curriculum. These methods spring from different needs, but I think they serve the same purpose. The most desired result of all is that *every* student grow and learn and experience a sense of accomplishment. That's the goal that teachers enter the classroom with at the start of their careers, and it's the one that keeps them going over the long term, especially when they collaborate. But wishing alone won't make it happen. It also takes caring. As I've tried to show in this and previous chapters, teachers' caring is manifested in thoughtful design—not only of the writing and literature curriculum, not only of the assessment system or the ongoing instruction in technology and basic skills, but also of the strategies that we use to make English accessible and relevant to all students, to feel included and valued, that we use to open their paths to success. Organization driven by compassion and hope is the best means I know of fulfilling my school district's motto: "Every student, every day."

Recommended Reading

Echevarria, Jana, MaryEllen Vogt, and Deborah J. Short. *Making Content Comprehensible for English Learners: The SIOP Model*. 2nd ed. Boston: Pearson, 2004. Print.

> Using positive and negative classroom examples, this manual provides instructions and an observation protocol for implementing "sheltered instruction" to support ELLs in the content classroom.

King-Shaver, Barbara, and Alyce Hunter. *Differentiated Instruction in the English Classroom: Content, Process, Product, and Assessment*. Portsmouth, NH: Heinemann, 2003. Print.

> This book includes a primer on differentiated instruction and explains how it can be implemented naturally in the English classroom. Examples of differentiated units and activities are included.

Nieto, Sonia. *The Light in Their Eyes: Creating Multicultural Learning Communities*. New York: Teachers College Press, 1999. Print.

> Nieto not only gives a thought-provoking theoretical perspective on culture and learning but also includes voices of teachers transforming practice.

Perry, Theresa, Claude Steele, and Asa Hilliard III. *Young, Gifted, and Black: Promoting High Achievement among African-American Students*. Boston: Beacon, 2003. Print.

> Each essay in this collection adds a key perspective to the achievement gap debate: a history of African American achievement, an analysis of stereotype threat, and a study of the features of effective schools.

Putnam, JoAnne W., ed. *Cooperative Learning and Strategies for Inclusion: Celebrating Diversity in the Classroom*. 2nd ed. Baltimore: Brookes, 1998. Print.

> Besides the Kagan essay cited earlier, this volume includes pieces on topics ranging from cultural diversity to conflict resolution to computers. The final chapter describes school programs that promote successful inclusion.

Afterword: Growing Professionally through Teacher Leadership

At the end of my first semester of teaching, I received a nice note from a parent who had appreciated my efforts on her son's behalf. I tucked the note into a folder, which I labeled "Kudos." Over the years I have used that folder to collect complimentary cards and letters from students, parents, and administrators, as well as a few newspaper stories about my classes. At some point, to keep the record balanced, I added "and Complaints" to the tab on the folder. Fortunately, the affirmative responses I've accumulated outnumber the negative ones. This isn't a thick folder, but it's important to me, especially during those periodic lows when I'm not feeling totally successful in my work. I value the letters from students above all. Many of them were written at graduation time, but some much later—in a few cases, almost thirty years later. While the details of these letters vary, their two most common themes are satisfaction at gaining new insights or skills and gratitude for individual attention and encouragement. Reading these mementos from time to time, I feel reassured that I am a pretty good teacher and that I made the right career choice; I also feel challenged to continually reflect on my practice and maintain my professional growth, to live up to the writers' generous praise.

The most astonishing letter I ever received came on official stationery: it informed me that the mother of two of my students had nominated me for Massachusetts Teacher of the Year. I was gratified, but I immediately thought of dozens of talented teachers I knew, in my own school and elsewhere, who were far more deserving of the accolade. The letter requested that I compile a variety of documents for the selection committee, and I almost didn't do it; but then I thought, if a parent had been thoughtful enough to honor me with this nomination, the least I could do was follow through. Several rounds of submissions and a couple of stressful interviews later, I was notified that I had been chosen for the award. Naturally, I was humbled and overwhelmed. What I had learned during the process, though, was that the title was given to me not because I was the "best teacher in the state" or anything like that, but because I had been a teacher leader in a variety of venues and because state officials thought I had the potential to represent the profession in a positive way. Like the complimentary letters in my folder, this honor has challenged me to keep growing, as a teacher and as a leader.

Over my career I have come to believe that professional growth goes hand in hand with teacher leadership, which I define as contributing to the professional conversation. The most talented teachers I know are living examples of this connection. It makes sense: sharing best practices with others—in institutes, workshops, meetings, or everyday discussions—prompts us to reflect on our work in a much deeper way than we can do on our own. As I have indicated several times, I have learned many of my best teaching techniques from colleagues, and I hope I have offered them some useful strategies in return. Professional discourse, within departments and schools and across the larger teaching community, is the key to improving education.

Unfortunately, some of the by-products of education reform—school improvement plans, in-house inservice training, and recertification requirements—however valuable they may be, have narrowed the scope of many teachers' professional development. More and more teaching resources are available online, but release time and financial support for participating in face-to-face opportunities to exchange ideas and best practices, such as workshops and conferences, are harder and harder to come by. Nevertheless, there are still some accessible avenues—and lots of compelling reasons—for English teachers to get out into the field and partner with peers.

Here I would like to make a case for pursuing professional growth *through* teacher leadership. Leading at the department or school level does not necessarily mean taking on a powerful position; sometimes it's easier to bring about meaningful change from the ranks. But it does mean feeling and acting responsible for all students' learning and sharing the work of improving curriculum and instruction throughout the program. Active involvement in networks such as NCTE and the National Writing Project enhances teachers' capacity for local leadership. Conferring with colleagues from outside our immediate contexts provides new perspectives on common problems and combats parochial thinking. Contributing to the larger conversation about teaching enriches us and ultimately benefits our students. I'll offer some suggestions for growing by participating in regional and national organizations as well as in local initiatives.

Going Deep in the Discipline

My first glimpse of the "big picture" of English teaching came when two of my mentors who were involved in the New England Association of Teachers of English encouraged me to attend the fall conference. Attracted by the big-name authors giving keynote addresses, I happily tagged along. What hooked me, though, were the sessions presented by fellow teachers. Some of them confirmed my own practices, while others opened my eyes to new approaches; all of them prompted me to think about why I was doing what I was doing in the classroom. I recall hoping that someday I would have the courage and the expertise to offer a conference workshop.

That day came sooner than I had imagined, at a small regional conference, and it was followed in due course by sessions at the NEATE and NCTE annual meetings, many of them collaborations with colleagues. I still get nervous presenting, but I value the connections I make with peers from other places, and I always end up learning as much as I teach. Getting to know people at the conventions eventually led to leadership positions in NEATE and in NCTE's Assembly on American Literature, although I had had no ambitions along those lines. I learned that professional organizations are always in need of people who can devote some time and energy to planning and problem solving, and here too I've found that I gain as much as I give.

The leadership experiences I have enjoyed the most were my stints as editor of two small professional publications: NEATE's journal *The Leaflet* and AAL's newsletter *This Is Just to Say* (now called *Notes on American Literature*). With encouragement from previous editors, I had published a few articles in these periodicals. Writing about my teaching practices had been beneficial for me, and I wanted to use the editor role to encourage others to write about theirs. College professors are expected to publish, but K–12 teachers get little encouragement to do so. I made it my mission to recruit new authors, especially at conventions, where presenters and participants alike are engaged in reflecting on their teaching. Coaching fellow teachers on their nascent ideas for articles and evolving drafts was an opportunity for me to practice at another level the writing process philosophy enacted in my classroom. Many contributors said that receiving feedback and revising made them feel more confident and competent as teachers and as writers. Readers certainly benefited from hearing new voices in the professional conversation. I say all this to dispel the myth that the world of educational publishing is hopelessly competitive or closed to "normal" folk. It's true that high-profile national journals receive more manuscripts than they can accept, but many fine regional and niche publications are far from overwhelmed, and their editors actively seek and are willing to work with first-time authors with promising ideas. Publishing articles about teaching, like presenting at conferences and taking on leadership roles in professional organizations, is an open and accessible path to professional growth.

Your turn. If you're not already involved in your state or regional affiliate of NCTE, find out what services it offers to English teachers in your area. Talk to colleagues who are members, and look at the organization's website. Then think about joining: most affiliates' annual membership dues are quite low, and they generally include a journal and/or newsletter, reduced conference fees, and other benefits. Consider how you might become involved in the work. What classroom practices could you (with a colleague, perhaps) present at a conference? What insights could you share in an article? What talents could you offer to committees or boards? Don't be modest—you have expertise that someone needs. If you are already active at the state or regional level and wish to extend your reach, research the opportunities provided by NCTE (www.ncte.org). Besides the annual convention and journals, there are numerous councils, committees, and assemblies, many with their own meetings and publications. Which would be right for you?

Networking Nationally and Regionally

A few years after finishing graduate school, I was looking for new opportunities to learn. Two of my colleagues had participated in National Endowment for the Humanities Summer Seminars & Institutes for School Teachers, and they strongly recommended that I apply. I did so and was lucky enough to be accepted into an institute in California on *Moby-Dick*. I can still hear my students' reaction: "How can you spend six weeks studying one book?" Blissfully. I learned so much that I later applied for a similar program at the National Humanities Center in North Carolina. I got in on the second try and again had a terrific experience learning with and from an outstanding group of colleagues. Both seminars ended with promises to stay in touch, but the connections faded over time as the participants became reabsorbed in their work.

The summer program that truly changed my teaching life was the Western Massachusetts Writing Project (WMWP) Invitational Summer Institute. Like all other local sites of the National Writing Project, WMWP gathers a group of teachers each summer to write together, share and respond, engage in professional reading and research, and give demonstrations of their teaching practices. This "teachers teaching teachers" model of professional development was developed by James Gray and his colleagues at the University of California, Berkeley, in 1974 as an alternative to top-down inservice programs (Gray 45–69); it is now in place at more than two hundred sites across the country. At the core of the program is respect for teacher knowledge and experience. Summer institute participants often say that for the first time in their careers they feel that they have ownership of their learning. They are strongly encouraged to adopt an inquiry stance toward their work: "Permeating the entire NWP culture is the idea that constant questioning and searching are fundamental to good teaching" (Lieberman and Wood 30). Another strength of the program is that it includes all grade levels, K–college, and all subject areas; good teaching is good teaching, and reflective practitioners from all contexts have valuable insights and strategies to share.

The best part of the experience is that it doesn't end with the summer. Built into the NWP model is the expectation that participants who enter as individuals will emerge as members of a network of *teacher-consultants*, committed to ongoing inquiry and reform and empowered to lead in their schools, districts, and regions. As Ann Lieberman and Diane R. Wood show, the network's entire approach to professional development "contradicts traditional practice":

> Instead of teachers passively listening to a speaker, who most often presents decontextualized, generic knowledge and skills, teachers become active participants in learning as they discover together new approaches to teaching literacy and then apply them in their classrooms. Instead of having to choose between theoretical and practical knowledge, they learn ways to connect the two. Instead of taking classes in leadership at the local university, NWP teachers have opportunities to actually develop leadership skills as they contribute to the professional development of other teachers. Instead of thinking of leadership as something a principal does, teachers are encouraged to facilitate learning for their peers, create and lead work groups, do research, share and discuss articles and books, read and write for publication, and so forth. (99)

The arc of teachers' NWP involvement bends constantly toward deepening inquiry, expanding leadership, and strengthening voice. I am not alone in calling it life-changing.

My NWP experience began with immersion in the 1994 WMWP summer institute. What attracted me initially was the opportunity to write among a community of writers. I had taught writing for more than twenty years, completed a dissertation on writing instruction, and published a few articles, but I still didn't feel entirely comfortable with my own writing process, nor did I write as regularly as I thought I should. Sometimes I felt like a hypocrite in class, asking my students for more and better writing than I was producing myself. As it turned out, many of my fellow participants in the summer institute were in similar circumstances; some hadn't written at all since college. The institute schedule provided time and support for us all to flex our writing muscles again. Among the pieces that I surprised myself by writing that summer was a long narrative poem about my father. Another was an article about my eighth-grade English teacher, who planted the seeds that germinated into my career. I don't think I would ever have completed these projects on my own; helpful feedback from my response group and the program facilitators made them possible.

By the end of the institute I felt capable of living up to the NWP creed that "teachers of writing must write" (Gray 143), and I had many new ideas for making my students' writing experience more pleasurable, authentic, and fulfilling.

Most of the summer institute "content" was provided by the participants themselves in teaching demonstrations. I gave a workshop based on my research on invention strategies, and other participants presented on topics ranging from considering the audience to improve revision to "creating" historical artifacts. The presentations were fascinating not only because they gave everyone the chance to experience a variety of teaching techniques but also because they let us in on the presenters' thinking, on *why* they believed their approaches were effective. Some of the workshops offered strategies I could apply directly, and all of them inspired me to reflect on my practices. Coupled with a hearty draught of reading in the professional literature, the daily doses of pedagogy offered in the demonstrations strengthened my philosophical constitution.

For me, as for many NWP teacher-consultants, the summer institute was the first step in a long journey into networking and leadership. I have had opportunities to co-facilitate programs for students and teachers at my site, to conduct inservice workshops in area schools, and to participate in site governance. Through these activities I have built working relationships with teachers from a wide variety of schools—urban to rural, elementary through college. Some of this work has led to presentations at NWP annual meetings and invitations to take part in state and national initiatives, all directed by teachers committed not only to writing improvement but also to social justice and education reform. The annual gathering of NWP teacher-consultants is a heady experience. The opening session, which is often likened to a revival meeting, gathers a thousand or more believers in the NWP cause to celebrate and rededicate themselves to the work. The meeting is dramatic evidence that NWP is more than an organization; it's a movement.

Your turn. Summer presents many opportunities for teachers to renew themselves and develop their knowledge and skills. Besides sponsoring the national Summer Institutes and Seminars for School Teachers (see http://www.neh.gov/projects/si-school.html for the current schedule), NEH funds a variety of regional workshops through museums and other institutions. Many colleges and universities offer programs for teachers as well. Be on the lookout for possibilities that might benefit you. To learn more about NWP, visit http://www.nwp.org/. Click on the interactive map and follow the links to your local site. Most sites offer writing retreats, study groups, workshops, conferences, and open institutes. Sampling these programs is a good way to decide if you want to commit to the invitational summer institute.

Becoming a Local Teacher Leader

Getting involved in professional networks is personally gratifying and career building, but its most important effect is its impact on teachers' local leadership capacity. Engagement with peers on the national and regional levels makes us more effective in the school community and the classroom, though the benefits also flow in the other direction. I would like to highlight some opportunities for teacher leadership at the local level other than those that come with a title, such as department head or curriculum coordinator. I've held those jobs, so I know how important they are, but here I'm thinking of quieter roles that can be just as influential as established leadership positions: mentoring new and prospective teachers, advising cocurricular activities, collaborating with colleagues in study groups, and serving on school or district committees. Working in any of these roles fosters professional growth while enriching the community.

Mentoring can be as casual as talking about teaching with a new department member over coffee or as formal as discussing observations of an assigned mentee using an analytical protocol. In either case the aim is to provide a safe, nonevaluative space for a colleague to air concerns and benefit from the mentor's wisdom and experience. That experience doesn't have to be long; the best advisers of first-year teachers may well be second- and third-year teachers, who have just been through the induction process. Mentoring isn't about solving problems for colleagues but rather helping them to see what their options are and how to make good choices.

My most sustained and thus most rewarding mentoring experiences have been with student teachers I've sponsored from the University of Massachusetts and nearby colleges. Their enthusiasm and curiosity are infectious, and it's always instructive to see the classroom and the students through their eyes. Helping them to figure out how to plan instruction and manage the learning environment gives me the chance to revisit and reassess my own values and beliefs, and I usually gain new insights and strategies as they share what they have learned in their courses. Knowing how important it is to renew the teaching force with talented young professionals, I try to make sure that my interns have a worthwhile, authentic teaching experience in my classroom, but the arrangement benefits me—and my students—as well as them.

Cocurricular activities may not seem at first glance to offer such rich opportunities for professional growth, but the experience of advising a club can be revelatory. It gives teachers the chance to develop deeper relationships with students than are often possible in the classroom; in casual circumstances they are more apt to share what's really on their minds. In addition, the cocurricular activities typically sponsored by English teachers—drama, yearbook, newspaper, literary magazine, debate—enable students and teachers to collaborate on using language arts skills "for real." Then, too, these activities give the English program a public face in the school and community, highlighting the importance and relevance of the subject and sometimes stirring up controversy. All of these aspects of advising give teachers occasions to learn and to lead.

I've worked with a number of clubs over the years, but none as long or as deeply as the newspaper staff. I became close to the students who worked many a late night editing stories and laying out pages. I was inspired by the determination of several of my editors, who didn't let disabilities (one was profoundly deaf, one legally blind) stand in their way. Together we puzzled over logistical problems, took on challenging projects, and even weathered some intense storms. All of my learning from these experiences came back to my classroom in the form of keener insights about students, sounder approaches to instruction, and more authentic assignments in classes. Cocurricular activities often lead the way to curriculum innovation.

Study groups, in my opinion, are among the best forms of professional development and teacher leadership going. I include in this category alignment task forces, data analysis teams, curriculum revision committees, professional reading clubs—any gathering of teachers, official or unofficial, around a specific question or goal. These groups can accomplish several purposes at once: everybody can learn (from one another and from the material being studied), everybody can lead (by presenting ideas for discussion and proposing resolutions to conflicts), and valuable work can get done (in the form of curriculum plans, teaching strategies, portfolio designs, and other common agreements). Study groups work best when they are small enough (four to six people) that all of the members feel responsible to one another and no one has to be "in charge."

For the past several years, the English department at Amherst Regional High has been using the study group model for most meetings, in lieu of traditional whole-group "discussions" in which some people speak too much (that would be me), some tune out, and little gets resolved. Our department chair, Jane Baer-Leighton, established study groups for a variety of purposes, from creating curriculum maps to looking at student work. For me, the most memorable was the ninth-grade teachers' group, which met regularly for two years and still reconvenes on occasion. The purpose of the group was to work out agreements on the ninth-grade writing and literature curriculum, which had been in place since long before many of the teachers had started at the school. Some squabbles had arisen over what books should be taught, and there was little consistency in the types of writing being assigned. The initial meetings were lively and even a little contentious as we shared our beliefs and passions and argued for this or that title or project. A few sessions ended with hurt feelings, but because the process had created a bond in the group, members followed up with each other and strived for consensus. In the end, we produced a goal-driven plan that ensured all students would be exposed to a variety of genres in both reading and writing. Some texts and assignments were listed as required, others optional, and teachers were allowed a good deal of flexibility in how they implemented the agreement. Developing this plan together has had enormous benefits. First, it has given the ninth-grade team collective ownership of the program and established a basis for exchanging materials and best practices. Second, it has produced a living document that can be shared with new teachers, parents, and counselors. Finally, it has established a higher level of consistency in the ninth-grade classes, facilitating vertical alignment within the department—probably forestalling mandates that might otherwise have been imposed from above. This work has benefited everyone, most of all the students.

School and district committees are likely the least glamorous options for local leadership, and teachers can be forgiven for trying to avoid serving on them. But the work that they do is often important, and they offer opportunities to forge ties across department and grade-level boundaries. In many, perhaps most, schools and districts, progress is sometimes poisoned by a culture of blame. English teachers are often the subjects of censure: students can't write social studies essays or read their science textbooks or learn Spanish syntax because we haven't done an adequate job of teaching writing, reading, and grammar. College students have to take remedial classes because we haven't prepared them well enough to analyze data and construct arguments. But we're guilty of playing the blame game, too: we have to spend valuable time teaching history because students didn't learn the basics in their social studies classes; we have to review the parts of speech because students didn't master them in middle school; and so on. Finger-pointing usually arises not from any real animus for other teachers but from frustration with trying to meet overwhelming curricular demands. Cross-discipline and cross-school committee work breaks down barriers to communication and helps teachers understand each other's jobs, even when the focus of the committee isn't the curriculum per se.

I can't even estimate the number of committees I've served on. The first was a K–12 language arts group whose job was to create a skills continuum. I'm not sure that the document we produced was all that useful, but we certainly learned a lot about how literacy was taught at the various levels, and we developed connections that lasted for a long time. Every ten years I have served on self-study committees as the high school has prepared for accreditation visits by outside evaluators. Although the charges to these committees always include tedious documentation tasks, they also provide opportunities to envision new directions for the school, and I've enjoyed having a voice in those discussions. The most challenging committee work I have done has been in groups tasked with evaluating and redesigning the high school's class schedule. Nothing hits teachers and students where they live like the arrangement of their work days, so schedule committees are often beset by intractable conflicts over the number and length and order of periods, endless debates over the merits of semesters and trimesters, principled disagreements over the needs of at-risk and advanced students, and the like. Members usually come to the initial meetings in full armor, on a mission to defend their departments' interests to the death. But over time, the discussions humanize the contending factions. For instance, in the last committee I served on, my opinion of "those stubborn social studies teachers" gradually changed as their representative, a person of great integrity, presented valid reasons for their views. Because schedule decisions ultimately require hard choices, consensus is nearly impossible, but in every case I have come away from the work with a better understanding of, a deeper respect for, and a stronger connection to my colleagues in other departments.

To lead is to learn. The professional activities I've discussed in this chapter are healthful stretching exercises that, along with a diet of good classroom organization, can help sustain and grow a successful career. There are, of course, many other leadership opportunities I haven't mentioned. The type doesn't matter as much as the choice to be involved, to seek intellectual challenge, and to reach out to other teachers in the school and in the broader educational context.

> **Your turn.** What formal or informal leadership roles have you taken in your department, school, or district? Have you mentored colleagues or student teachers? Advised a cocurricular activity? Participated in a study group? Served on a committee? What have you learned from these experiences? What influence do you think you have had? What other kinds of teacher leadership would you like to try? If you haven't yet been in a leadership role, where do you think you might start? Is there a new teacher who could use some support? A club that needs an advisor or co-advisor? A topic that needs exploring in a department study group? A committee that's looking for English department representation? How can you help? What can you learn?

Four Final Words

I began this book with the goal of sharing some strategies that I have found successful for managing what often seems like an unmanageable job. Organizing instruction in the numerous disciplines that fall within English, responding meaningfully to mountains of student work, and accommodating the needs of diverse learners require ingenuity, skill, and determination, plus a generous spirit and a lot of flexibility. I hope my observations and suggestions have been helpful to you and encouraged you to experiment with a variety of organizational strategies to figure out what works best for you and your teaching situation. I'd like to leave you with four key words that have guided me throughout my career and that I have used frequently in this book:

- *Collaborate*. Despite being surrounded by students every day, teachers often feel all alone in the classroom. That isolation can be scary. All teachers need support from their colleagues to sustain themselves, so make a point of seeking it out, within your department and school and in professional networks.

- *Plan*. Students, parents, colleagues, and administrators are more apt to have faith in you if they can see that what you do day by day is not arbitrary or capricious but part of a larger design. Long-range and big-picture planning is hard, but it's essential for doing right by your students and feeling good about your work.

- *Reflect*. Lessons don't always go as planned, and even when they do, they need to be questioned occasionally. It's important to examine what's happening in your classroom. To do that, you need to carve out some private time. As you ponder how to fix whatever may be going wrong, don't forget to name your successes.

- *Believe*. Teaching often feels like a roller coaster ride, with hard climbs, giddy highs, frightening plunges, and long glides, even after years in the classroom. It never gets easy. But you can enjoy it if you believe in yourself, your students, and the messy process of education. Teaching is the ultimate act of faith.

That's my advice—collaborate, plan, reflect, and believe. Teachers who practice these skills thrive and grow and lead, and together with their students they build successful classrooms.

Works Cited

"About Project Outreach." *National Writing Project.* NWP, 2008. Web. 29 June 2009.

Achebe, Chinua. "An Image of Africa: Racism in Conrad's *Heart of Darkness*." *Hopes and Impediments: Selected Essays.* New York: Anchor-Doubleday, 1988. 1–20. Print.

Appleman, Deborah. *Critical Encounters in High School English: Teaching Literary Theory to Adolescents.* New York: Teachers College; Urbana: NCTE, 2000. Print.

Aronson, Elliot. Home page. *Jigsaw Classroom.* Social Psychology Network, n.d. Web. 29 June 2009.

Beck, Isabel L., Margaret G. McKeown, and Linda Kucan. "Choosing Words to Teach." Hiebert and Kamil 209–22.

Beers, Kylene. *When Kids Can't Read, What Teachers Can Do: A Guide for Teachers 6–12.* Portsmouth: Heinemann, 2003. Print.

Bizzell, Patricia. "Negotiating Difference: Teaching Multicultural Literature." *Rethinking American Literature.* Ed. Lil Brannon and Brenda M. Greene. Urbana: NCTE, 1997. 163–74. Print.

Bloom, Benjamin S., ed. *Taxonomy of Educational Objectives: The Classification of Educational Goals. Handbook I: Cognitive Domain.* New York: Longmans, 1956. Print.

Booth, Tiina, and Bruce M. Penniman. "Multicultural Literature in a Multi-Level Class." *Tracked for Failure/Tracked for Success: An Action Packet to Derail the Negative Effects of Ability Grouping.* Ed. Task Force on Grouping and Tracking. Urbana: NCTE, 1993. 104–09. Print.

Britton, James. "Writing to Learn and Learning to Write." *Prospect and Retrospect: Selected Essays of James Britton.* Ed. Gordon M. Pradl. Montclair: Boynton, 1982. 94–111. Print.

Broad, Bob. *What We Really Value: Beyond Rubrics in Teaching and Assessing Writing.* Logan: Utah State UP, 2003. Print.

Broad, Robert L. "'Portfolio Scoring': A Contradiction in Terms." Huot and O'Neill 301–14.

Burke, Kenneth. *A Grammar of Motives.* 1945. Berkeley: U of California P, 1969. Print.

Chekhov, Anton. "A Nincompoop." *Selected Stories.* Trans. Ann Dunnigan. New York: Signet-New American Library, 2003. 20–22. Print.

Christensen, Linda. *Reading, Writing, and Rising Up: Teaching about Social Justice and the Power of the Written Word*. Milwaukee: Rethinking Schools, 2000. Print.

Cohen, Elizabeth G. *Designing Groupwork: Strategies for the Heterogeneous Classroom*. 2nd ed. New York: Teachers College, 1994. Print.

Collins, James L. *Strategies for Struggling Writers*. New York: Guilford, 1998. Print.

Conrad, Joseph. *Heart of Darkness and The Secret Sharer*. New York: Signet-New American Library, 1983. Print.

Coogan, Michael D., ed. *The New Oxford Annotated Bible, with the Apocryphal/Deuterocanonical Books. New Revised Standard Version*. 3rd ed. New York: Oxford UP, 2001. Print.

Culham, Ruth. *6+1 Traits of Writing: The Complete Guide, Grades 3 and Up*. New York: Scholastic, 2003. Print.

Damrosch, Leopold, et al., eds. *Adventures in English Literature*. Heritage ed. Orlando: Harcourt, 1980. Print.

Daniels, Harvey. *Literature Circles: Voice and Choice in Book Clubs and Reading Groups*. 2nd ed. Portland: Stenhouse, 2002. Print.

———."What's the Next Big Thing with Literature Circles?" *Voices from the Middle* 13.4 (2006): 10–15. Print.

Day, Deanna, with Glenna Ainley."From Skeptic to Believer: One Teacher's Journey Implementing Literature Circles." *Reading Horizons* 48.3 (2008): 157–76. *Wilson Education Abstracts*. ProQuest. Web. 16 March 2009.

Dean, Deborah M."Muddying Boundaries: Mixing Genres with Five Paragraphs." *English Journal* 90.1 (2000): 53–56. Print.

Dean, Deborah. *Strategic Writing: The Writing Process and Beyond in the Secondary English Classroom*. Urbana: NCTE, 2006. Print.

Dellinger, Dixie."Portfolios: A Personal History." *Teachers' Voices: Portfolios in the Classroom*. Ed. Mary Ann Smith and Miriam Ylvisaker. Berkeley: NWP, 1993. 11–24. Print.

Delpit, Lisa."The Silenced Dialogue: Power and Pedagogy in Educating Other People's Children." *Other People's Children: Cultural Conflict in the Classroom*. New York: New, 1995. 21–47. Print.

Devitt, Amy J."Generalizing about Genre: New Conceptions of an Old Concept." *College Composition and Communication* 44.4 (1993): 573–86. Print.

Dickinson, Emily. *The Poems of Emily Dickinson: Reading Edition*. Ed. R. W. Franklin. Cambridge: Belknap-Harvard UP, 1999. Print.

Dressman, Mark, and Mark Faust."Poetry and Its Teaching in *English Journal*, 1912–2005: Ten Watershed Articles." *English Journal* 96.1 (2006): 76–78. Print.

Echevarria, Jana, MaryEllen Vogt, and Deborah J. Short. *Making Content Comprehensible for English Learners: The SIOP Model*. 2nd ed. Boston: Pearson, 2004. Print.

Eckert, Lisa Schade. *How Does It Mean? Engaging Reluctant Readers through Literary Theory*. Portsmouth: Heinemann, 2006. Print.

Elbow, Peter. "High Stakes and Low Stakes in Assigning and Responding to Writing." *Everyone Can Write: Essays Toward a Hopeful Theory of Writing and Teaching Writing.* New York: Oxford UP, 2000. 351–59. Print.

———. "Ranking, Evaluating, and Liking: Sorting Out Three Forms of Judgment." *College English* 55.2 (1993): 187–206. Print.

———. "Teaching Two Kinds of Thinking by Teaching Writing." *Embracing Contraries: Explorations in Learning and Teaching.* New York: Oxford UP, 1986. 54–63. Print.

———. *Writing with Power: Techniques for Mastering the Writing Process.* 2nd ed. New York: Oxford UP, 1998. Print.

Elbow, Peter, and Pat Belanoff. "Portfolios as a Substitute for Proficiency Examinations." Huot and O'Neill 97–101.

———. *Sharing and Responding.* 2nd ed. New York: McGraw, 1995. Print.

Ellison, Ralph. *Invisible Man.* 1952. New York: Vintage, 1990. Print.

"English Language Arts, Grade 10." *Release of Spring 2008 MCAS Test Items.* Malden: Massachusetts Dept. of Elementary and Secondary Educ., 2008. 199–229. *Mass.gov.* Web. 22 June 2009.

Finn, Patrick J. *Literacy with an Attitude: Educating Working-Class Children in Their Own Self-Interest.* Albany: State U of New York P, 1999. Print.

Fisch, Karl, and Scott McLeod. "Shifthappens." *Wikispaces.* 25 April 2008. Web. 29 June 2009.

Flower, Linda, and John R. Hayes. "The Cognition of Discovery: Defining a Rhetorical Problem." *College Composition and Communication* 31.1 (1980): 21–32. Print.

Freeman, Yvonne, and David Freeman. "School Success for Secondary English Learners." *Reading and Writing in More Than One Language: Lessons for Teachers.* Ed. Elizabeth Franklin. Alexandria: TESOL, 1999. 1–28. Print.

Gardner, Howard. *Multiple Intelligences: New Horizons.* New York: Basic, 2006. Print.

Golden, John. "Literature into Film (and Back Again): Another Look at an Old Dog." *English Journal* 97.1 (2007): 24–30. Print.

Goulden, Nancy Rost. "Implementing Speaking and Listening Standards: Information for English Teachers." *English Journal* 88.1 (1998): 90–96. Print.

Gray, James. *Teachers at the Center: A Memoir of the Early Years of the National Writing Project.* Berkeley: NWP, 2000. Print.

Guinee, Kathleen, and Maya B. Eagleton. "Spinning Straw into Gold: Transforming In-formation into Knowledge during Web-Based Research." *English Journal* 95.4 (2006): 46–52. Print.

Hamp-Lyons, Liz, and William Condon. "Developing a Theory for Portfolio-Based Writing Assessment." *Assessing the Portfolio: Principles for Practice, Theory, and Research.* Cresskill: Hampton, 2000. 115–64. Print.

Harrington, Colin. "Re: co-teaching." Message to the author. 6 Feb. 2009. Email.

Harris, Violet J. "Multicultural Literacy and Literature: The Teacher's Perspective." Miller and McCaskill 187–204.

Hartwell, Patrick. "Grammar, Grammars, and the Teaching of Grammar." *College English* 47.2 (1985): 105–27. Print.

Heritage, Margaret. "Formative Assessment: What Do Teachers Need to Know and Do?" *Phi Delta Kappan* 89.2 (2007): 140–45. *Wilson Education Abstracts*. ProQuest. Web. 1 Dec. 2008.

Herrington, Anne, Kevin Hodgson, and Charles Moran, eds. *Teaching the New Writing: Technology, Change, and Assessment in the 21st-Century Classroom*. New York: Teachers College; Berkeley: NWP, 2009. Print.

Hiebert, Elfrieda H., and Michael L. Kamil. *Teaching and Learning Vocabulary: Bringing Research to Practice*. Mahwah: Erlbaum, 2005. Print.

Hitchcock, Chuck, et al. "Equal Access, Participation, and Progress in the General Education Curriculum." *The Universally Designed Classroom: Accessible Curriculum and Digital Technologies*. Ed. David H. Rose, Anne Meyer, and Chuck Hitchcock. Cambridge: Harvard Education P, 2005. 37–68. Print.

"How to Evaluate a Web Site." *Amherst Regional High School Library*. Amherst Regional Public Schools, n.d. Web. 19 June 2009.

Hunt, Russ. "What is Inkshedding?" May 2004. *St. Thomas University*. St. Thomas U, Fredericton, NB, Canada. Web. 28 Oct. 2008.

Huot, Brian, and Peggy O'Neill, eds. *Assessing Writing: A Critical Sourcebook*. Boston: Bedford; Urbana: NCTE, 2009. Print.

Jago, Carol. *Papers, Papers, Papers: An English Teacher's Survival Guide*. Portsmouth: Heinemann, 2005. Print.

———. "Understanding Literature: Reading in the English Language Arts Classroom." *Content Area Reading and Learning: Instructional Strategies*. 3rd ed. Ed. Diane Lapp, James Flood, and Nancy Farnan. New York: Erlbaum, 2008. 303–26. Print.

Jenkins, Henry, et al. *Confronting the Challenges of Participatory Culture: Media Education for the 21st Century*. Chicago: MacArthur Foundation, 2006. *National Writing Project*. Web. 29 June 2009.

Kagan, Spencer. "New Cooperative Learning, Multiple Intelligences, and Inclusion." *Cooperative Learning and Strategies for Inclusion: Celebrating Diversity in the Classroom*. 2nd ed. Ed. JoAnne W. Putnam. Baltimore: Brookes, 1998. 105–36. Print.

Kajder, Sara B. *The Tech-Savvy English Classroom*. Portland: Stenhouse, 2003. Print.

Kauer, Suzanne M. "A Battle Reconsidered: Second Thoughts on Book Censorship and Conservative Parents." *English Journal* 97.3 (2008): 56–60. Print.

Keene, Ellin Oliver, and Susan Zimmermann. *Mosaic of Thought: Teaching Comprehension in a Reader's Workshop*. Portsmouth: Heinemann, 1997. Print.

Keil, Katherine. "Rediscovering the Joy of Poetry." *English Journal* 95.1 (2005): 97–102. Print.

King-Shaver, Barbara. *When Text Meets Text: Helping High School Readers Make Connections in Literature*. Portsmouth: Heinemann, 2005. Print.

King-Shaver, Barbara, and Alyce Hunter. *Differentiated Instruction in the English Classroom: Content, Process, Product, and Assessment*. Portsmouth: Heinemann, 2003. Print.

Ladson-Billings, Gloria. *The Dreamkeepers: Successful Teachers of African-American Children*. San Francisco: Jossey, 1994. Print.

Lane, Barry. *After the End: Teaching and Learning Creative Revision*. Portsmouth: Heinemann, 1993. Print.

Lederer, Richard. "Question & Answer." *National Review* 31 Dec. 1995: 38. Print.

Lent, ReLeah Cossett. "Facing the Issues: Challenges, Censorship, and Reflection through Dialogue." *English Journal* 97.3 (2008): 61–66. Print.

Lester, Julius. "On the Teaching of Literature." *English Journal* 94.3 (2005): 29–31. Print.

Lieberman, Ann, and Diane R. Wood. *Inside the National Writing Project: Connecting Network Learning and Classroom Teaching*. New York: Teachers College, 2003. Print.

Lyon, George Ella. "Where I'm From." *George Ella Lyon, Poet and Writer*. n.d. Web. 12 Jan. 2009.

Mack, Nancy. "The Ins, Outs, and In-Betweens of Multigenre Writing." *English Journal* 92.2 (2002): 91–98. Print.

Massachusetts English Language Arts Curriculum Framework. Malden: Massachusetts Dept. of Educ., 2001. *Mass.gov*. Web. 29 June 2009.

McMahon, Robert. *Thinking about Literature: New Ideas for High School Teachers*. Portsmouth: Heinemann, 2002. Print.

Melville, Herman. "To Nathaniel Hawthorne, June 17, 1851." *Moby-Dick: An Authoritative Text, Reviews and Letters by Melville, Analogues and Sources, Criticism*. Ed. Harrison Hayford and Hershel Parker. New York: Norton, 1967. 556–60. Print.

Miller, Suzanne M. "Why a Dialogic Pedagogy? Making Space for Possible Worlds." Miller and McCaskill 247–65.

Miller, Suzanne M., and Barbara McCaskill, eds. *Multicultural Literature and Literacies: Making Space for Difference*. Albany: State U of New York P, 1993. Print.

Moffett, James. "Learning to Write by Writing." *Teaching the Universe of Discourse*. New York: Houghton, 1968. 188–210. Print.

Moran, Charles. "One Teacher, Two Cultures: A Study of Influence and Change." *When Writing Teachers Teach Literature: Bringing Writing to Reading*. Ed. Art Young and Toby Fulwiler. Portsmouth: Boynton, 1995. 34–46. Print.

Moran, Charles, and Cynthia L. Selfe. "Teaching English across the Technology/Wealth Gap." *English Journal* 88.6 (1999): 48–55. Print.

Moynihan, Karen E. "A Collectibles Project: Engaging Students in Authentic Multimodal Research and Writing." *English Journal* 97.1 (2007): 69–76. Print.

Mungai, Anne. "Collaboration for Inclusion among General and Special Educators: Problems and Solutions." *Pathway to Inclusion: Voices from the Field*. Ed. Anne Mungai and Esther Kogan. Lanham: UP of America, 2005. 29–45. Print.

Nagy, William. "Why Vocabulary Instruction Needs to Be Long-Term and Comprehensive." Hiebert and Kamil 27–44.

National Writing Project, and Carl Nagin. *Because Writing Matters: Improving Student Writing in Our Schools*. San Francisco: Jossey, 2003. Print.

Nieto, Sonia. *The Light in Their Eyes: Creating Multicultural Learning Communities*. New York: Teachers College, 1999. Print.

Penniman, Bruce M. *Prodding the Muse: The Effects of Instruction in Rhetorical Invention on the Composing Processes of Ninth Graders*. Diss. U of Massachusetts Amherst, 1985. Ann Arbor: UMI, 1985. AAT 8509591. Print.

Perl, Sondra. "Understanding Composing." *College Composition and Communication* 31.4 (1980): 363–69. Print.

Porter, Andrew J., Jr., Henry L. Terrie, Jr., and Robert A. Bennett, eds. *American Literature*. Lexington: Ginn, 1981. Print.

Redd, Teresa M., and Karen Schuster Webb. *A Teacher's Introduction to African-American English: What a Writing Teacher Should Know*. Urbana: NCTE, 2005. Print.

Romano, Tom. *Blending Genre, Altering Style: Writing Multigenre Papers*. Portsmouth: Boynton, 2000. Print.

Rose, Mike. "Rigid Rules, Inflexible Plans, and the Stifling of Language: A Cognitive Analysis of Writer's Block." *College Composition and Communication* 31.4 (1980): 389–401. Print.

Rous, Emma Wood. "Opening the Doors of Perception." New England Association of Teachers of English Annual Conference. Sheraton Nashua Hotel, Nashua, NH. 20 Oct. 2000. Address.

"RubiStar." *4Teachers.org*. Advanced Learning Technologies in Educ. Consortia at U of Kansas, 2008. Web. 29 June 2009.

"School/District Profiles: Amherst Regional High." Malden: Massachusetts Dept. of Elementary and Secondary Educ., 2008–09. *Mass.gov*. Web. 15 June 2009.

Schuster, Edgar H. "A Fresh Look at Sentence Fragments." *English Journal* 95.5 (2006): 78–83. Print.

Sebranek, Patrick, and Dave Kemper. *Daily Language Workouts 9*. Wilmington: Great Source, 1996. Print.

Sembene Ousmane. *The Money-Order with White Genesis*. Trans. Clive Wake. London: Heinemann, 1987. Print.

Shafer, Gregory. "Tell Me a Story." *English Journal* 92.2 (2002): 102–06. Print.

Shakespeare, William. *The Tragedy of Romeo and Juliet*. Ed. J. A. Bryant, Jr. New York: Signet-New American Library, 1987. Print.

Shanahan, Timothy, and Cynthia Shanahan. "Teaching Disciplinary Literacy to Adolescents: Rethinking Content-Area Literacy." *Harvard Educational Review* 78.1 (2008): 40–59. Print.

Shaughnessy, Mina. *Errors and Expectations: A Guide for the Teacher of Basic Writing*. New York: Oxford UP, 1977. Print.

Shelley, Percy Bysshe. "A Defence of Poetry." 1819. Indianapolis: Bobbs, 1904. *Google Book Search*. Web. 18 June 2009.

Smith, Michael W., and Jeffrey D. Wilhelm. *"Reading Don't Fix No Chevys": Literacy in the Lives of Young Men*. Portsmouth: Heinemann, 2002. Print.

Smith, Thomas B. "Teaching Vocabulary Expeditiously: Three Keys to Improving Vocabulary Instruction." *English Journal* 97.4 (2008): 20–25. Print.

Sommers, Nancy. "Revision Strategies of Student Writers and Experienced Adult Writers." *College Composition and Communication* 31.4 (1980): 378–88. Print.

Strunk, William, Jr., and E. B. White. *The Elements of Style*. 4th ed. Boston: Allyn, 2000. Print.

Sumaryono, Karen, and Floris Wilma Ortiz. "Preserving the Cultural Identity of the English Language Learner." *Voices from the Middle* 11.4 (2004): 16–19. Print.

Swardson, H. R. "The Use of the Word *Mistake* in the Teaching of Poetry." *Teaching Literature: A Collection of Essays on Theory and Practice*. Ed. Lee A Jacobus. Upper Saddle River: Prentice, 1996. 159–75. Print.

Tennyson, Alfred Lord. "The Charge of the Light Brigade." *The Poems of Alfred Lord Tennyson*. Roslyn: Black's Readers Service, 1932. 235–36. Print.

"This I Believe in the Classroom." *Thisibelieve.org*: This I Believe, n.d. Web. 29 June 2009.

Thoreau, Henry David. *Walden, or Life in the Woods, and On the Duty of Civil Disobedience*. New York: New American Library, 1960. Print.

Tovani, Cris. *I Read It, but I Don't Get It: Comprehension Strategies for Adolescent Readers*. Portland: Stenhouse, 2000. Print.

Tyson, Lois. *Critical Theory Today: A User-Friendly Guide*. New York: Garland, 1999. Print.

"US Historical Immigration Trends." *MPI Data Hub: Migration Facts, Stats, and Maps*. Migration Policy Institute, 2009. Web. 29 June 2009.

Vreeland, Susan. "The Judith Paintings." *Books by Susan Vreeland*. Official website for Susan Vreeland, n.d. Web. 7 Jan. 2009.

Vygotsky, L. S. "Interaction between Learning and Development." *Mind in Society: The Development of Higher Psychological Processes*. Ed. Michael Cole et al. Cambridge: Harvard UP, 1978. 79–91. Print.

Weaver, Constance. "Teaching Grammar in the Context of Writing." *Lessons to Share on Teaching Grammar in Context*. Ed. Constance Weaver. Portsmouth: Boynton, 1998. 18–38. Print.

Whicher, George Frisbie. *This Was a Poet: A Critical Biography of Emily Dickinson*. 1938. Hamden: Archon, 1980. Print.

Wiggins, Grant, and Jay McTighe. *Understanding by Design*. Expanded 2nd ed. Upper Saddle River: Pearson, 2006. Print.

Wilhelm, Jeffrey D. "Thoughts on the Twenty-First Century Classroom: An Interview with Jeffrey D. Wilhelm." *Teaching the Neglected "R": Rethinking Writing Instruction in Secondary Classrooms*. Ed. Thomas Newkirk and Richard Kent. Portsmouth: Heinemann, 2007. 10–16. Print.

Willis, Arlette Ingram, and Marlen Diane Palmer. "Negotiating the Classroom: Learning and Teaching Multicultural Literature." *Teaching and Using Multicultural Literature in Grades*

9–12: Moving Beyond the Canon. Ed. Arlette Ingram Willis. Norwood: Christopher-Gordon, 1998. 215–50. Print.

Wilson, Maja. *Rethinking Rubrics in Writing Assessment*. Portsmouth: Heinemann, 2006. Print.

Yancey, Kathleen Blake. "Looking Back as We Look Forward: Historicizing Writing Assessment." *College Composition and Communication* 50.3 (1999): 483–503. Print.

Young, Richard E., Alton L. Becker, and Kenneth L. Pike. *Rhetoric: Discovery and Change*. New York: Harcourt, 1970. Print.

Index

standardized tests, 168–71, *170*
   in writing grid model, 26, 30
high-status knowledge, 9
historical criticism, 123, *124*
Hitchcock, Chuck, 204–5
holistic scoring, 61–62
homosexuality, 196
Honors/AP program
   critical theory in, 124–25
   curriculum mandates and, 53
House on Mango Street, The (Cisneros), 32
hovering, 128
How Does It Mean? (Eckert), 117
Huckleberry Finn. See Adventures of Huckleberry Finn, The (Twain)
Hudson River School, 126
humor in tests, 85–86
Hunger of Memory (Rodriguez), *48*
Hunter, Alyce, 203
Hurston, Zora Neale, 164, 181
Hwang-Carlos, Malia, 34

identities, cultural, 201
IEPs (Individualized Education Plans), 199, 205
Ikiru (Kurosawa), 193
immigrant interview assignment, 30, *31*, 47
Incidents in the Life of a Slave Girl (Jacobs), *7*, *128*, 187
inclusion practices, 202–3, 217
Individualized Education Plans (IEPs), 199, 205
inkshedding, 29
inquiry strategies, 96
inspiration, creating, 94
intelligences, multiple, 199, 203–4, 207
intensity, 160
Internet research, responsible, 141, 147–50
interpretation, 41–43, 55
interpretative presentations, 150–51
intertextuality, 118–19
interventions, 205
Into Africa unit, 190–93
invention, 94, 97–102, *100*, *102*
Invisible Man (Ellison), 47–49, *48*, 50, 142, 146, 208
Irving, Washington, 52
Iverson, Kristen, 117

"Jabberwocky" (Carroll), 162
Jacobs, Harriet, *7*, 187
Jago, Carol, 63, 159
jigsaw technique, 120, 121, 122, 125
Joffe, Roland, 142
journalism classes, 145–46
Joy Luck Club, The (Tan), 50, *166*
Judith (biblical book), 186–87

Kagan, Spencer, 203–4
Kajder, Sara B., 147–48
Kasal, Alan, 215–16
Kauer, Suzanne M., 54
Keene, Ellin Oliver, 119, 130
Keil, Katherine, 55, 56
Kesey, Ken, 54
King Lear (Shakespeare), 132
King-Shaver, Barbara, 118–19, 203
Kingston, Maxine Hong, *48*, 187
knowledge
   declarative, procedural, and conditional, 95–96
   high-status, 9
Koehler, Gene, 188
Kurosawa, Akira, 193

Ladson-Billings, Gloria, 201–2
Lane, Barry, 108
language
   diversity in, 162, 164
   expressive, transactional, and poetic, 21–22, *22*
   Shakespearean, 167–68
leadership. *See* professional development and teacher leadership
learning disabilities and special education, 199, 202–3, 211, 215–18
Leaves of Grass (Whitman), 196
Lederer, Richard, 85–86
Lent, ReLeah Cossett, 54–55
"less is more" approach, 157, 165
Lester, Julius, 41
Levinson, Barry, *48*
Lewis, Marilyn, 179
Lieberman, Ann, 225
Life in the Iron Mills (Davis), 121–22, 187
Life is Beautiful (Benigni) (film), 143, *144*
linguistic terminology, 162

censorship and, 54

contact zones and Western Civilization course strategies, 188–94, *189*

definition and overview, 179–80

difficult discussions, 194–97

educational equity and heterogeneous classes, 182–83

literary conversations, 185–88

literature instruction, 39–40

as ongoing inquiry, 197

pitfalls, 183–85

See also diversity in the classroom

multiculturation, 201

multigenre writing, 25, 34

multiple intelligences, 199, 203–4, 207

multiple narration, 33

Mungai, Anne, 217

music, 50, 126

My Ántonia (Cather), 196

Nagy, William, 160, 165

Narrative of the Life of Frederick Douglass (Douglass), 7, 187

National Council of Teachers of English (NCTE), xiii, 222, 223

National Endowment for the Humanities Summer Seminars for School Teachers, 224, 226

National Public Radio, 32

National Writing Project, xiii, 29, 222, 224–26. *See also* Western Massachusetts Writing Project

"Nature" (Emerson), 7, 207

NCTE (National Council of Teachers of English), xiii, 222, 223

NCTE Assembly on American Literature, 223

Neihardt, John, 7

networking, national and regional, 224–26

New Criticism, 41–42, 55, 134

New England Association of Teachers of English (NEATE), 222–23

news, balance and bias in, 145–46

Ngũgĩ wa Thiong'o, 183, 193

Nieto, Sonia, 202

Night (Wiesel), 143, *144*

"Nincompoop, A" (Chekhov), 122–23

Northwest Regional Educational Laboratory, 64

note-making process, 149

objective criticism, 41

"object-of-value" speech, 172, *173*

Odyssey, The (Homer), 50, 83, *84*, 186–87, 207–8

One Flew over the Cuckoo's Nest (Kesey), 54

oral communication, 160–61, 171–74, *173*. *See also* performance

Oral Communication course, 135

Orlando (Woolf), 196

Oroonoko, or the Royal Slave (Behn), 189

Ortiz, Wilma, 201

outcomes, focus on, 4–5

outlines for courses

American Literature and Nature example, 6–9, *7–8*

Course Requirements section, 67

in planning process, 5–6

parental involvement, 211

parental objections, 53–55

partial drafts, 109, *110*

partial works, 50

participation gap, 139–41

participatory learning, 135–37

passage analysis, 131–32, *133*, 169

Paton, Alan, 193

pedagogical goals, 6, 9

peer response for writing, 103–7, *106. See also* feedback and response; group work

performance, 56, *83. See also* oral communication

periodical articles, publication of, 223

Perl, Sondra, 92

personal essays, 12, 32, 69

philosophy of assessment, 66–69

plagiarism, 148–49

"plan," 231

planning, long-range

overview, 3–4

backward design and, 4–5

big-picture planning, 10–13, *11*

goal setting and course outlines, 5–10, *7–8*

learning modes and, 207

macro to micro, 19

revision and progress assessment, 18

unit plans and weekly schedules, 13–16, *14–15*, *17*

writing assignments, 35–36

play in language study, 163–64

Rosenblatt, Louise, 120
rubrics
    criticism of, 64–65
    for portfolios, 77, *78*
    6+1 Trait model, 64, 65
    student-generated, 72–74, *73*
Rubyfruit Jungle (Brown), 196

Sartor Resartus (Carlyle), 39
sayback strategy, 104
scaffolding of tests, 83
Scarlet Letter, The (Hawthorne), 18, 127
schedule committees, 229–30
schedule grids, *11*, 12
scheduling. *See* planning, long-range
scoring, holistic, 61–62
scoring guides. *See* assessment; rubrics
second chances principle, 67
"Second Coming, The" (Yeats), 56
selection for portfolios, 63
self-assessment, 72–74, *73*
Selfe, Cynthia L., 140
self-reflection, 66, 70–72, 77–80, *79*
Sembene Ousmane, 192–93
sexual orientation, 196
Shafer, Gregory, 161
Shakespeare, William, 132, 134, 135, 167–68, 196
Shanahan, Cynthia, 158
Shanahan, Timothy, 158
"sharing: no response" strategy, 103
Shaughnessy, Mina, 157
Shaw, George Bernard, 164
Shelly, Percy Bysshe, 55
sheltered instruction (SI) model, 200–201
Sheltered Instruction Observation Protocol (SIOP), 201
short passages, analysis of, 131–32, *133*, 169
Short Stories (Hawthorne), 7
short works, 49–50
Silko, Leslie Marmon, 52, 183
6+1 Trait model, 64, 65
skeleton feedback, 105
skills vs. process debate, 94–95
Smith, Michael W., 43, 49
Smith, Thomas B., 160

social action approach to multiculturalism, 181
social justice issues, 146. *See also* diversity in the classroom; multiculturalism
social skills and media literacy, 140
Sommers, Nancy, 93
Song, Cathy, 52, 56
"Song of Myself" (Whitman), 74
Song of Solomon (Morrison), 50
sonnet challenge, 29
sonnet performance evaluation form, *83*
sonnets and specialized language, 134
Souls of Black Folk, The (DuBois), 210
speaking, 160–61, 171–74, *173*
special needs and special education, 199, 202–3, 211, 215–18
specificity in student writing, 130–32
stakes
    audience linked with, 26–32
    Elbow on, 24
    in writing grid model, 26
standardized tests, 168–71, *170*
Steinbeck, John, 125
stereotyping, 146, 184, 195
Stranger, The (Camus), 189
Strategic Writing (Dean), 96
Strategies for Struggling Writers (Collins), 95–96
strategies for writing. *See* writing process
stress and planning, 3
structuralist criticism, *124*
study groups, 228–29
Sumaryono, Karen, 201
Summary of Basic Questions, 118
summative assessment, 74–75, *76*
Summer Institutes and Seminars for School Teachers (NEH), 224, 226
summer seminars and institutes, 224–26
Sweardson, H. R., 55–56
syllabus development, 43–49, *48*
system view, 100

tagmemic heuristic, 100–101
teacher-consultants, 225–26
teacher-leaders. *See* professional development and teacher leadership
teachers teaching teachers model, 224

Wright, Richard, 184
Writer's block, 93
writing, student
    big-picture planning and, 13
    creative, 12, 24, 29, 33
    critical interpretation of literature and, 42
    curriculum organized around, 20
    evaluation-free, 23–24
    expressive, *26*, 27, 32
    freewriting, 23–24, 29, 99
    genre organization of curriculum, 46
    high-stakes, 26, 30, 35
    low-stakes, 24, 26, 28–29, 35, 56
    medium-stakes, 26, 29–30, 35
    multigenre, 25, 34
    poetic, xii, 22, *26*, 27, 32–33, 58
    profile writing, 30
    revision, 25, 72, 93, 107–12, *110, 111*
    transactional, 22, *26*, 26–27, 33–34
    voice and specificity in, 130–32
Writing and Literature course, 46, *46*
writing assessment. *See* assessment
writing folders, 69–75, *71*, 77
writing grid model
    curriculum organized around writing, 20
    frequency and variety, 36

grid format, 25–27, *26*
modes and genres, 32–35
planning with writing, *35*, 35–36
stakes linked with audience, 27–32, *28*
theory of writing process and, 21–25, *22*
writing process
    invention strategies, 94, 98–102, *100, 102*
    peer response, 103–7, *106*
    publication projects, 112–14
    research on, 93–97
    revision as re-vision, 107–12
    strategies vs. steps, 91–92, 98, 114
writing-to-learn activities, 58
"Writing to Learn and Learning to Write"
    (Britton), 21–22

Yeats, William Butler, 56
Yellow Raft on Blue Water, A (Dorris), 12
Yezierska, Anzia, *48*, 215

Zeffirelli, Franco, 142
Zimmerman, Susan, 119, 130
zone of minimal effort, 159
zone of proximal development, xiv, 159

About Bruce M. Penniman

Bruce M. Penniman taught English for thirty-six years at Amherst Regional High School, where he also held the positions of department chair and instructional director. In 1999, he was named Massachusetts Teacher of the Year and was a finalist for National Teacher of the Year. A past president of the New England Association of Teachers of English, he has also edited NEATE's journal, *The Leaflet*, and the NCTE Assembly on American Literature newsletter, *This Is Just to Say* (now *Notes on American Literature*). A teacher-consultant with the Western Massachusetts Writing Project since 1994, he served as the site's co-director from 1994 to

2002 and director from 2003 to 2007. Currently semiretired, he is still active in the National Writing Project, facilitating inservice workshops, co-coordinating the Massachusetts Writing Project network, serving on the State and Regional Networks Leadership Team, and assisting with National Reading Initiative projects. He serves on the NEATE Executive Board and is active in the Teacher Leadership Academy of Massachusetts. He also teaches courses at the University of Massachusetts Amherst and is co-teaching an interdisciplinary African Studies course at ARHS.

Photo credit:
Ulrika Gavér Gerth/Sviensklararen

This book was typeset in TheMix and Palatino by Barbara Frazier.

Typefaces used on the cover include Trebuchet and Franklin Gothic Medium.

The book was printed on 50-lb. Williamsburg Offset paper by Versa Press, Inc.